PIONEER DAYS
IN BRITISH COLUMBIA

volume two

Edited by Art Downs

© 1975-1979 Heritage House Publishing Company Ltd. and the authors

ISBN 0-9690546-2-9

FRONT: Throughout the province are reminders of our pioneer heritage, including wagons which once hauled hay from the fields and produce to the market.

TITLE PAGE: The 83 Mile House on the Cariboo Wagon Road in 1912. See Page 80 for an article on a famous roadhouse.

BACK: Framed in the doorway of this collapsing Chilcotin ranchhouse are a dirt-roofed cabin and a high-peaked barn, monuments to an abandoned venture.

Books by Art Downs

WAGON ROAD NORTH:
Historic photographs from 1863 of the Cariboo gold rush

PADDLEWHEELS ON THE FRONTIER:
The story of British Columbia-Yukon sternwheel steamers

Edited by Art Downs

PIONEER DAYS IN BRITISH COLUMBIA
Volume One

PIONEER DAYS IN BRITISH COLUMBIA
Volume Two

PIONEER DAYS IN BRITISH COLUMBIA
Volume Three

PIONEER DAYS IN BRITISH COLUMBIA
Volume Four

Heritage House Publishing Company Ltd
5543 - 129 Street
Surrey, British Columbia
V3W 4H4

Design by John Moutray
Printed in Canada by Evergreen Press

CONTENTS

	THE AUTHORS	4
1	WE PIONEERED by Arthur Shelford	6
2	POPLAR CREEK AND THE COLONEL OF THE KOOTENAYS by Elsie G. Turnbull	16
3	LAST VOYAGE OF INTERIOR B.C.'s LARGEST CANOE by E. M. Cotton	22
4	PIONEER FENCES by Donovan Clemson	26
5	THE BRIDGES AT HAGWILGET by Sperry "Dutch" Cline	32
6	OUR LOG CABIN HERITAGE by Donovan Clemson	36
7	PIONEER DAYS IN NELSON by Dr. L. E. Borden	42
8	HISTORIC NOOTKA SOUND by Peggy Young	48
9	ORDEAL ALONG THE LIARD by F. H. Ellis	54
10	THOSE CARIBOO CAMELS by Bruce Ramsey	60
11	THE LIFE OF PIONEER MINERS by George P. Stewart	70
12	EARLY GILLNET FISHERMEN by Walter Wicks	76
13	HISTORIC COTTONWOOD HOUSE by Emelene Thomas	80
14	DOG DAYS IN HAZELTON by Wiggs O'Neill	90
15	ALICE ELIZABETH JOWETT: GRAND OLD LADY OF LARDEAU by Elsie G. Turnbull	92
16	STOP OF INTEREST—Apostle in the Rockies	95
17	THE COMING OF THE STEEL by Blaine Boyd	96
18	THE HOMESTEADERS by Ferdi Wenger	106
19	CAPE BEALE—GRAVEYARD OF THE PACIFIC by W. J. Betts	110
20	STOP OF INTEREST—Southern Crossroads	115
21	JOHN B. RAY: WILDERNESS PIONEER by Nigel Pooley	116
22	STERNWHEEL DAYS ON THE PEACE RIVER by Harold Fryer	120
23	BARD OF BARKERVILLE by R. M. Thorburn	128
24	THOMAS ELLIS: OKANAGAN PIONEER by Eric D. Sismey	136
25	NEW YORK-SIBERIA: THE ASTONISHING HIKE OF LILLIAN ALLING by Francis Dickie	140
26	DAVID DOUGLAS: PIONEER BOTANIST by Robert F. Harrington	146
27	TALES THE TOTEMS TELL by B.C. Government Travel Bureau	150

BENNETT
ATLIN
25
9
FORT NELSON
ALDOUS-ROBERTSON REAL ESTATE
CIGAR STORE
SANDON
FORT ST. JOHN
22
DAWSON CREEK
5
HAZELTON
14
TERRACE
SMITHERS
FORT ST. JAMES
PRINCE RUPERT
12
KITIMAT
BURNS LAKE
1
VANDERHOOF
17
PRINCE GEORGE
23
3
QUESNEL
BARKERVILLE
BELLA COOLA
13
WILLIAMS LAKE
4
21
10
GOLDEN
15
18
LILLOOET
FERGUSON
QUATSINO
6
KAMLOOPS
11
2
VERNON
CAMPBELL RIVER
SANDON
POWELL RIVER
MERRITT
AINSWORTH
7
8
NOOTKA SOUND
KELOWNA
YALE
24
NELSON
16
FERNIE
NANAIMO
VANCOUVER
HOPE
PENTICTON
TRAIL
27
26
20
19
VICTORIA
CF-AOW

The Authors:

WESTON J. BETTS, 1895-1973, arrived in the Pacific Northwest in 1898 with his parents. His father bought property at Stone's Landing on Puget Sound, re-named it Redondo Beach and developed a picnic-amusement area. During World War One, Weston served overseas for twenty-one months then returned to the family business. After a $300,000 fire destroyed the complex in 1958, he built and operated a marina. He enjoyed writing about the marine history of the Pacific Northwest and his boat, *Thunderbird,* was a frequent visitor to British Columbia waters.

In 1907 three prominent doctors gave **L. E. BORDEN,** M.D., 1877-1963, three months to live. Next year he went to Nelson where he practiced for forty-seven years, in addition to serving as a major in the Medical Corps in both World Wars and representing Nelson as an MLA from 1928-33.

In 1903-4 Dr. Borden was surgeon and botanist on the first Canadian Government Expedition to the Eastern Arctic. During this cruise Captain A. P. Low officially took possession of Ellesmere and Southampton Islands on behalf of the Canadian government and asked Dr. Borden to keep one of the Proclamations of Sovereignty in his diary. A half century later a question was raised on an international level about Canada's ownership of the Arctic Islands. Dr. Borden heard about this doubt and sent his documents to Ottawa. In August 1956 the Proclamation and correspondence were presented to the House of Commons by H. W. Herridge and accepted as proof that the Islands were, indeed, part of Canada.

DONOVAN CLEMSON was born in Warwick, England in 1907 and arrived in B.C. in 1924. Since then he has been engaged in rural pursuits, first on farms, then on ranches and after that in remote mountain mines. He later acquired a farm in the North Okanagan and at the same time contributed photographs, articles and photo-stories to many magazines and newspapers.

"I have a feeling for isolated places and admiration for the backwoods dwellers," he admits, "especially the prospectors, the away-back ranchers, the lonely fire-watchers in their remote mountain-top eyries, and the sheepherders who spend their solitary summers in the high mountain pastures. All these have been subjects for pen and camera and have lured me into many out-of-the-way places in Interior British Columbia."

SPERRY "DUTCH" CLINE was one of the most colorful members of the old B.C. Provincial Police. Born in St. Thomas, Ontario, he left home early and by 1896 was fighting the fierce Matabele natives in South Africa, and during the Boer War won the Distinguished Conduct Medal. In later years in B.C. this South African service plus the fact that he tended to combine his English with Dutch, Swahili and Chinook earned him his nickname "Dutch."

In 1914 Mr. Cline became a policeman and served in many communities, including Hazelton. One of his most memorable patrols was mushing with dogs 170 miles to a lonely cabin on the Yukon Telegraph Line to bring in the frozen body of an unfortunate operator. Mr. Cline retired as sergeant in 1946 and died at Vancouver in May 1964.

LES COOK, 1912-1970, was a civil servant closely involved in provincial historic interpretation programs. In 1957-58 he was one of those given the responsibility of selecting and erecting the initial thirty-five Stop-of-Interest plaques along the provincial highways system.

With the inception of the Barkerville restoration project in 1958 he went to the gold community as supervisor and remained until 1965. Then he was transferred to Victoria to supervise the accelerated Stop-of-Interest program. He died at fifty-eight, taking with him a wealth of knowledge of the history and development of British Columbia.

The late **E. M. COTTON** was a native son of New Westminster with a strong interest in B.C. history. The story of his trip from Fort St. James to Quesnel in what is believed to be Interior B.C.'s largest canoe began in September 1911 when he and his brother, Walter, set out to join their father at Stuart Lake.

So isolated was the region that they travelled from Vancouver to Prince Rupert in the steamer *Prince George*. Then they ascended 180 miles of the Skeena River to Hazelton by sternwheel steamer and proceeded overland to Babine Lake. They paddled down the eighty-five-mile-long lake to Babine Portage, walked ten miles to Stuart Lake then paddled thirty-five miles to Fort St. James.

FRANCIS DICKIE is originally from Manitoba, born in Carberry in 1890. After leaving school in 1906 he worked with survey parties for three railways, Canadian Pacific, Grand Trunk Pacific and Canadian Northern.

He began writing at an early age, selling a short story to *Cassels Magazine* when he was fifteen. In 1911 he became a reporter on the *Calgary Herald,* then later joined the *Edmonton Daily Capital,* first as a reporter then editor. After World War One he free-lanced in Vancouver, B.C. until 1923 when he forsook the city for Heriot Bay on Quadra Island where he built a home in the wilderness and has lived for over fifty years.

FRANK ELLIS is the last surviving Canadian pilot who flew in Canada before the outbreak of World War One. He and a partner, Tom Blakely, built a Curtiss-type pusher biplane at Calgary in 1913-14 and taught themselves to fly. Ellis' first solo flight was July 2, 1914.

He served in the Royal Flying Corps and the Royal Air Force during the last two years of World War One. Afterwards he became actively engaged in civil aviation in Canada, barnstorming, parachuting and wing-walking. In Ontario on July 15, 1919, he became the first Canadian to make a parachute jump from an airplane flying in Canada, then a year later he was one of two crewmen to make the first flight into the Canadian north, flying a passenger from Winnipeg to The Pas.

In later years Mr. Ellis began researching the flying history of Canada and has written over 300 magazine articles and four books, including the best selling *Canada's Flying Heritage*. In 1972 his historical work was recognized when he was awarded the Order of Canada, the highest acknowledgement the government can bestow for service to the country at large.

HAROLD FRYER is a courageous and determined writer. After service with the Canadian Army overseas during World War II he settled in the B.C. section of the Peace River. Here he met his wife and here their three children were born. Then in October 1953 he contracted polio.

The next four years he spent in an Edmonton hospital, two of them in an iron lung. Today, he is almost completely paralyzed from the neck down and depends on some form of mechanical help for breathing. Despite this handicap he learned to type with the aid of a mouth stick and the weak fingers of his right hand. It took several years of practice to build a modest speed.

"Whatever success I've had I owe to my wife," he wrote. "For without her getting me up, setting up my typewriter, placing paper in and taking it out of the machine, helping with research, taking photos and so on, I wouldn't be able to write at all."

BOB HARRINGTON lives quietly in a scantily populated section of the Kootenays, between the upper end of the Arrow Lakes and the tiny village of Trout Lake. His interest in the outdoors has led to deeply rooted convictions about the necessity for greater environmental comprehension as an essential part of modern life. For the past three years, his weekly letters to Radio Noon, Calgary, have emphasized man's role as an integral part of the natural world, rather than as lord and master. Bob has given university short courses in ecology for the Canadian Wildlife Federation and has prepared several texts for schools.

When **C. P. LYONS** was four his family moved to the Okanagan, and a boyhood spent ranging the hills around Penticton resulted in a deep-seated love of the outdoors. After graduation he joined the B.C. Forest Service, then switched to the Parks Division. As a result he was closely connected with the development of many provincial parks.

Now a free-lance photographer and lecturer, he spends most of his time producing television programs and on National Audubon Society Film Tours. He has written several books, with one of them, *Trees, Shrubs and Flowers to Know in B.C.*, a steady best seller.

WIGGS O'NEILL, 1882-1964, was one of the best-known pioneers of Smithers. He was born in Barkerville but his family moved to the Queen Charlotte Islands, then to Port Simpson where his step-father was a Hudson's Bay Company factor.

Wiggs worked on sternwheel steamers on the Skeena River, finally owning his own boat on the Skeena and also operating a Packard truck in the freight and passenger business between Hazelton and Aldermere. He eventually settled in Smithers where he was a General Motors dealer for forty-three years. His hobby was history and he wrote many articles on his experiences and old-timers he had known. Many of his stories were collected into two soft-cover books, *Steamboat Days on the Skeena* and *Whitewater Men*. He also collaborated on a third book, *Along the Totem Trail*.

NIGEL R. C. POOLEY, 1912-1968, was born in the Okanagan Valley where his father was one of the early pioneers in the fruit industry. Mr. Pooley had a strong interest in provincial history and in the late 1930's travelled through central and northern B.C. writing stories about old-timers. When he returned from the Second World War in 1945 and took over the family orchard in Kelowna his interest in history continued. He was an active member of the Okanagan Historical Society for many years, serving as president of the Kelowna Branch and editor of the Society's annual report.

BRUCE RAMSEY is a B.C. newspaperman with a deep interest in provincial history. For years he was librarian of the *Vancouver Daily Province* and assisted with the paper's editorial page. Because of his desire to record material on our pioneers, the editorial page frequently had a decided historical flavor.

Mr. Ramsey, now a newspaper editor in the East Kootenay, has written many articles, radio scripts and books. Among the latter are *PGE—Railway to the North*, *Barkerville*, and *Ghost Towns of British Columbia*. His *Ghost Towns*, published in 1963, has remained a popular book that is now in its fifth printing.

In 1966, when **ARTHUR SHELFORD** and his wife, Millie, left Central B.C., they retired to an apartment in Victoria. He was then eighty-one and, after a lifetime in the outdoors, his friends wondered how he could stand an apartment. "It is not a case of enduring it," he wrote, "but of accepting it as the best solution in our remaining years. We miss many of the amenities of country life, especially the genial warmth of our old wood-burning stoves and heaters.

"If we were young we should at once hit out again for the north. But since we are not young any longer we are quite happy and content to live in beautiful Victoria."

ERIC D. SISMEY was something of a wanderer for the first years of his life. He was born in Halifax, Nova Scotia and educated in England, Tasmania and New Zealand. He arrived in Vancouver, B.C. in 1911, and for a number of years worked at various jobs before moving to California in 1923.

In 1957 Mr. Sismey retired and returned to B.C. He is a member of the Sierra Club, the Okanagan - Similkameen Parks Society, Canadian Nature Federation, and has filled several offices in the Okanagan Historical Society, including editor of the Okanagan Historical Society's annual report from 1971-73.

Mr. Sismey and his wife, Christine, now live in the community of Naramata high above Okanagan Lake. Eric's favorite hobbies are photography and fishing, with salmon his main interest.

GEORGE P. STEWART was born in the old mining town of Sandon in 1907 and lived there almost continuously until 1942.

"My schooling was in Sandon where I completed Grade 8," he notes. "When you finished grade school your education ceased since there was no high school in the community and with the low wages paid at that time very few parents could afford to send their children away for additional education. As a consequence, most of us went to work early. I worked in the mines from the time I was sixteen until the 1960's. After leaving the mines I was employed at New Denver until my retirement in 1972."

ELSIE G. TURNBULL has had a lifelong interest in our past that began when she studied history at the University of Toronto. After marriage to a metallurgist, she moved to Trail, British Columbia and became interested in local and regional history. This led to the formation of the West Kootenay branch of the B.C. Historical Association and getting down on paper as much as possible about life in earlier days. She served for some years on the council of the B.C. Historical Association and was president in 1955.

She has written numerous magazine articles, booklets on Trail's sixty years of development, and the United Church in Kootenay Diocese. Her book, *Topping's Trail,* published in 1964, is an account of the start of the world-famous smelter.

FERDI WENGER, a native of Switzerland, came to Canada in 1956 when he was twenty. During his first years in Canada he worked as a farmhand, a lumberjack, and a cowboy, spending his spare time learning English and the craft of writing. He returned to Switzerland twice, the last time for three years, but missed B.C. so much that he had to come back.

He now lives at Heffley Creek where he teaches canoeing and conducts guided canoe tours. In winter he combines writing with canoe building, the latter activity earning grocery money until he can support himself by writing full time.

In 1900, **WALTER WICKS** came with his family from Germany to the Skeena River country and became a commercial fisherman in the halibut fisheries off Hecate Straits and the Alaska coast. Later he learned carpentry and helped clear and build the first portion of the city of Prince Rupert. He moved to that city after the railroad arrived, married and raised three children.

After 1922, the family moved to Washington where he continued to work as a carpenter. He retired in 1958 and since then has written an autobiographical history of the Skeena River country.

PEGGY YOUNG was born and educated in Vancouver and has lived since 1960 in Campbell River. Her husband, Captain Henry Young, operates a shipping service on the west coast of Vancouver Island.

Mrs. Young has published over 100 illustrated articles, mostly on natural history subjects, in magazines throughout Canada, U.S. and abroad. She is currently making a series of portraits of British Columbia wildflowers, a project she has been working on intermittently for years. She sees no end to it in the near future — a happy state of affairs since taking pictures is her favorite activity and she hopes to publish a book of flower portraits.

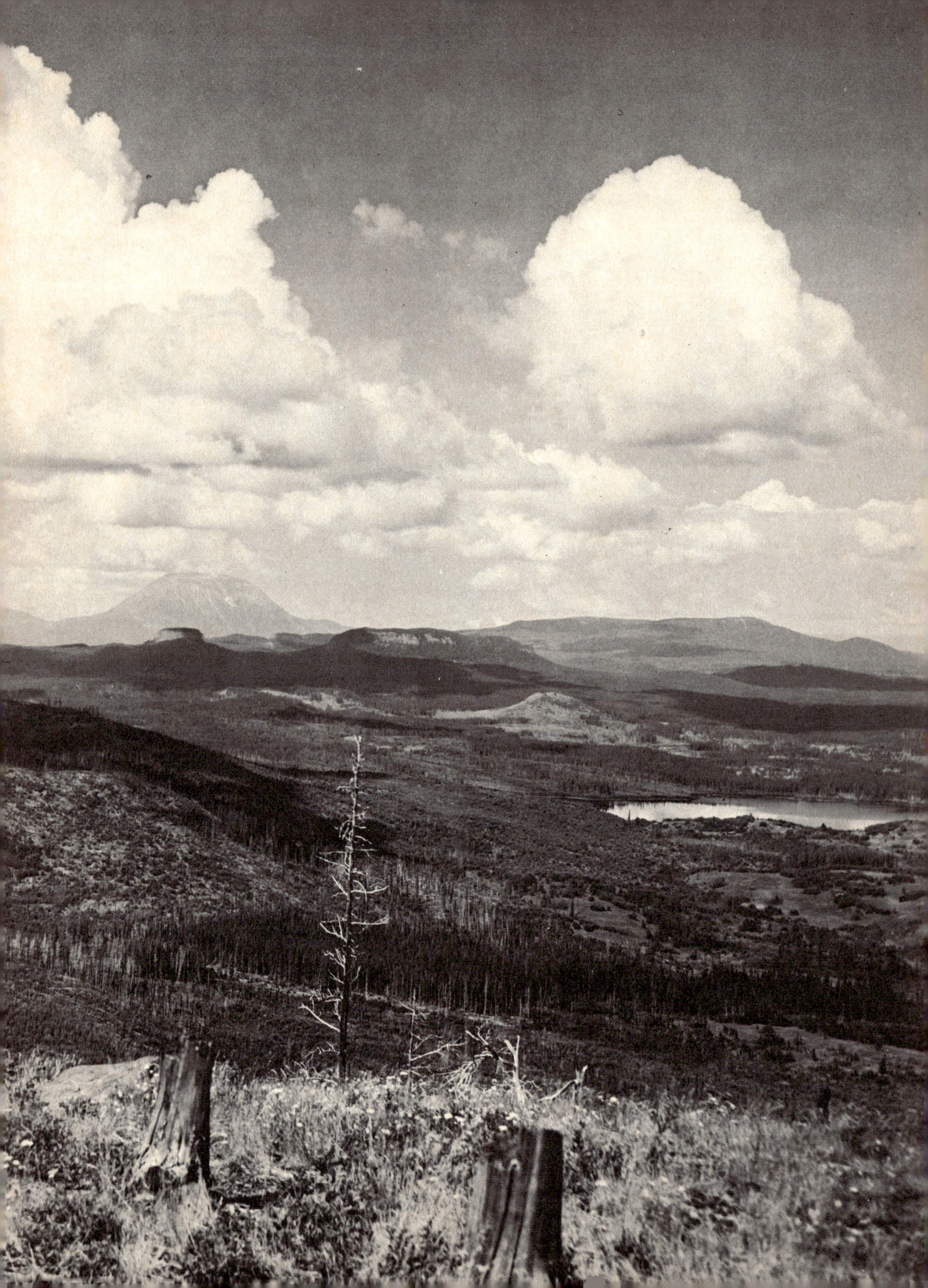

We Pioneered

by ARTHUR SHELFORD

A pioneer farmer recalls people and events during fifty-six years spent on the land in the Ootsa Lake district of Central British Columbia.

In 1908 the author left his position with the post office in England and immigrated to Canada. For two years he worked at various jobs then with his brother, Jack, decided to go farming in the Ootsa Lake country of Central British Columbia. Access to this beautiful, but remote, lake-dotted region was by sternwheel steamer 180 miles up the Skeena River to Hazelton, then 150 miles by trail through virtually uninhabited wilderness. With a packhorse carrying their tent and basic necessities, the brothers hiked into the district and selected two parcels of land. Since Hazelton was then the nearest government administrative centre, they had to walk back the 150 miles to register their land.

With our land recorded, we now had to purchase an outfit of food and all other necessary supplies to carry us through the coming winter and get them to our new "home." It was fortunate that Jack had had lots of experience buying outfits during his years of trapping in Alaska. I am afraid I would have left out a lot of necessary things and, when your nearest store is about 150 miles away, you can't pop in for something you have forgotten.

Our grub supply was entirely staples: 600 lbs. of flour, 200 of beans, 200 of rice, 200 of sugar, 100 of bacon, enough rolled oats and cornmeal for breakfast cereals, with dried apples for fruit, and then odds and ends such as baking powder, baking soda and salt. Last, a good supply of tea, with a limited amount of condensed milk and a little canned butter.

For other supplies we had candles, our only source of light, and a good supply of traps for Jack had done a lot of trapping in Alaska and this was one means we intended to use to bring in money. Jack had sufficient carpenter's tools, but we had to take in cross-cut saws and, for cutting lumber, a never-to-be-forgotten whipsaw. Cooking utensils, winter clothes such as moccasins, rubbers and mitts, different size nails, a couple of knock-down sheet-iron stoves and a few odd tools just about completed our outfit. Then came the matter of getting it transported. We decided to buy two more packhorses and soon became the owners of Billy and Romeo.

But three horses were not enough for our stuff, so we hired an Indian, Tom Campbell, with several packhorses, to take the greater part of the load for the first ninety miles. After Tom Campbell left us we had to relay three times with our three horses for the last fifty miles. Altogether, we hiked another 300 miles on this trip—800 in all during the summer.

It was now September 7th and we had to hustle to get

Arthur Shelford, his wife, Millie, and Laddie about 1950. By then he had already spent forty years in the Ootsa Lake country.

Opposite is Nadina Mountain and the country typical of the region where the author spent a happy fifty-six years.

everything in shape for winter. First we cut slough hay with a scythe to carry our horses through the winter. Fortunately, the weather turned to a beautiful period of Indian summer, and for three weeks we had warm days and cloudless skies.

With the hay up, we started building a cabin of jackpine logs. About this time, we got our first experience with a form of torture called "whipsawing." We had to have lumber for doors, windows, the floor, and enough to make a small boat which was needed for net fishing on Ootsa Lake. Since the nearest sawmill was over seventy miles away in the Bulkley Valley, with no road for the first fifty, we cut our lumber by hand.

I had seen several saw-pits in our village in England, but in Canada pits are not used. Instead, a stand about seven feet high is made right in the timber with trees as posts. The saw logs are rolled up on it after being squared on opposite sides. Then one man stands on top and pulls the saw up, while the other stands below and pulls it down. It is commonly said that on the frontier whipsawing has broken more partnerships than anything else.

By the time we had got our cabin in shape it was the end of October. We had by now thoroughly looked over the land and decided that there was plenty for both of us. It was therefore necessary that I make another trip to Hazelton to abandon my first pre-emption and stake on one almost adjoining Jack's.

Away I went on another 300-mile round trip. I have wondered since why I didn't use one of the horses, but I didn't and just hoofed the whole way. Averaging fifteen to twenty miles a day, it took about three weeks, but the last fifty miles were tough since there was nearly a foot of snow to trudge through. Fortunately, three of our future neighbors were ahead of me with packhorses, so the trail was fairly well broken. Even so, it was pretty hard going for I was carrying over fifty lbs., besides two blankets and a pair of snowshoes. The snowshoes were the real joke since I didn't realize the labor they would have saved me. Also I did not know how to use them, so ignorance was not bliss in this case.

Jack soon put me wise to the proper use of snowshoes and the general methods of trapping for he had spent about four years in Alaska, where he had trapped every winter. While his trapping lore was most useful, there was one part of his Alaskan experience much the reverse. In Alaska the country he travelled was mostly flat and over muskeg with little timber. He therefore used a dog-sleigh or a hand-sleigh for his winter transportation. When I returned from my 300-mile walk to Hazelton, I found that he had already made a hand-sleigh and, since I was to do most of the trapping away from home, I had to slash out a sleigh trail. This was quite a job since the timber was often thick. But I soon learned that trail cutting was nothing compared to pulling the sleigh over the rough, rolling country, heavily loaded as it was with stove, traps, tent, bedding, and grub.

My first tent camp was at Peaked Hill, about five miles from home. From there I cut more trail and got my first taste of winter muskrat trapping. We had a cold spell early in January when it got down to fifty-five below zero. Believe me, playing with traps in water at that temperature is no picnic. I had to carry a towel and use it at every muskrat house but it soon got wet and frozen. Some nights when I returned from cutting trail I would go right into the tent in my snowshoes and light the fire, and then look around for something to eat. Alas, everything was frozen — bread, beans, even the condensed milk. However, a tent soon warms up and it was not long before I ate.

Some people might think that life in a tent in such temperatures is a great hardship, but it really isn't. A thick layer of spruce boughs kept my bed and the rest of the floor insulated from the snow, and I could light a fire in the morning while lying in bed and thus warm the tent before getting up. Winter life in a tent, however, isn't the essence of comfort and anything lower than forty below is miserable. At this temperature even a candle won't function properly since the heat cannot melt the outside wax and the flame burns down the centre until it goes out for lack of air. Fortunately, cold spells seldom lasted longer than two weeks, and usually less than that.

While life on a trapline may seem lonely and monotonous, it is neither to a person of the right temperament. There is plenty of work, what with walking fifteen to

A form of torture called "whip-sawing," or cutting lumber by hand. The photos on the opposite page show Hazelton in 1910 and packhorses in the Bulkley Valley, part of the route followed by the author on the two round trips he made to Hazelton the first year. To stake and record his land he walked some 600 miles.

twenty miles a day to check traps, stretching pelts, cooking, cutting firewood, repairing snowshoes and similar chores. I had no reading matter on the trapline except the directions on the condensed milk cans, which were read and re-read a great number of times.

I didn't see Jack very often that winter. I went home only every three weeks or a month, even then sometimes he was away on a trapline of his own. We did not get mail all winter since our nearest post office was fifty miles away and didn't see our neighbors until spring. Jack, however, was used to such loneliness. In Alaska he spent all one winter trapping on the Kuskokwim River in the shadow of Mt. McKinley without seeing a single person.

During the following summer we learned that quite a few people had settled before we arrived in 1910 and we got to know them.

I believe that the first man to spend a winter in the Ootsa country was Jake Henkel, but the next year he moved to the north shore of Francois Lake where he spent the rest of his life and established a fine home and farm. The government ferry which operates on Francois Lake is named in his memory.

The first permanent settlers on Ootsa Lake were three men who in 1904 came via Kemano, an Indian village on the Coast where today the huge hydro-electric generating station of Alcan is situated. They had to climb the Coast Mountains, drop down to Tahtsa Lake, then follow the Tahtsa River and continue for miles along Ootsa Lake, where they staked land. One of them was Harry Morgan, who remained till his death in 1936. He was one of our most colorful settlers, engaged in the early years in bringing supplies by pack train over the Bella Coola trail.

In our neighborhood, which later was called Wistaria, were two Northern Irishmen, Bob and Jim Nelson, and their Irish-Canadian partner, Kelly, who came in 1908, and who are now all dead. Olaf Anderson arrived in 1907 and as I write is still going strong at seventy-nine, doing lots of work and really enjoying life. Mark Brennan, a little Newfoundlander, George Lawson and Shorty Matheson completed our population in 1910. But since most of them were

The upper two photos show caribou above timberline and Eutsuk Lake in what is today Tweedsmuir Provincial Park. During his early years in the country the author trapped in this lofty region. The other photo is of the fledgling community of Burns Lake on the Grand Trunk Pacific Railway in 1917. From Burns Lake, the author's farm was over sixty miles away by wagon, boat and packhorse.

away part of the year earning grub-stakes at different jobs along the Grand Trunk Pacific Railway then being constructed across Central B.C. to Prince Rupert, we saw them infrequently.

At Ootsa Lake was another small pocket of about twenty settlers. Not a very big population stretched over thirty miles, but what we lacked in numbers was made up for by the friendliness and hospitality of everyone.

It is unfair to pick out anyone special for it was just about the same wherever one went and, even today, that spirit of hospitality is still strong. One reason for this spirit is those pioneer women who braved the long hard trails into the country, then settled to make the best homes they could for their husbands and children.

Mrs. Mitchell of Oklahoma and Mrs. Eakin from the Fraser Valley were both quite middle-aged when they came in together over the Bella Coola trail. For the greater part of the way those two women walked, one of them packing a stable lantern the whole distance. Horses could not be spared for riding, and Bill Eakin even put a pack on one of the cows they were bringing in.

Then there was young, slight Mrs. Morgan who came in over the same trail with husband and little son, Jimmy. Not long after she gave birth to the first white child in the entire district. The nearest doctor and hospital were 150 miles away, and the only attendant at little Lulu's birth was her father. In 1912, another pioneer woman, Mrs. Sandy Thompson of Tatalrose on the south shore of Francois Lake, tried to reach Hazelton hospital by saddle horse to have her first baby. However, the stork arrived early and little Jacobina had the distinction of being born under a spruce tree in lonely Buck Flats, the only midwife her father. Anyway the children seem to have suffered no harm and they are now not only mothers, but also grandmothers.

In 1911 a girl from an English Midlands town arrived at Hazelton to marry the eldest of the Bennett boys, and she had to make the journey of 150 miles to Ootsa Lake by saddle horse. A little later a Scottish girl from the Orkney Islands made the same trip from Hazelton. She was Mrs. George Lawson, a near neighbor and friend for many years. I never forgot her story of when she first arrived in Hazelton.

"When Geordie and I went to breakfast at the Omineca Hotel the first morning I was there," she recalled, "the waitress came and asked me if I wanted mush. I didn't ken what she was talking about and I said 'What's mush, anyway?' And I found out it was porridge.

"Then, later, we were around town talking to folks and when one man learned I was going to Ootsa Lake he said, 'How you going to get there, are you going to mush in?' Well, I was all muddled up again until I found out that he meant was I going to walk in.

"The same day Geordie and I were walking up the street past the Ingenika Hotel and there was a crowd watching two men fighting and we stopped to take a look. Pretty soon one of the lookers-on shouted, 'Hit him in the mush, Jake.'

"And right there," she concluded, "I figured Canada must be all mush."

None of these women had an easy life, but they took it in their stride and left a host of kindly memories with the folks who knew them.

During the summers of 1911-12, Jack and I were kept more than busy building fences and outbuildings, packing supplies from Hazelton, tending the garden, clearing land and similar labor. But in 1913 we concentrated on building a house for Jack was considering marrying a girl in England. We got out logs and squared them on three sides for a two-storied house thirty-two by twenty-six feet. The logs gave us plenty of trouble, for neither of us had used a broadaxe, and big spruce logs, about sixteen inches at the butt end, take a lot of hewing to square on three sides. On top of that, we had to skid each of them over a mile and a half.

By fall we had the log part of the house built and enough lumber whip-sawed for the roof, floors, and partitions, so Jack was able to get away just after Christmas. But since the Grand Trunk Pacific Railway was not yet completed, he walked over one hundred miles before he made contact with the necessary transportation.

Jack returned in early June 1914, having successfully concluded his matrimonial arrangements which called for his bride-to-be, Safie, to come over in the summer of 1915. The house now became a priority item and our time, other than that spent packing supplies and haying, was concentrated on getting the house ready. It was quite a job since our whip-saw lumber was usually not of an even thickness and the edges needed a lot of planing. Also the floor and ceiling joists and partition uprights had to be hewn out with axes, while Jack made all the windows and doors from our own lumber.

In August, the outbreak of World War I complicated matters. Since we were busy haying and never left the farm, and our nearest neighbors lived about ten miles away, it was six weeks before we learned that war had been declared.

What to do now had to be decided. Finally, in view of the work to be done to prepare Jack for his coming venture into matrimony and to enable him to look after our growing herd of cattle, we decided that, for the time at least, we would stay put. Everyone felt that the war would last only a short while, and the meagre news that we got didn't give us much information on which to act. We just kept on with a view to getting Jack settled and in shape to take care of things on his own.

When spring came and the time was nearing when Safie was to sail, the *Lusitania* was sunk. This, of course, brought a great deal of uncertainty into her plans. But, after an exchange of cables, which in itself was not easy since our nearest telegraph office was over sixty miles away, it was decided that she should take the chance.

Jack went to Montreal to meet her where they were married and, in due course, arrived at Burns Lake station on the newly completed railway. From there Safie was introduced to the rougher side of life in our country. First, fifteen miles by wagon to Francois Lake, followed by a night in an empty cabin, then a trip of forty miles in a little boat powered with a small outboard to Nadina at the head of Francois Lake. Here I met them with packhorses for the remaining miles of the journey to Safie's new home.

After Safie's arrival we continued work on the house and by the spring of 1916 had Jack's place fixed up so that he could manage. I decided to enlist and with Alan Blackwell, the youngest son of a neighbor, walked forty-five miles to Houston in one day. Since there was no train we continued thirty miles along the track to Telkwa and caught the train to Hazelton.

Alan passed his examination without trouble, but when I came before Dr. Wrinch he wanted to turn me down because of flat feet. I asked him what flat feet implied with regard to a soldier. "Why," he said, "you can't march."

"I may not be able to march," I said, "but I walked the forty-five miles to Houston over a rough, muddy road in twenty-five hours."

"Yes" he replied, "but you couldn't move the next day."

"Maybe, but I walked thirty miles along the track to Telkwa that day and I will take an eighty-pound pack on my back and walk up the Bulkley Valley against any man you like to choose."

"Well," said the pioneer doctor, "if that is the way you feel about it I guess I had better pass you."

Editor's note: During his military service, the author rose from private to Company Sergeant-major and took part in several of the bloodiest battles of World War I, including Vimy Ridge, Passchendaele and Arras. Here, on September 2, 1918, he was wounded in the shoulder. He spent the winter of 1918-19 in various English hospitals and met a nurse whom he eventually married. He left for Canada early in April.

On Easter Day I finally arrived back at Houston and next morning set out for home, using the familiar "shanks pony" since there was no other transportation. The trip was tough for soon after leaving the Bulkley Valley I struck snow up to eighteen inches deep and walking was not easy. It was a relief to reach home and receive a warm welcome from Jack and Safie and two tiny nephews I had never seen.

There was one sad side to my homecoming. Alan Blackwell, who had walked out with me to enlist, did not return. He was killed near Mons six days before the war ended.

The period of World War I and just after were not kind to our district. With the completion of the Grand Trunk Pacific Railway, very little work was available. Also, the market for even the small amount of farm produce had dwindled. Nevertheless, there was steady progress in

In the top photo three pioneer families—Shelfords, Blackwells and Larsons—pose outside the author's home after church service in 1937. The other photo, taken in 1915, is of the last team of oxen to be used in the Francois Lake district. On the opposite page are the author's brother, Jack, and sister, Flora, in 1940 and Jack's farm in 1922. The cabin which the brothers built in 1910 is at right foreground. The lower photo shows the Francois Lake ferry *Jacob Henkel*, named after a pioneer who settled on the north bank of the lake.

many ways: cattle herds were reaching sizeable proportions, trapping still provided many with an income, a few mining prospects supplied some work, and, about 1922, the timber industry began to develop.

The population on Ootsa Lake also received a boost with the influx of several large families, notably the Mohrs, Priests and Van Tines. As usual, these new settlers consisted mostly of people who took the rough with the smooth, the only kind of much use in a country like ours.

For instance, there was the mother, two sisters, and girl cousin of Charlie Hinton who came right from London, all of them knowing nothing about life outside a city. "Old Lady Hinton," as the mother was always termed, was well into her sixties when she came. The journey of more than fifty miles from Houston, in a wagon over rough roads, must have been a trial for she was of heavy build and somewhat lame. But she took it like a thoroughbred, as she did, too, the often far-from-easy life afterwards.

The biggest boost to the population was the arrival of Mr. and Mrs. Harrison with eleven children from just over twenty to babies. This influx of young men and women gave community life quite a shot in the arm.

At this period, public utilities began to appear. A Post Office had been established at Ootsa Lake and in 1916 Wistaria also got one, with mail coming in once a week from Burns Lake.

Later, another Post Office was established between Wistaria and Ootsa Lake. Since this one was in the vicinity where the Hinton family lived, it was named Streatham in memory of the London suburb where they came from.

Another Post Office was later established on Francois Lake and first run by Mr. and Mrs. Newgard. Since their christian names were Lee and Nora, it was called Noralee.

About this time, too, stores were established at Ootsa Lake and Nadina, at the head of Francois Lake. They were another big step forward. Previously, I had had to make three or four trips by sleigh each winter to Houston, trips that were far from pleasant if the weather did not cooperate. There were only about three habitations on the whole fifty miles and each trip usually took a week.

Meanwhile, we all were searching to find the best way of making a living. When cattle prices slumped badly in the early 1920's, many turned to shipping cream and then to growing different kinds of grass seed for which our district proved suitable. Several high awards were won for timothy seed at the Chicago and Toronto Winter Fairs. Another line of effort carried on quite strongly from the late 1920's was fur-farming, mostly fox and mink. This industry did well until the start of World War II when it declined and finally died. The chief reason was that fresh meat, mostly snowshoe rabbits and fish, became so hard to get that too much time had to be spent hunting and fishing.

The district also moved ahead in other ways. About 1920 we got our first doctor at Southbank, on the south side of Francois Lake, and a few years later a small hospital. In the midst of all this change and general progress I also started a new way of life. In 1922 I married one of the Nursing Sisters of the Lord Derby Hospital in England. By now, Millie had taken a post in a hospital at Kuala Lumpur in Malaya, and I ended up meeting her at Victoria where she landed from one of the Empress boats.

A Victoria friend who had taught school at Wistaria the previous year generously arranged for us to be married from his sister's house, and Millie was made to feel really at home. My friend's thoughtfulness gave our wedding that homey touch which it would otherwise have lacked, and we have been everlastingly grateful.

When we finally arrived at Wistaria Post Office we had a noisy reception from nearby residents who welcomed us with jangling cow bells, tin pans and any other contraption that made a good row. Also there was brother Jack with the democrat to take us to his home until our own was ready. Millie landed into a real bunch of Shelfords, for Jack now had four sons aged from six years to eighteen months. Sister Flora was there also, for she had decided to

Except for the lumber, which he and his brother sawed by hand, the author constructed his house and outbuildings single-handed. In the 1930's he built his barns, lower photo, the same way, hewing the timbers for the roof trusses with a broadaxe.

come and see how she liked British Columbia.

The summer of 1922 proved to be the driest on record, with no rain between April 15 and August 15, when we had a heavy shower, then no more until September 15. Most of our crops were light, especially those on land which had been broken and planted to tame hay. Fortunately, the growth of wild hay on unbroken land was reasonably good and Jack had to take horses and machinery to some natural slough-hay meadows at the head of Ootsa Lake, about eight miles away, and put up as much as we still needed.

This left me alone to look after the farm and progress as well as I could with my house-building, a slow job for one man. Our house was twenty-six by twenty-six feet inside, with seven rooms and a cellar. I have mentioned that we now had a sawmill in the district, but only rough lumber was available. This meant that lumber for floors, doors, window casings, and similar parts all had to be planed by hand, entailing a vast amount of work. Added to this was the fact that the lumber was green and had to be tacked into position and left to dry before being permanently nailed. But by early spring our home was sufficiently complete for us to move in, with further work proceeding as opportunity arose.

When I see the ease and speed with which the modern generation can build a house with dressed lumber, plywood, tiles of all descriptions for floors and ceilings, and windows and doors and their fittings ready made, I wonder how we pioneers found time and energy to build the houses we did. But we did, and those houses are still lived in, and though maybe not as stylish as the newer type, still contain all the elements for comfortable living.

The years from the time of our marriage to 1939 passed in a routine manner but then came a string of upsets in our quiet and secluded way of living. The first change — and the greatest — was the outbreak of World War II. Most of our young folk joined the armed forces, including three boys of my brother, Jack, leaving one son to help Jack and Safie keep the farm running.

On the whole, casualties were not heavy among the boys of the district. Jack's three boys came home safely, though Hugh lost most of his left arm.

He was taken prisoner in Normandy the day after D-Day, and while being marched between two points near Tours our Air Force unknowingly strafed the column of prisoners. Hugh was wounded in the leg, but not too seriously. Later, the Germans made an effort to get a trainload of prisoners to Germany. Again our Air Force came into the picture, strafing the train and doing serious damage to the prisoners. This was where Hugh got his arm so badly injured that it had to be amputated, the job being well done by the German doctor.

Another unfortunate casualty happened to a young Scot, Jock MacIvor, who had lived and worked with us through the depression of the 1930's. He joined the Army but spent most of his time of service in England, in due course marrying a Scots lass. Returning home in September 1945, he spent two days with us and then went to visit other friends. A few days later, while on a hunting trip, he accidentally shot himself and died.

Our family group also suffered casualties. My brother-in-law died in 1944 and Jack's wife followed in 1945. This was the first bad break amongst us oldsters, and was further increased in 1951 and 1953 when brother Jack and our good neighbor, Ed Blackwell, passed on.

Thus, in a few short years, our group of families was badly broken up. When my sister moved to the south of the province, only Mrs. Blackwell and ourselves were left of the early settlers.

But great as were those changes, a far greater one was in the offing for us. In 1965 Millie and I decided that it was time we got off our old farm and moved to a place where life would be easier. As many people know, the life of a wife on a pioneer farm is a very busy one. Besides the routine work around the home, three days a week can be written off for washing, churning, and bread-making, while the chickens take a lot of attention, as does the lone pig kept for home consumption. But, in addition to all this, Millie did most of the work in the garden and helped often with the milking when we kept several cows. She always gave a lot of help in the hayfield and in harvesting potatoes and turnips and in other lines of endeavor too numerous to mention.

For many years I had to go to Victoria as a member of the Advisory Board of Farmers' Institutes, and was usually absent for over two weeks. During that time, Millie looked after the farm herself, preferring to do so rather than have anyone to help her.

But it was often not a bit easy for her, with all the feeding, the waterholes to chop and the hundred and one other chores to attend to. Sometimes the temperature dropped to twenty below and lower; at other times considerable snow fell to make moving around difficult. I think the toughest break she had was the winter when several of our cows decided to calve while I was away. I returned to a very proud wife for she had six calves to show from five cows, one cow having twins.

In 1965, however, Millie developed a nasty attack of arthritis, while I, at over eighty, was beginning to feel that the work was more than I wanted. Our farm of over 480 acres needed a lot of fencing and since many of the fences were, like myself, getting rather ancient, replacement work was necessary. This work, added to the routine of the farm, was too much. For instance, in a summer with pitch forks and horses we put up sixty tons of hay, besides harvesting three tons of potatoes, seven of turnips and a half ton of carrots, as well as other vegetables.

Added to this was the fact that we were sixty miles from the railway, doctors, hospital and other necessary services, while our Post Office was four miles away and our nearest store thirty-five miles.

We listed the farm with a real estate firm and sold it early in 1966. On July 28, after being on the farm for fifty-six years, we left for Victoria where we planned to spend our retirement.

It might be expected that we would feel the break of leaving our old home very much. I can truthfully say, however, that when I drove the pickup through the gate with our few personal belongings, I left everything behind and have scarcely given a thought to the old place. We had spent all those happy years there but it was now a thing of the past. Our life lay ahead — not behind.

We arrived in Burns Lake after having a flat tire on the journey out. We spent two days at the home of our nephew, John, and finished all our business. Then, in the evening of my eighty-first birthday we boarded the train for Prince George. Thus ended our long life in the north. ■

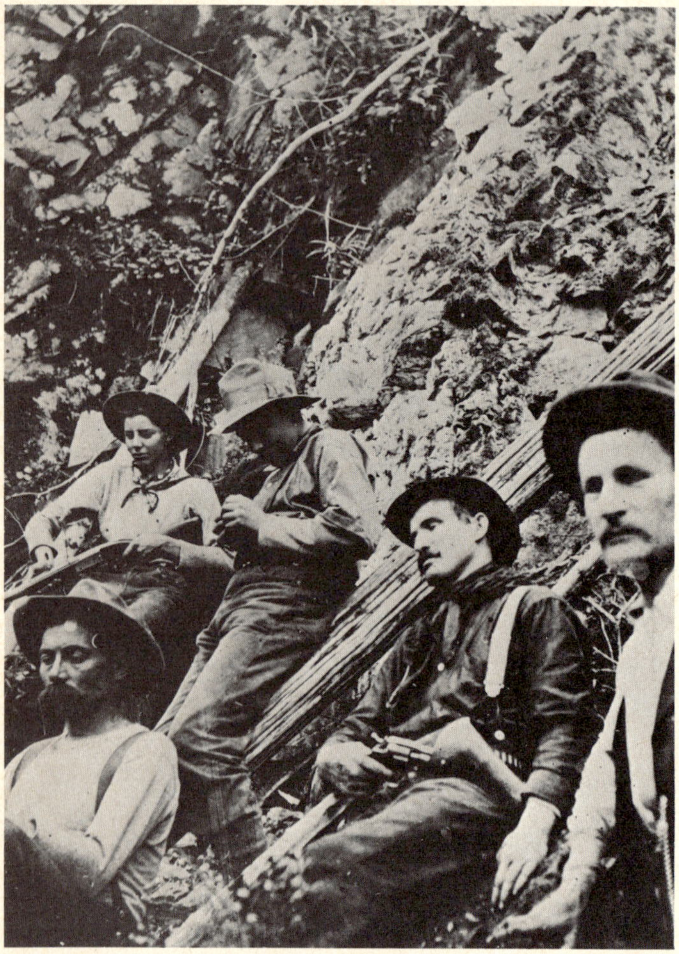

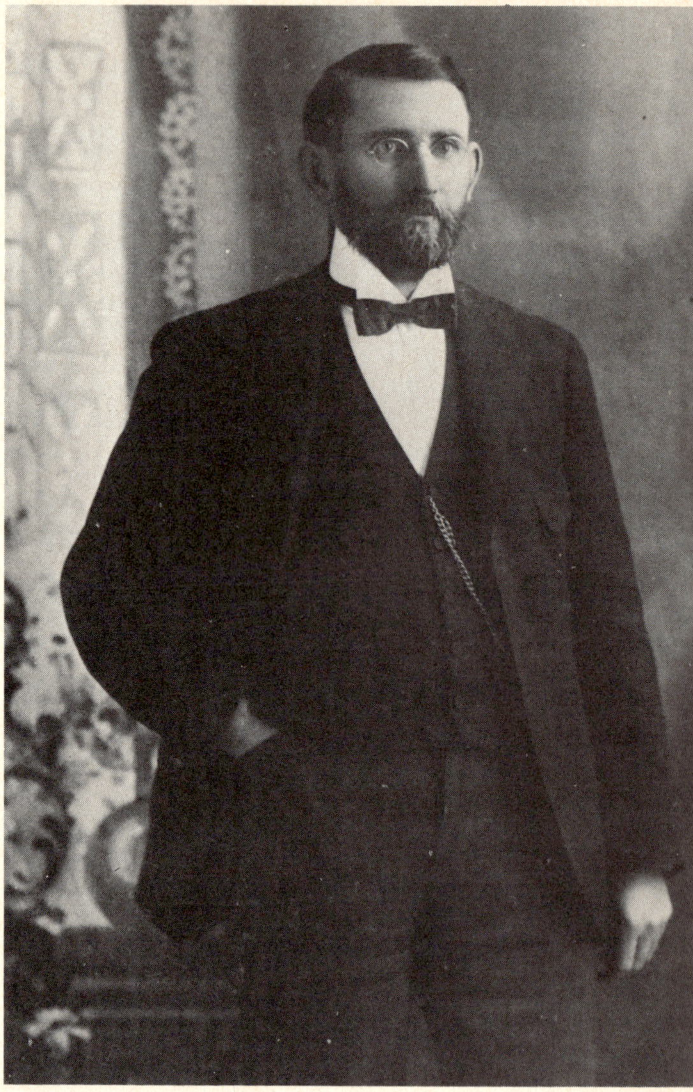

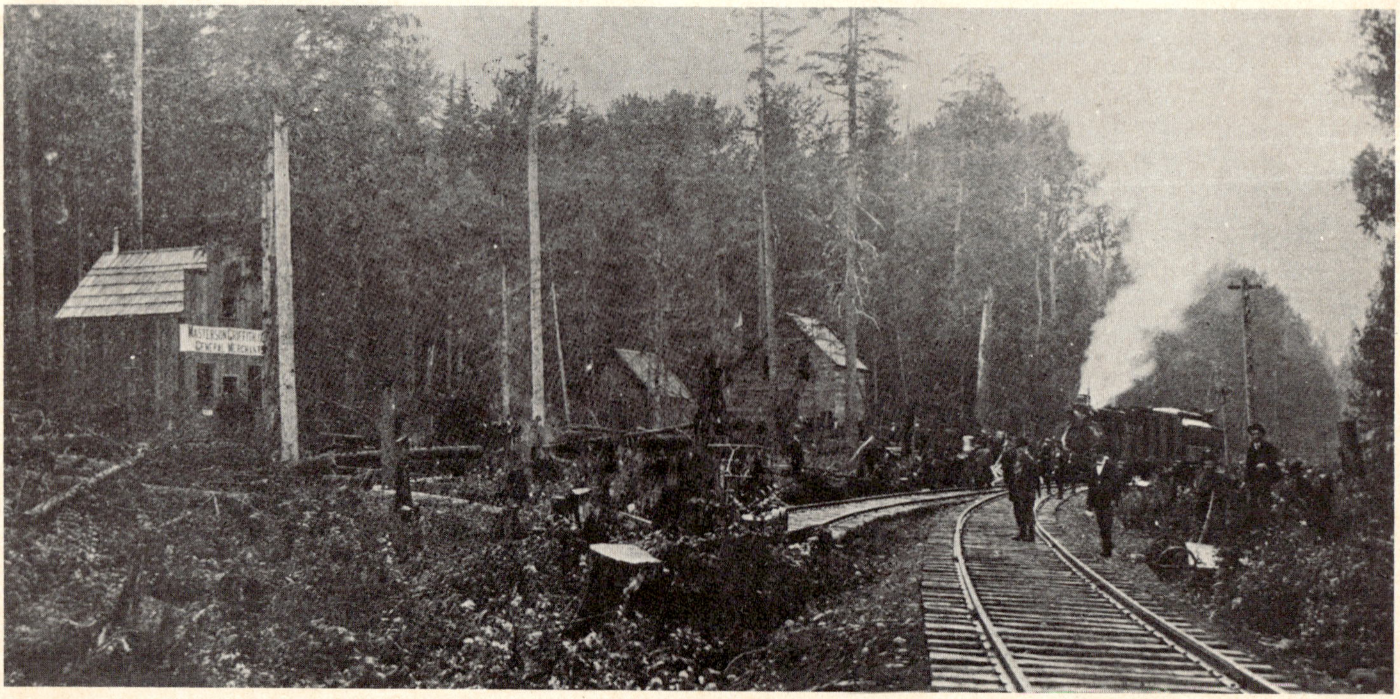

POPLAR CREEK and the COLONEL of the KOOTENAYS

In the early 1900's a roving journalist named R. T. Lowery started papers in several Kootenay-Lardeau mining towns. Their pages are an uninhibited account of people and events in communities which frequently boomed into life then quietly faded into history.

by ELSIE G. TURNBULL

In the early 1900's gold-seekers swept into the rugged Lardeau country of southeastern British Columbia, searching for precious metals in the steep glacier-crowned peaks above Trout Lake and the Lardeau River. Promising claims were staked along many tributary streams and several mining communities sprang up. Chief among these were Ferguson, Camborne, Trout Lake City and Poplar Creek. Of them, only Trout Lake City has survived. The others have been reclaimed by the forest but in their heyday all flourished and were hailed as great mining centers.

Poplar Creek, also referred to as Poplar City, Poplar Creek Camp and plain Poplar, was located on a turbulent stream that joined the lower Lardeau River about fifteen miles above the head of Kootenay Lake. It was born in 1903 when three prospectors, finding nuggets "large enough to hang your hat on," located a claim they called Lucky Jack.

The *Kaslo Kootenaian* newspaper noted that gold particles were "sticking out in plain sight all along the lead" and that "one can leave the cushions of the passenger coach on the A & K Railway and after a stroll of half a minute be upon the ground claimed by the locators."

The Lucky Jack lay less than 100 yards from the Kaslo and Lardo-Duncan Railway (a branch of the CPR) which ran from the head of Kootenay Lake to the foot of Trout Lake. Scores of other claims were quickly staked, and a store built on the creek. By September a townsite had been laid out and thus was born Poplar Creek. In October the *Kootenaian* noted that the community is "thoroughly imbued with the idea of incorporation at once under the Speedy Incorporation of Towns Act and putting in their own water works and electric light plant without the intervention of companies." The paper also noted that growth was "solid, sound and without the appearance of that detestable disease called boom."

By December the community had its own newspaper, *The Nugget*. Its purpose, stated editor-owner Robert Thornton Lowery, was to tell "the world about the glories of the new El Dorado."

In his first issue he noted: "As a rule we like to get into a camp before the pianos and canary birds, but on our arrival last week we found these things had preceded us, in addition to a large number of birds that are not canaries. The camp is a little over 100 days old and has six hotels, five of which are producing every day, four stores, a livery stable, a laundry etc., and more gold in the hills around the burg than we have ever got close to since we first planted a set of stakes in the shadow of the grand old mountains of the Great West. So, seeing that Poplar was in need of a paper to make known its wonderful resources and fight for its rights, we have hoisted our flag on the banks of Poplar Creek and printed upon it the immortal words of Macbeth. The Nugget is small but like the camp from which it hails it will soon grow so large that all the world can see it without straining their eyesight."

While *The Nugget* didn't reach the optimistic heights envisioned by its founder it did gather, as Lowery noted, "local concentrates from the editor's upper stope." (Stope is a mining term meaning a working from which ore is extracted.) Lowery himself was a small, bearded man who had acquired the nickname "Colonel" during his travels and was always given this title. He was bespectacled and mild mannered, but this outward appearance concealed an acid wit and sharp perception. It was not long before his reading public was either titillated or shocked by his uninhibited comments, especially about religion and what he considered injustice to the miners.

He was born in Ontario and arrived in the Slocan area of the West Kootenay at the age of 34. He soon made his presence felt in the journalistic world. Starting with the *Kaslo Claim* in the spring of 1893, he published a paper at one time or another in most of the Slocan camps. When hard times forced closure of the Kaslo paper he moved his press

---

R. T. Lowery, upper right on the opposite page, was a mild looking man with an acid wit who either shocked or titillated his readers.

At far left, opposite page, miners guard the Lucky Jack claim at Poplar Creek, May 1903.

In the photo opposite are the first buildings at Poplar Creek in the summer of 1903. By December, business places included six hotels, four stores and a newspaper.

to Nakusp and began printing *The Ledge,* a news sheet which he described as "the leading excitement" and which he moved to New Denver, to Nelson, to Fernie and finally to Greenwood.

During his sojourn in the Kootenays he also initiated the *Sandon Paystreak,* the *Slocan Drill* of Slocan City and the *Poplar Nugget.* Not content with the weekly *Ledge* he published a monthly periodical which he heralded in advance: "Tomorrow *Lowery's Claim* will be shot into the journalistic sky. The light from it can be easily seen with a dollar." A couple of years later he "wrote, compiled, published and shipped a literary blend" called *Float* which, in his words, "tells about booze in Nelson, poker in the Silvery Slocan, gospel at Bear Lake and rain in New Denver."

Once he was forbidden to send *Lowery's Claim* through the mails because (as he said) "Authorities considered the prospector in charge of it was using too explosive a powder and became alarmed for fear that he would blow a hole through the universe." Another time an outraged churchgoer bought an entire issue and burned it in the stove. However, Lowery's brief stay in Poplar was free of controversy and *The Nugget* presents a candid picture of a short-lived mining camp.

First issues carried advertisements for several hotels:
"The Poplar Hotel.
Is the oldest hotel in Poplar and adjoins the Canadian Pacific Railway depot. The wet grocery department contains pure goods, any brand of which will produce optimistic results.
Armstrong & Almston.

"The Kaiser House.
Is convenient to the depot and has accommodation for 50 quiet guests. The nerve-bracers in the bar are free-milling and an orchestra provides music while the guests are at dinner. The landlord has studied human nature from Brazil to Alaska and knows the way to make a stranger feel at home.
Fred Kaiser, Proprietor.

"The Royal Hotel.
Has cocktails for the nervous, beer for the delicate, whiskey for the hardy mountaineer, and cigars for those who prefer narcotic to alcoholic stimulants.
August Buffalo, Manager.

"Hotel Inn.
The only hotel in town that is plastered. Rates $1.50 a day and up.
Hanson & Ostby."

"Poplar can boast of the nicest little Swede waiter girls in the world," Lowery noted, in offering his personal comments on the hotel service. "There is Gussie at the Grand who smiles on all alike, whether they are 'star' or otherwise; Ole at the Inn who affects the intellectual, wears glasses and is too bashful to speak; Martie at the Dominion, a new arrival who will get the grub to the table on time even if the soup does occasionally go down the customer's back."

In January 1904 *The Nugget* reported: "School will open in Poplar next week if the furniture arrives. J. J. Cameron is moving his school plant from Lardo here. Mr. Cameron is perhaps the only man in Canada who is owner of a complete school outfit. When school was opened in Lardo some years ago he had to put up cash for all necessary furniture. As he has never been re-imbursed for his outlay and as Lardo has about run out of population he has decided to move his school plant from Lardo to Poplar where it will run full time.

"The schoolteacher is expected on the Wednesday train. There is no necessity for young men appearing at the station in their best. She will, sooner or later, have to become accustomed to them in their digging clothes."

On June 10, 1903, that same J. J. Cameron and his wife became parents of the first child born in Poplar. In Lowery's words: "They are the proud possessors of the most valuable nugget yet found in the camp. It is a boy and tips the scales at ten pounds."

Lowery also commented on the state of religion in the new town: "Rev. George Findlay of Ainsworth went up on Wednesday's train to Trout Lake where he will preach and then go on to Camborne for Sunday services, returning next week. Missionaries in Kootenay have to work two shifts on weekdays and three on Sunday while the sleek, chicken-fed parson in the East has nothing to do but look wise and say 'Gee' and 'Haw.'"

"Church services will be held in the reading room of the Grand Hotel on Tuesday evening by Rev. S. J. Green of Kaslo Methodist Church."

"Gus Anderson of the Grand is not quite sure whether he is running an hotel or a church. He believes that it is up to some of the other hotel men to mix a little religion with their booze."

"The church is the only 'bust' business in Poplar. While we support seven saloons not even a parson can negotiate three squares daily. It can be said of western mining camps: 'Before the Lord erects a house of prayer, the devil builds a dozen taverns there.'"

Although he was caustic about church affairs, Lowery exuded optimism about the future of the settlement. "Poplar and Paradise are similar," he commented. "Both have gold in the streets, although the latter place beats us out on angels.

"Prosperity is pushing Poplar pretty well past the pessimistic period. Push, pluck and perseverance are bound to win out.

"The people of Poplar can now render medical, surgical, notorial, horological assistance to everyone requiring it for we have a physician and surgeon, watch and clock manufacturer, notary public, drug store, post-office, record office, meat market, grocery and clothing stores."

Early September was brightened by an unusual celebration. "Last week there were 'doings' in this burg," Lowery wrote. "It was one of the occasions on which every pros-

In addition to Poplar Creek, settlements born in the Lardeau during the 1895-1905 era included Ferguson, Comaplix and Camborne, opposite page in 1905. Their survival depended on mining or lumbering, but both industries proved unstable economic props and most of the communities disappeared. The photo below, taken in the early 1900's, shows the crew of the Lardeau mill.

pector drops down from the hills to spend a few days. There does not appear to be any prearranged time for these gatherings. It is just a 'swarming' time. On Monday without any apparent reason for it, the Rapid Creek contingent quit work and came to town. Tuesday, Poplar Creek commenced to move, the disturbance extending as far up as the Spyglass and on Wednesday, Tenderfoot, Cascade and Meadow Creeks began to move. On Thursday the town was pretty well filled with prospectors. Before Sunday there will probably not be a single prospector in town. It is strange that men working over a district, without any prearranged plan, will quit work and gather at a common centre within a few hours of each other. This frequently occurs in a mining camp."

"An alcoholic wave hit the camp," he noted, "and many there were who fell by the wayside. There were Gaelic and French and Swede and Norwegian and Dutch and Italian and United States so badly tangled up in the atmosphere that the dogs took to cover and Charlie Hanson's bear had convulsions. Justices of the Peace took to higher levels and Chataway's mules retired to the seclusion of the banks of the Tenderfoot. And yet the supply of exhilarants is more than equal to the demand."

As the year wore on, the editor's tone became less jaunty. At one time he remarked: "Although business does not appear very brisk, eight pack animals are kept busy every day taking supplies to creeks. The town seems dead but the hills are alive with men working claims." Before the approach of winter he estimated the season's assessment work as quite successful in regard to the showing of ore bodies but disappointing in the number of claims taken up. Reason for this lay in litigation involving the Lucky Jack claim.

Although the Lucky Jack originally sparked the rush to Poplar Creek, it was plagued with misfortune. It was staked as a lode deposit carrying gold values and was sold by the three locators to Great Northern Mines Ltd. But before the deal had been completed a placer claim was staked on the creek by a prospector whom the other men considered a claim jumper. They removed his posts and persuaded the Gold Commissioner to throw him into jail.

Feelings ran high and armed men stood guard over the Lucky Jack for a time. Rumor was rampant. The so-called claim jumper filed suit in the Supreme Court and obtained judgment in his favor. In the meantime, Great Northern Mines could not get a clear title to the property and development of the mine was delayed. Disparaging reports by the Provincial Mineralogist did nothing to relieve the gloom and Poplar's boom gradually collapsed. The Colonel left the creek in October and waved a sad farewell to the former Paradise.

"This week the Nugget, editor, printer, pressman and devil, hies himself to the railroad track and takes as nearly a southern course as the transportation companies have furnished for the convenience of those who work for the public and take their pay in the next world. The camp is all right but no camp can stand both claim jumpers and the supreme court of B.C. monkeying with it all the time. Vale, The late Nugget."

An out-of-court settlement was finally reached late in the year 1904 and Great Northern Mines began development, but by then it was too late to help the newspaper. At any rate gold values in the Lucky Jack and other properties proved to be pockety and irregular, not sufficient to make a mine.

Poplar disappeared from the mining scene but continued for a number of years as a small logging center. Today the bush has taken over and only the tumbledown remains of a cabin or two stand beside the highway on the banks of Poplar Creek.

After he left Poplar, the Colonel moved to Nelson, Fernie, and, in 1906, to Greenwood. He published his *Ledge* in all four communities, calling it "the oldest mining camp newspaper in British Columbia." He died of dropsy in 1921 at the age of 62.

Had he been asked to select an epitaph from his writings he would probably have chosen the following passage from the *New Denver Ledge* of August 9, 1906. It is the type of material that delighted or angered his readers.

"I have my own ideas in regard to religion, but I ask no one to accept them. I believe that every mind should be free to act according to the light within or without. I have located a short trail over the divide to the great beyond, but unlike creed trails, heaven is along mine at every step, and it is not necessary to die in order to get some of it. Other trails, said to lead where Peter takes the tickets, have all kinds of tolls and restrictions. The travellers along my trail each carry a pass that entitles them to all privileges at the end of the journey. None of them believe that the Creator is a fool or a demon....

"My trail has plenty of the sunshine of love, mercy, gentleness, kindness and other rays of light that bless and sweeten those who travel it. None of the pilgrims believe that God runs for the elect an eternal picnic of song, honey and harps on a golden floor up-stairs, while in the basement a heavenly Cape Nome is in operation, where the ice never clinks in the glass, and everybody has teeth, while the sulphur smokes eternally. They could not believe that God, represented as being all-powerful, would be so wicked as to keep untold millions in torment when a wave of his hand would close up hell forever. Only man, poor, weak, cowardly, unregenerate man could ever have created such a place. Poor man! what a sucker he is sometimes.

"Along my trail there are no costly churches built by people who live in poverty, and whose children often suffer for food, let alone education, while bishops and lesser clerical lights live on the tenderloin steaks of the land. None of my pilgrims wear their pantaloons out at the knees praying for God to change his program to suit their ideas or desires. No parson urges soldiers on my pike to throw lead and religion into pagans at the same time. It is a pleasant road that I have built, with others, to that great territory from whence no prospector has ever returned...."

Some of the mining communities such as Rossland, opposite page about 1900, flourished and developed into major communities. Others weren't so fortunate. Phoenix, for instance, in the early 1900's had a population of nearly 2,000, a newspaper, and buildings that included a hospital, three-storey Miners' Hall, hotels, banks, four churches and twenty-eight saloons. But after producing some $100 million in ore, local mines closed in 1919 and today only the graveyard and war memorial remain. Poplar Creek, too, has all but vanished. A few tumbledown buildings, below, are the only indication of a townsite largely overgrown with trees.

The canoe on the river bank at Quesnel in 1920. In the photo opposite a packtrain prepares to leave Fort St. James with supplies for Fort McLeod in 1914.

The top photo shows the sternwheel steamer *B.X.* at Fort George Canyon in 1911. Since the canyon was frozen over when the author and his party arrived, they had to manhandle their massive log canoe over the ice.

What was it, wondered Quesnel residents as the strange craft approached, a full-sized cookstove belching smoke and nine unshaven men manning the oars. It was the

LAST VOYAGE OF INTERIOR B.C.'S LARGEST CANOE

by E. M. COTTON

In 1911 the author was a member of a survey party working at Stuart Lake in Central B.C. At the time access to the area was extremely difficult. From the west it involved a 180-mile journey by sternwheeler steamer up the Skeena River to Hazelton, overland by horse or foot to 110-mile-long Babine Lake, then down the lake by rowboat to Babine Portage and across to Stuart Lake, about 350 miles in all.

The other access was by train from Vancouver to Ashcroft, up 215 miles of the Cariboo Wagon Road to Quesnel then northwest through some 150 miles of wilderness. An alternative route from Quesnel was 170 miles of water via the Fraser, Nechako and Stuart Rivers to Fort St. James.

When winter halted surveying, the party decided to return by the rivers to Quesnel. This account of their hazardous journey is courtesy of B.C. Historical Quarterly: The approach of cold weather early in November warned us that it was time to break camp and head down river for "Outside," or run the risk of being frozen in where we were for the winter. The camp's only means of travel was an old river scow, which unfortunately was not large enough to carry us all with safety. We decided that eight, including myself, would remain behind and try to find some other means of getting away before the freeze-up came. Failing that we would winter in Fort St. James.

We did our best to locate a boat but could find none large enough to carry eight men and equipment. We had almost given up when we heard about a large Indian dug-out canoe near Fort St. James. We were told that this canoe would more than fill our needs, in size at least.

It was certainly large enough! In fact it was believed to be the largest ever built in the Interior of British Columbia — fifty-five and one half feet long, and four feet wide. It was of the dug-out type, hewn from a single huge log. Strangely enough, it was made of cottonwood instead of the usual cedar. It had been used by the Hudson's Bay Company as a freighter on Takla Lake and, besides being old, it was almost paper thin in places. We realized that we were taking our lives in our hands to venture into those ice-filled rivers in such a craft. But beggars can't be choosers, and we felt that we had no alternative. We either had to take our chances with the river or stay where we were for the winter. Of the two we preferred the river. We took the precaution, however, of hiring as our pilot Jimmy Alexander, an Indian guide with the reputation of being the best fast-water canoeman in the country.

Our nine-member party must have been a memorable sight that cold December morning as we left Fort St. James in our odd craft. It was propelled by six large oars, three on each side, and steered by a huge fifteen-foot sweep at the stern (the canoe was too large for paddles). It was jammed with equipment, and with smoke pouring from the full-sized stove that we had erected on a platform at the rear, we must have looked like something left over from the flood.

For all its unsightliness, that stove certainly proved a comfort since it rained and snowed most of the time and, because we had no covering over the canoe, we felt the cold bitterly. We travelled without stopping all day and

In the photo on the opposite page H.B.C. employees unload freight at Fort St. James in August 1909. At the left of the men is a dug-out canoe but whether it is the one used by the author and his party two years later is unknown.
The photo below shows a dug-out canoe on Fraser Lake in 1905. These canoes were used extensively on the waterways of Central B.C.
In the lower photo the sternwheel steamer *Charlotte* is winched up Cottonwood Canyon in 1909. The Canyon was one of two dangerous stretches of water on the 170 miles between Fort St. James and Quesnel.

camped on shore at night. At intervals during the long cold day the men would leave their places at the oars and make their way back to the stove, where cook Harry Reid always had a steaming pot of soup or tea ready. This, followed by a comforting smoke by the fire, soon had us ready for another turn at the oars.

We had little or no trouble until we neared the Fraser River at Fort George. There we ran into large quantities of pancake ice which kept rubbing through the soft cottonwood of the canoe, forcing us to go ashore and find spruce gum to patch the leaks. In the ice area we were forced to stop for repairs five or six times a day. In sub-zero weather this was anything but a pleasant task.

Arriving at Fort George Canyon we found it completely frozen over, and the ice piled so high that we were forced to go ashore and carry, or rather slide, our huge canoe along the river bank to open water.

After clearing this obstacle we had smooth sailing until we reached dangerous Cottonwood Canyon. Here the water is exceedingly swift and foams and churns through the narrow rocky canyon at a great rate. Even the light and easily-handled river canoes seldom tried to run this tricky and extremely dangerous canyon. We knew that to attempt it in our clumsy fifty-five-footer was out of the question. We went ashore, and Jimmy Alexander went on ahead to size up the possibilities of portaging our equipment along the river bank. After some time, he came back to report that it would be impossible to carry the canoe on the shore, as the banks along the canyon were too steep, and covered with several feet of snow. That left us no alternative. We must run the canyon, fifty-five-footer or no.

This decided, we wasted no time in starting lest we lose our nerve, for we needed steady nerves for the task ahead. With our hearts in our mouths we started, and it seemed that we had no sooner left the shore than we felt the rush of the canyon. We gained momentum like a falling stone. Faster and faster we sped, cutting through the angry waters like an arrow. From the bow rose showers of spray to drench the feverishly straining oarsmen, whose oars seemed to barely touch the rushing waters.

Had it not been for Jimmy Alexander we never would have made it. He did a wonderful job of steering our clumsy craft through the dangerous maze of huge rocks. Time and again, by what seemed only inches, we missed great jagged rocks which would have torn gaping holes in the sides of the canoe, and in an instant consigned us to swift, certain death in the icy waters.

The swift maneuvering almost cost the life of Harry Reid. A sudden lunge of the canoe caused a section of the stove pipe to fall overboard. Harry made a wild grab for it, and was saved from falling overboard by Jimmy Alexander, who pulled him to safety by the seat of his trousers. After what seemed a lifetime, we finally got through. That ride was the fastest and most thrilling I ever had. It is great to look back upon. But never again!

After that, pancake ice was our only trouble. We made good progress, and at nightfall on the sixth day camped just a few miles from Quesnel, and were off to an early start the next morning. As we approached Quesnel we were surprised to see a large crowd lining the river bank awaiting our arrival. We were at a loss to explain the unexpected welcome until Mr. Collins, of the Hudson's Bay store, explained. We had been sighted as we rounded the bend of the river, about three miles above Quesnel, by Mr Allison, a druggist. The odd appearance of our craft, with the smoke pouring from our stove, aroused great curiosity as to just what was the queer type of ship approaching. Soon the whole village gathered to witness the arrival of the mysterious craft. We must have been a great sight at that, nine woefully tired and unshaven men in a giant six-oared, stove-cluttered canoe.

We soon had the canoe unloaded on the bank, and, having enjoyed the open-handed hospitality of the good people of Quesnel, we continued our journey homeward, traveling overland. We were sorry to leave our great canoe behind. It had served us faithfully and carried us through dangerous waters to safety. After we had gone the people of Quesnel erected a shelter over the canoe, and I believe it is still there.

The canoe remained on display for over thirty years but since cottonwood is not as durable as cedar, it gradually decayed and was finally pushed into the river. ∎

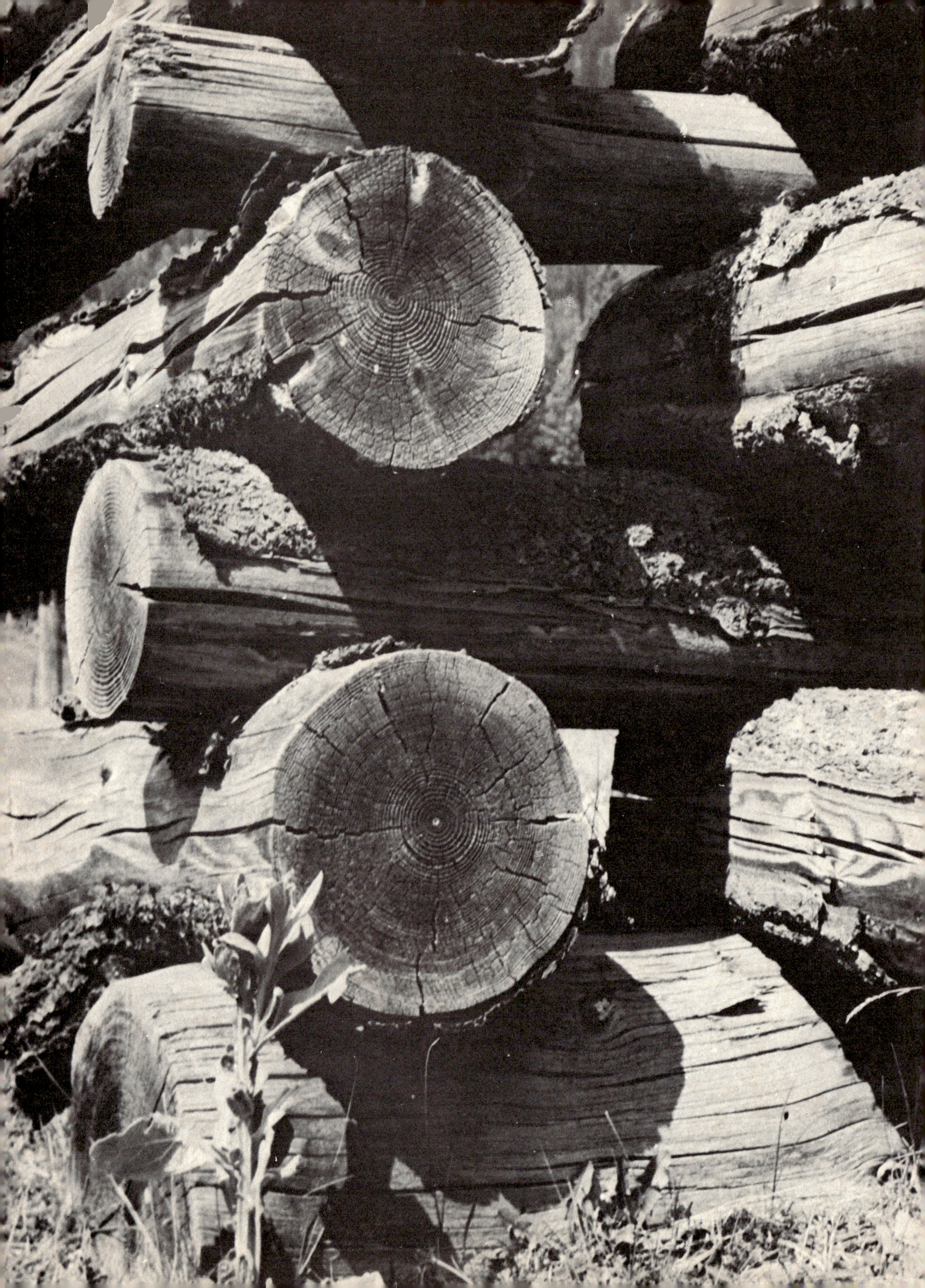

pioneer fences

Solid and durable, log fences form a picturesque pattern on the
British Columbia countryside, their variations in structure and design
reflecting the personality and ambition of the people who built them.　　by DONOVAN CLEMSON

Quite apart from their sentimental value as picturesque landmarks of the ranching landscape, log and rail fences are supreme from a pioneer's standpoint. No other fence can equal them in solidity, durability, and ease of maintenance. They are individualistic, too, since they come in a variety of patterns with modifications to suit the personality of the builder. On the whole, however, they have evolved into a few basic designs: post and rail, snake rail, stake and rider, log, and Russell. A common characteristic is that they are built almost entirely of wood, some of them without a nail or inch of wire for mile after mile.

To many people, the Russell fence is the most picturesque, although it wasn't designed to add charm to the scenery. It is a rancher's fence, long-lasting and trouble free, seldom seen outside ranching country. It straddles the ground and is easy to erect on all types of terrain since there are no posts to plant. Of rather ingenious construction, it is quickly set up and can be made into a very substantial fence. Some of the spidery looking samples, however, are poor recommendation for the design, being built of too slender rails which soon sag and give a flimsy appearance to the structure. There are many miles of Russell fence in the Cariboo and Chilcotin, some of them no doubt being converted snake-rail fences. The Russell, being economical of material, can be made from the remains of a snake-rail which zig-zags along, eight or ten rails to a panel, enough material for a Russell fence twice the length.

In building a Russell fence the initial rail, the second from the top, is carried along for a few panels on temporary supports. Then the stakes for each section are set crossways over the rails where they overlap and are secured by passing a loop of wire around the stakes and under the rail. A loop of wire is suspended from the fork of the stakes to hold the three bottom rails which are inserted weaver fashion, a twist of the loop for each rail. The top rail, the last to be added, is carried in the fork of the stakes. Now the whole thing is trussed up firmly by the use of a couple of stakes called "binders" at every panel. A figure eight loop of wire is threaded around the top of the stakes, the binders inserted and levered around until they can be wired to one of the rails. The resulting tension draws the top wire loop so tight that the frame of the fence is rendered quite rigid.

Fences contrived solely from the materials available at the site were naturally popular in pioneer days of ranching and included several variations of the log fence, the snake-rail fence and the stake and rider, all of which are to be seen today in more or less serviceable condition.

The stake and rider is an uncommon fence and only the occasional devotee to the design makes use of it now. It is seen at its best on the open flats of the Anahim Lake country where it stretches for miles, but elsewhere in British Columbia is seldom met with. A serious drawback with this fence is its tendency to collapse like a house of cards when badly breached. This weakness, inherent in the design, has been overcome by the Anahim Lake ranchers through use of occasional binders and wire ties.

The stake and rider made a cheap temporary fence in situations where the bush provided the right material for rails — the kind of bush generally referred to as "the sticks." In such groves of slender and limbless trees a man can build a fair stretch of stake and rider in a day with no tool other than his axe. I recall a story that was going round in the Chilcotin in 1928 about a stalwart denizen of Big Creek who claimed to have cut 400 rails in an hour. It excited admiration among the ranch hands, although no one expressed a desire to deprive the Big Creek resident of his record. However, the mere fact that the story was accepted without question is an indication of the density of rail timber in those regions.

In areas where timber is bigger, log fences are the most practical, being easy to construct, sturdy, and long lasting. They are also adaptable, as I learned when I worked on the Chilco Ranch in the Chilcotin.

It was in 1928, long enough back, I hope, to permit a safe disclosure of a little incident illustrating the usefulness of log fences and the resourcefulness of cowboys. All winter Tex, the head rider, and I had been feeding cattle on Chilco's Whitewater Meadows about fifty miles back from the ranch. In spring we moved the bunch down to what we

The log fence, opposite, has stood in the Turtle Valley near Chase for many years and is still in perfect shape.

called New Meadows, an opening in the jackpines where a solitary stack of hay would provide sustenance over the short period remaining until there would be grass on the range. Tex figured the steers could go on the range and rustle; we'd keep the hay for the cows. So we sorted them out and drove the steers back to some open country where the grass was beginning to show. Next morning they were all back at the meadow bawling their heads off around the stackyard fence. "I'll fix those critters," said Tex.

This time we drove them south through the sticks for a couple of hours when we came to a log fence snaking through the trees. We opened a panel, pushed the bunch through and closed the gap after them. "Best darn fence ever invented," said Tex with a grin as we replaced the top log. Beyond the fact that this was "Newton's Pasture" I could gather little from Tex about the mysterious fence, but we were certainly not bothered with the steers again.

I was a greenhorn at the time, new to the country, but the following year I was able to gain some insight into such Chilcotin manoeuvers by getting a job on the very ranch that owned the conventional log fence. Newton's Ranch lay at the confluence of the Chilko and Chilcotin Rivers, and about twenty-five miles north on the plateau were the wild hay meadows. Enclosing the meadows and a tract of grazing land was the snake log fence, roughly circular and eight miles in circumference. It formed a perfect holding ground as the astute cowpunchers of Chilco Ranch were quick to realize.

One of the first spring jobs at Newton's Ranch was to ride this fence and replace top logs where necessary. The owners were always puzzled at the number of stray cattle they had to chase out. I could have enlightened them but I had already learned that discretion is a highly desirable quality — even in a ranch hand.

Tragedy struck both Chilco and Newton's Ranches and they have changed hands since, while Tex drifted on as cowboys do. But I expect the old log fence is still serviceable, for, as Tex said, "It's the best darn fence invented." Solid and durable, it is easily maintained and repaired and has the advantage of being easily opened and

The Russell is one of the few split rail fences to be patented. The above example is in the Cariboo near 150 Mile.

The photo opposite shows a well-built stake and rider fence in the Chilcotin ranching country near Alexis Creek.

closed at any point. Perhaps the above incident would indicate that the last feature is not always an advantage.

Even in those days before the great depression the contract price for building log fence ran up to $400 a mile, while the lighter, five-rail Russell fence would cost no more than $150 plus wire. Most ranchers would agree that the extra cost of the logs was worth it, though, and many of those sturdy barriers four and five logs high can be seen in the ranching areas of the Cariboo, Douglas Lake and Nicola country where they have decorated the landscape since pioneer days.

A good deal of improvisation is resorted to by ranchers where local situations dictate some modification of standard fence design. I knew one once who used to excuse his unconventional methods by remarking "Good enough for Chilcotin," an unflattering insinuation which I thought was unwarranted. But however outlandish his modifications they were certainly effective. This rancher used to insist on a huge log for the top of a log fence. "To hold it down," he said, but we hands thought he did it because he liked to see us straining ourselves.

Among the novel ways of solving fencing problems an original effort at Upper Hat Creek deserves a prominent place. Faced with a situation where absence of timber ruled out rails and extremely rocky terrain made digging post holes impracticable, a rancher devised a unique system of tripods with a platform on which he piled the rocks so plentiful on his land. These solid units served in lieu of fence posts and carried five strands of taut barb wire just as effectively as planted posts would have done — with the added advantage that the tripods would outlast posts.

Other uses of rock in connection with fencing are to be seen in Deadman Valley in the dry-belt where slender stakes of juniper serve as fence posts. Such stakes are obviously too small to be fitted with the corner braces customary at the angles of a wire fence so a huge rock — maybe 200 pounds — is slung on the outside of the corner post. This provides the necessary rigidity, and somehow it looks all right, too, in the rugged and picturesque locality.

To lessen the chore of replacing posts, some ranchers

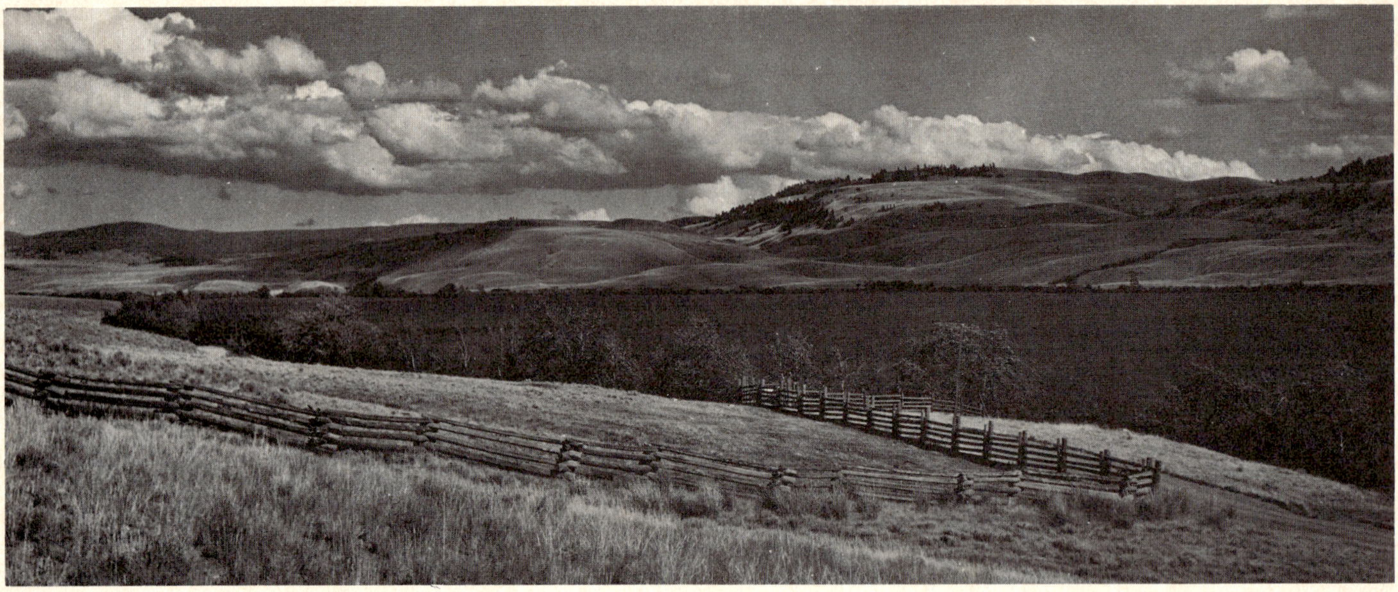

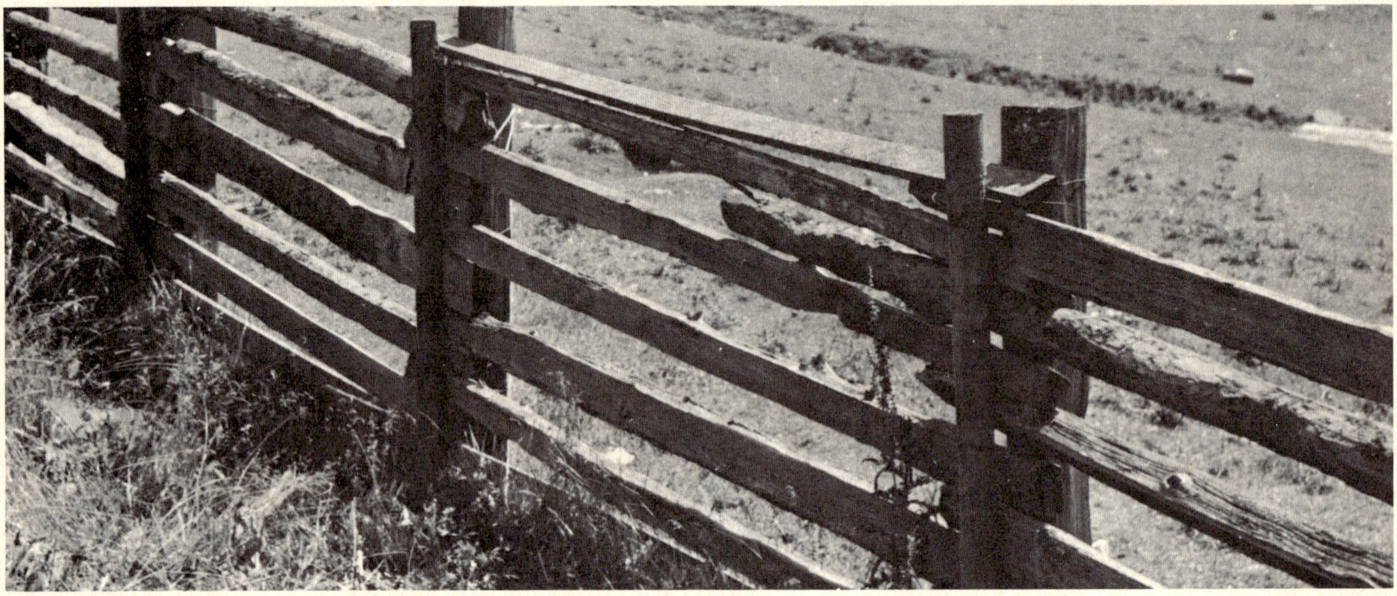

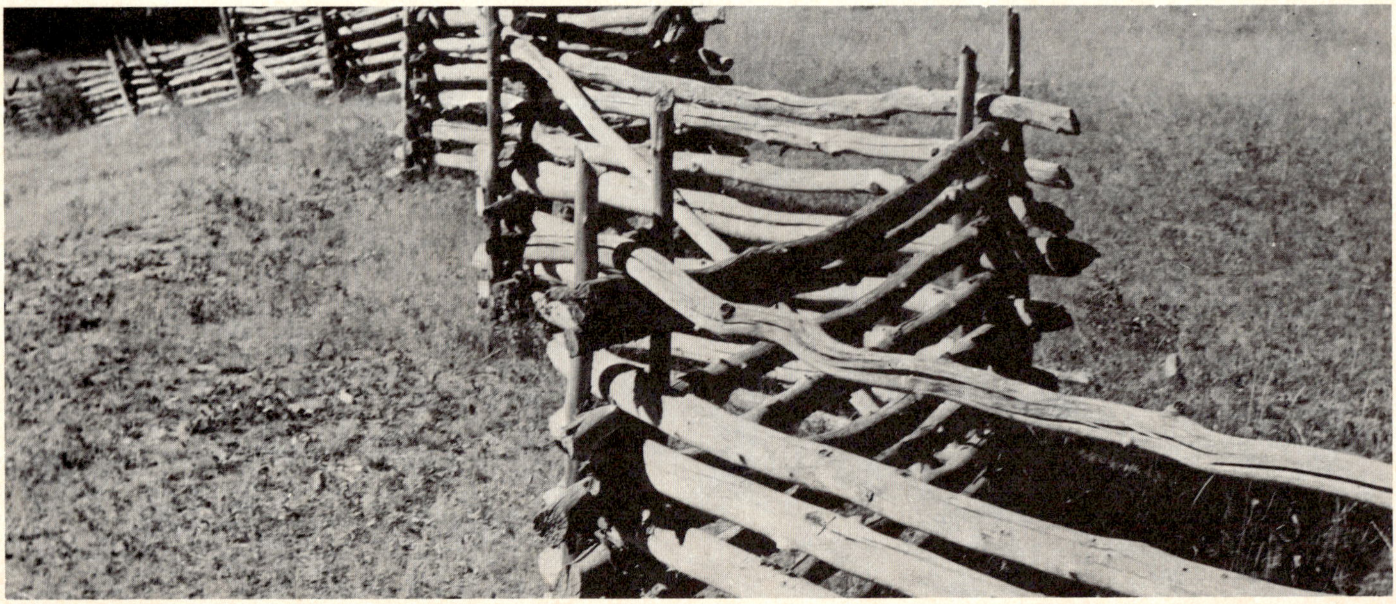

hunt for pitch pine which outlasts the usual fir or cedar many times. But since pitch-pine posts are scarce, they are set as gate or corner posts where the gnarled and knotted specimens endure for years. Perhaps even better than pitch pine for durability is juniper. On the J. Allan Ranch, north of Savona, there is a wire fence attached to juniper posts which have remained standing and sound for at least sixty-five years according to Jim Allan, who didn't know how long they had been in the ground when he first saw them. Naturally, the ranchers in the district all use juniper. Some of it is pretty small, too, little bigger than stakes, but it does the job and stands up year after year.

It is doubtful if wire will ever oust log and rail fences from the ranching scene where the raw material is in plentiful supply. Wire is chiefly used in open country where rails and logs are hard to come by. It is an expensive fence to maintain, for posts have to be renewed frequently, and there are constant repairs to be carried out to keep it effective. A new stretch of wire fence becomes a sorry sight once breached, and it is an unpleasant fact that many range cattle have no respect for wire. An additional hazard throughout Interior B.C. is that moose also have no respect for a wire fence — probably because they don't see it until too late — and barge through, ripping out yards at a time.

At present wooden fences appear to be holding their own, especially in the Chilcotin where they seem to be more plentiful than they were thirty years ago. Unfortunately, in recent years modern highway construction with its demands for a wider swath over the terrain has swallowed some of the old log fences—thus disappeared a fine old relic at Ashcroft Manor on the Trans-Canada Highway. But on backroads throughout B.C. the log and rail fences wander for miles, picturesque and practical landmarks that I hope will be with us always.

The photos opposite, top to bottom, show a log fence at Douglas Lake in the Merritt area, a post and rail fence on a farm near Lumby, and a snake rail fence near Alexis Creek.

In the photo below, the late cowboy-author Rich Hobson works on a fence of his own design at River Ranch near Vanderhoof.

The Bridges at HAGWILGET

of which the first two were homespun structures that had little reason for defying gravity and it was permissible for horseback riders to dismount and walk across.

by SPERRY "DUTCH" CLINE

Probably nowhere else in the world has there been such a contrast in bridge building techniques as in the structures which spanned Hagwilget Canyon over the Bulkley River near Hazelton in the past 120 years. During this period four bridges have spanned the chasm, two built by Indians and two by white men. The most unique were those built by the Indians, homespun structures that looked as fragile as a spider's web and had little apparent reason for defying gravity. Yet they served the area for upward of half a century, and in the process caused many travellers to pale at the mere thought of venturing onto them.

I don't know when the first of them was built but it was about 1856. It was there a decade later when Colonel Charles S. Bulkley, the man in charge of constructing the famous Collins Around-the-World Telegraph Line that was to link North America and Europe via Siberia, reached the forks of the Skeena River. No doubt this bridge had been used by the fur-traders but, being all in a day's work, they were not impressed by the ingenuity of the primitive people who had constructed it. Not so Colonel Bulkley, however, who was impressed.

He was faced with the task of finding means of crossing hundreds of such canyons from Hazelton north through B.C., Yukon and Russian Alaska. He was glad to be able to glean knowledge of bridge building from whomever he could. I was told by one of the veterans of his party that he supplied the press of that day in eastern America and Europe with an account of his discovery. I haven't seen what he wrote, but J. L. Waddell in his *Bridge Engineering* later described it as "a most creditable piece of work for entirely uneducated men, it is one of the romances of bridge building."

The structure was built on a more or less cantilever principle with poles cut in the immediate vicinity and held in place by ropes made by the Indians from the inner bark of cedar. It was about six feet wide with a span of 150 feet with the ends butted into the shoulders of the cliff some 100 feet above the water. I became acquainted with several of the older Indians who remembered using this bridge.

One of them was called Old Chickens, who had the rep-

At left is the second Indian bridge. As the author noted: "For strength the Indians used telegraph wire; nevertheless, I don't mind admitting that each time I crossed I dismounted and led my horse."

The Indians built the first bridge in the 1850's, using poles and rope made from cedar bark to hang a 150-foot span some 100 feet above the water. It is shown above in 1872.

utation of being one of the strongest backpackers of his day. He told me of packing 300-pound packs across this structure. He also mentioned that when one of the early Roman Catholic Missionaries reached Hagwilget, he expressed a desire to cross the river. When taken to the bridge he hesitated and Chickens, wishing to accommodate the new priest, offered to carry him across piggyback. The reverend gentleman declined his offer and walked several miles downstream where he could be safely taken across by canoe.

When Colonel Bulkley arrived he evidently wanted to build something of a more substantial nature across the Canyon but the Indians refused since their medicine men predicted it would stop the run of salmon on which the Indians depended for survival. They did consent to having their bridge strengthened with wire. It played a part in helping construction of the Collins telegraph line, although in 1866 the project was abandoned when a cable was successfully laid under the Atlantic Ocean.

In time the original bridge passed out of being and another was built at a higher level. When the Collins line was abandoned, large quantities of telegraph wire and other materials were left behind and Indians and the few others in the country were free to use such materials at will. The Indians soon learned to make use of wire in place of their limited amounts of cedar rope.

Some excellent photos of this bridge give a much clearer view of their manner of construction. Again the cantilever principle is shown. Long trees were used and put into place by balancing the butts over crudely constructed abutments and weighing them down with loads of rock. These trees were slowly and laboriously shoved out from both sides — a feat worthy of consideration since the Indians knew nothing of mechanical power. Above midstream the ends of the trees overlapped for several feet and were securely bound together with telegraph wire. At each end were rough towers over which wires were passed and fastened to the body of the bridge below. These towers also suggest a knowledge of the suspension bridge, although where the Indians acquired this knowledge was

The Craddock bridge, above, was the first replacement for the Indian one, center left, but it never became popular because of its narrowness and tendency to sway in the wind.

On the opposite page is the present bridge, built as part of a projected highway to the Yukon. Now over forty years old, its grace and symmetry rival modern counterparts.

always a mystery to me.

The men who constructed this bridge well knew the strength of their cedar bark ropes but had only a faint idea of the strength of the white man's wire. Neither did they have any scientific means of testing the strength of building materials, although they realized that a stronger bridge must now be built than formerly since horses and mules were being used for packing.

They completed their test by sending the women of the tribe across in a body and the new construction stood the test satisfactorily. Since that time, many white men have told the story of the testing of this bridge and have inferred that the women were used to test it because the Indians valued the lives of the male members of the tribe much higher than the lives of the females. I learned that this was not the reason.

Indians who worked on the construction told me that the entire available male population was engaged in construction. When the women were sent across, the men all stood by with the necessary material to strengthen any portion of the bridge that might show sign of collapse.

This bridge served the community for years. I crossed it many times, both on foot and with a saddle horse. I am not ashamed to admit that each time I dismounted and led the horse. During its life the bridge became quite an attraction and was visited by nearly every traveller who came to the Hazelton district.

The bridge was used until the 1908-14 boom, caused by construction of the Grand Trunk Pacific Railway across Central B.C. to the Pacific Ocean at a new port called Prince Rupert. This development resulted in three additional bridges. The first was a low-level structure farther down the Bulkley River and built in 1913. However, it was not satisfactory since the approaches to it were very steep, prohibiting the hauling of heavy loads of freight. Also the bridge was so narrow a team of horses could barely get across, a remarkable case of oversight by some government official.

By now four townsites were being promoted in the district. These were Larkton, Ellison, South Hazelton and New Hazelton, the last being developed by Robert Kelly of the wholesale firm of Kelly Douglas and Company. In order to make his townsite more attractive, Kelly decided to put in a high bridge across the Bulkley at the site of the original Indian suspension bridges. At the time, an English firm, Craddock and Co., were extending their wire and cable trade in Western America. Kelly approached them and they took the contract at a very low price, considering it good advertising for their wares.

It was completed in the autumn of 1913 but there was one problem — it couldn't be used since no roads led to it. The Provincial government was still satisfied with the route to Hazelton over the low-level bridge, so to get his bridge into operation Kelly also had to build the connecting roads.

The bridge was very narrow, just wide enough for a car if the owner was an expert driver and cold sober. Since most of us were just learning to drive cars of the Model T variety, nearly every car in the country showed signs of contact with the side railings of the bridge. The structure was 266 feet above the water and swayed gently in the mildest of summer breezes. When the gales of autumn and winter roared through the canyon its gentle swaying motion changed dramatically. Many cases of seasickness were reported — or was it just fright? In any event, these and other reasons caused this bridge to become unpopular with the public.

It lasted until 1931 when the Tolmie government, considering the construction of a highway to the Yukon, replaced it with the graceful span that is still a landmark. When opened it was the highest suspension bridge in Canada, some 262 feet above water with a main span of 460 feet and a 16-foot roadway. It contains over a million pounds of steel and cable and six miles of 1½-inch wire rope in the suspension cables and hangers. The Craddock bridge, to the regret of none, was moved up the Bulkley to a point near Quick and rebuilt as a footbridge.

The Indian's bridge, meanwhile, had fallen into disuse. People began to realize its future value as a tourist attraction but the tourist trade was in its infancy. No action was taken and the structure that never ceased to amaze those crossing for the first time — or the fortieth — quietly collapsed into the river. ∎

Some had wooden chimneys and no windows; others were three stories high, their smooth-hewn logs and accurate cornering proclaiming the work of expert axemen. Most have burned but a few survive, weather-stained structures that have withstood a century of winters, a tangible link with

OUR LOG CABIN HERITAGE

by DONOVAN CLEMSON

The photo at upper left shows broadaxe work on a mountain cabin near Sardis. At left is an old cabin at Dutch Lake near Clearwater, part of the original homestead of two German settlers.

The photo above of the Colonial Hotel at Soda Creek in the Cariboo was taken in 1868 by frontier photographer F. Dally. It is an excellent example of pioneer craftsmanship with logs.

The log cabin was universally used for shelter by the pioneer trappers, prospectors, miners and settlers in the remote areas of British Columbia. Many of the early cabins were intended for temporary use and were of rough and ready construction; others were homes built with care and pride, their sturdy walls and shake roofs in some cases surviving more than a century of weathering. One such building is Cottonwood House, originally built in 1864 as a stopping place on the Cariboo Road between Quesnel and Barkerville. This fine old structure is now preserved in Cottonwood Provincial Park and every year is visited by thousands of people. (See page 80.)

One of the best examples of cabins built for temporary use was a trapper's cabin in the Chilcotin country in which I once spent a night. Like the beaver and muskrat, the trapper had built his tiny but cosy home with the materials at hand, all collected within a radius of fifty yards. Logs, the universal pioneer building material in British Columbia, formed the walls. These were jackpine, found in plentiful supply throughout the Chilcotin plateau, and perfectly adapted to building purposes on account of the straight and limbless trunks which are produced in the characteristic dense stands of the region.

The dirt floor of the cabin was dug down about a foot below ground level, and the height of the outside walls was no more than five feet. Inside, the dimensions of the cabin were about six by eight feet, one end of this tiny room occupied by a bed made of small poles on which the trapper laid his blankets. The roof was constructed with small poles laid close together, over which a layer of spruce boughs was spread to receive the thick blanket of soil which is, even at the present time, a not uncommon roofing material in the Chilcotin.

There were no windows, and the door, a small affair not more than three feet high, was skillfully made from the wooden cases in which the trapper had packed in his supplies. But the most curious contrivance was the chimney which projected from one corner of the building. It was triangular in shape, built with short sections of small poles laid horizontally, like the larger logs of the building. This wooden chimney was well lined with clay which rendered it proof against the trapper's winter fires. Unable to indulge in the luxury of a stove, the builder had constructed a hearth of stone, with large flat slabs to back his corner fireplace and protect the walls of the cabin. On this primitive hearth his fire supplied light and heat, and the wherewithal to cook his flapjacks and coffee. So, by the intelligent use of the materials available, he was able to winter without hardship.

One of the remarkable and effective features of such cabins is the dirt roof, especially if it is kept in good repair. Dirt is generally found on cabins in the dry Interior areas of the province, and while it is good insulation against heat and cold, it is not absolutely waterproof, although it does provide protection against normal rainfall. Some leaking may be expected under exceptional conditions, and the unwary householder who neglects to shovel the snow off in winter will be suitably baptized at the onset of a sudden thaw.

The early cabins were made tight and windproof by caulking the spaces between the logs with moss and lichen on the inside and clay mixtures on the outside. Maintenance consisted of simply renewing these materials when necessary. A stove and a few lengths of pipe supplied heating and cooking facilities. The inside furnishings of the single room, nearly always of the simplest kind, reflected the peculiar needs of the occupants.

A dirt-roofed cabin in which I once spent a winter was furnished for the accommodation of a couple of ranch hands winter-feeding cattle, and was typical of the cabins built for seasonal or occasional use in the area. The door was four feet high, the dirt floor dug down about a foot, and one small window admitted a dim light within. The furniture consisted of one small table and two rough pole bunks. There were no chairs, and two boxes nailed to the walls served as cupboards. A few pegs driven between the logs accommodated saddles and riding gear, while a camp stove with small oven completed the furnishings.

Such simple homes were sufficient for prospectors, trappers and cowboys, but the demands of a growing population as the British Columbia Interior opened up stimulated the production of more elaborate log buildings. The route of the old Cariboo Road, started in 1861 to provide access for wheeled traffic to the gold creeks, was soon dotted with large log buildings, many of them roadhouses to accommodate travellers. Some of these edifices were several stories high and had many rooms, their smooth-hewn logs and accurate cornering proclaiming the work of expert axemen. Roofed with shakes or shingles, these large buildings were resistant to weathering, but not, unfortunately, to fire and many of them burned down.

The Chilcotin ranchers used to say that to finish a log house one had to build a frame house inside it. This was because the bare logs used to be considered too crude a finish for a permanent home, so various kinds of panelling were used to cover them. Consequently, many of the old log houses in the region exhibit the smooth, conventional inside walls associated with more modern houses. The rancher's log house was usually long and low, which gave rise to the designation "ranch type" applied to a popular style urban house. It was comfortable to live in during winter when the thick walls retained the heat from several stoves, and provided a cool retreat in summer.

The more pretentious log houses of two stories with many bedrooms on the upper floor were common along the Cariboo Road. Here, in the days of horse transportation on that much travelled route, nearly every ranch was a stopping place or hostelry of some kind. Today, many fine specimens are still seen, and while a few of them are occupied, the majority stand forlorn and deserted. The stucco bungalow, which the modern rancher finds more convenient, has invaded the open landscape of bunchgrass and solitary yellow pine, bringing the taint of the city. The old log houses were country houses that grew into the landscape and mellowed along with the rocks and the trees and the old rail fences to become essential features of the scenery.

In large log house and single-roomed cabin the principles of construction are the same — the walls being

The main tools used to build a log cabin were the broadaxe and froe. The broadaxe was used for squaring logs and the froe for splitting cedar blocks into shakes for the roof.

erected with entire logs and openings for doors and windows sawn out afterwards. With a house it was usual to devote more time and attention to corners, making as neat a job as possible. Broadaxe work is evident in many of the houses built in the early period, with inside, and sometimes outside, walls being hewn flat. This hewing represented an enormous amount of labor. Each log would be marked with a chalk line, scored with an axe, then hewed flat with a broadaxe. This tool is practically unknown today, but at one time left its unmistakable mark on thousands of bridge timbers, millions of railway ties and countless log houses.

Probably the most excellent workmanship to be seen in the log buildings of B.C. can be attributed to Norwegian and Finnish settlers who established themselves in rural communities and applied their traditional skills in the erection of log houses and barns. Their houses in particular are fine examples of hewn log construction, close fitting with dovetail cornering, exhibiting the smooth exterior wall generally associated with sawn lumber. Such solidly constructed buildings will stand indefinitely if well roofed and set on good foundations. Well preserved examples can be seen in the Bella Coola Valley, Eagle Valley and the White Lake district near Salmon Arm. I once expressed my admiration for a log community hall in one of these settlements and was told that it was just a rough job, put up in a hurry. In this case the logs were left in the round while all the houses of the settlement were hewn.

Nowadays, people seem to like their logs in the round, a preference which probably springs from necessity since good broadaxe men and even broadaxes are not easily found. The modern log house fancier likes his house rugged and is not ashamed to have the bare, peeled and oiled logs constitute the walls of his rooms. He is also not so fussy about the corners. The ordinary inter-locking join with the ends of the logs projecting a foot or so is good

A dirt-roofed cabin at Chezacut in the Chilcotin. Throughout Interior B.C. such cabins still provide winter comfort for trappers and others who work in the outdoors miles from the nearest community.

enough for him. In fact he will claim that the effect is more picturesque, an argument that is supported by the Christmas card which never fails to depict this type of log house. This is the simplest form of construction, the work of notching for the corners requiring no more tools than an axe.

Such construction was practiced by trappers and prospectors who frequently carried all their equipment on their backs, and would naturally refrain from burdening themselves with articles not absolutely necessary. The more sophisticated homes of the settlers built with hewn logs neatly dovetailed at the corners required the use of a broadaxe, square, spirit level, adze and saw, as well as the axe, all of which were part of the settlers' normal equipment.

Perhaps the most notable of present-day log house fanciers is Mr. H. W. Herridge of Nakusp, who for many years represented the federal riding of Kootenay West in parliament. He was fond of boasting that he was the only MP who lived in a log cabin. Actually, his home is more than a

Although pioneer structures such as the center photo of the Log Cabin Hotel at Williams Lake in 1921 have disappeared, many log buildings still stand. Included are summer cabins typified by the one at top, the H. W. Herridge home near Nakusp on the Arrow Lakes, above, and the Indian Church, opposite, aging in the sun-baked hills just off the Trans-Canada Highway near Ashcroft Manor.

cabin, being a two-storey house with the principal room on the ground floor measuring about twenty-six feet square. The whole house is of honest log construction, though, built of fine straight timbers cut on the Herridge mountain-side property on Upper Arrow Lake a few miles from Nakusp.

With the building of the Columbia River treaty dams and the conversion of Arrow Lakes into a reservoir, a rising water level of forty feet threatened to drown the fine log house. However, B.C. Hydro crews, with great skill, succeeded in moving the large and heavy structure several hundred yards to its present position above high water. Also moved to safety was an original Arrow Lakes log cabin fitted by Mr. Herridge for an office. In this quiet retreat whose ancient log walls are almost completely covered with bookcases, he spends much time dealing with his large correspondence.

Mr. Herridge loves his log buildings, the product of his woods and the skilled workmanship of friends and neighbors. They are mellowed now and blend happily into the landscape as all log buildings do. He likes to tell a story of an American guest who observed with critical eye the splendid ceiling beams, hand hewn, with the inimitable texture produced by the broadaxe. "Too bad you couldn't have had those beams run through the planer," the man said.

Perhaps this story illustrates the difference in outlook between the genuine lover of log houses and those who regard them only as interesting curiosities, outdated relics of pioneer days not at all suitable for modern living. But the story also emphasizes that every log house is an original, which, like a wooden ship, cannot be duplicated. Its character reflects both the skill of the axeman and the care of the builder, and the logs themselves can tell much about the circumstances of construction. Fortunately, the forested nature of British Columbia ensured us a heritage of these individual buildings which adequately fulfill the old — but not always observed — axiom of the architect: that to fit harmoniously into the landscape a building should be constructed with local materials.

∎

PIONEE

The Hume Hotel, above, was Nelson's largest and most popular stopping place during pioneer days. The opposite photo shows the elaborate ladies' entrance.

The Manhattan Saloon, opposite page, was typical of the well-stocked drinking places which were open day and night until closed by prohibition.

DAYS IN NELSON

"This is not a community history," emphasized the author, a doctor in Nelson from 1908 to 1955. "It is, instead, recollections of memorable characters and personal experiences during my early years of practice."

by DR. L. E. BORDEN

When I arrived in Nelson in 1908 it had a population of about four thousand; a mining town beautifully located at the head of the West Arm of Kootenay Lake. Even then it was becoming known as the "Queen City of the Kootenays," a title it still wears proudly. During my early days in the community, however, it could also have called itself the "Saloon Capital of the Kootenays" for among its business places were eighteen hotels and an almost equal number of saloons, besides two breweries and a wholesale liquor store. While this may seem a large number of liquor establishments, the town was the center of a rich mining region and hundreds of miners came to the community on weekends and holidays. Since the old-time miner spent long hours in dark and dangerous underground shafts or in lonely bunkhouses miles from habitation, it was not surprising that the saloon was a favorite stopping place when he reached town.

In those days the saloons—Manhattan, Glue Pot, Bodega, Office, and many others—were open day and night. They all disappeared when prohibition came in but left in their passing many tales ranging from tragic to humorous.

The Office, for instance, was one of the better-class saloons. Public gambling was not permitted but rooms were set aside for private parties to enjoy poker and similar games. No charge was made or house rake-off taken for the proprietor had decided that his profit from the liquor covered the extra service. Since the name was a unique and subtle one for a saloon, it was quite a little time before housewives figured out why so many husbands had to go "back to the office" at night. At last the light dawned on one bright lady who marched into the Office. Sure enough her husband was engaged in a game of poker. She gently (so it is said) took him by the ear and led him out. History does not tell whether he was winning or losing.

On another occasion at the same saloon an old friend, Jeff Steele, came into the bar early one morning after a prospecting trip to the hills. He had his packsack and in it samples of ore which he had brought to have assayed. The bartender, a rather heavy drinker and in need of his "morning's morning," asked "What luck have you had?"

Without replying, Jeff opened his pack and dumped the contents on the counter. Besides the ore samples there was a beautifully colored garter snake which started to wiggle towards the bartender. He promptly let out a yell, waved his hands in the air and fled. It was some time before he could be assured that the snake was real and not the beginning of delirium tremens.

The Manhattan was on a side street and supposed to be

one of the quieter saloons. But about nine o'clock one evening a man entered the bar. Without bothering to order a drink he drew a revolver and shot two people dead. As I recall, there was no motive for the slayings, but the trade of this saloon diminished rapidly thereafter and was soon closed. The building stood unoccupied for many years and just before I left Nelson in 1955, I saw it being demolished to make room for business expansion. I looked at the old hand-hewn timbers and they were as firm and solid as when the building was built over fifty years before.

None of the other saloons gained any special notoriety but all made money for their proprietors. I think the same statement can be made for the hotels which, as I have mentioned, were as numerous as the saloons.

One I well remember was the Hume, built and owned by J. Fred Hume, once a member of the Semlin government of British Columbia. This was a well-run hotel and since a great many commercial travellers made it their headquarters, it was a very busy place.

After Mr. Hume's death the hotel was sold to a man who had made at least a quarter million dollars in the lumber business. He was a widower with two spendthrift sons, a contrast to their father who was careful of the pennies. It was said that he never bought a morning paper but waited in the rotunda until a customer discarded one. Unfortunately his boys and lack of knowledge in running an hotel forced him to abandon it. The last I heard of the unfortunate gentleman he was in an old men's home in Victoria, his quarter million dollars gone.

Three or four blocks up the hill was the Strathcona Hotel which catered to the non-commercial travelling public. It was well run and "Old Pop," the proprietor, was a good hotel man. He set an excellent table much appreciated by many of the business people who usually had lunch there. But Old Pop had a sharp tongue that at times lost him customers.

I lived there for over a year when I first came to Nelson and remember one night when a member of a group of evangelists wanted a room. He was given accommodation on the third floor—a tiny room with comfortable but small bed. In the morning the customer came to the office, full of complaints. Pop looked at him momentarily and quietly said, "I believe the man you are supposed to work for was born in a manger." The evangelist left without further discussion.

At the east end of the town was an hotel run by an old friend of mine, a character who drank three bottles of scotch daily but whom I never saw drunk. I consider him fortunate he didn't live with the present price, although he had great difficulty during prohibition when liquor was obtainable only by a doctor's prescription. In his case, special consideration was made by the government.

There were many other characters in Nelson, although I am not using the word "character" in an invidious manner. Some of the people considered a bit oddball had sterling qualities that in most cases included some little quirk by which they are remembered. Nor do I wish readers to feel that the whole population was peculiar. To the contrary, Nelson produced able men such as lawyers, doctors, and engineers—some of whom gained national stature.

One of those considered a local character was Silver King Mike, a secondhand dealer who could neither read nor write. Despite this lack of schooling he made lots of money, a fact I had on reliable authority since a friend of mine did his banking.

On one occasion he bought a large pile of blankets from the Silver King Mine when it gave up its boarding house. A woman thinking of starting a boarding and rooming house for miners came to the shop looking for supplies. As she walked beside Mike and inspected the blankets, she observed, "Those blankets smell."

"No, Ma'am, tain't dem, dat's me," replied Mike. He was probably telling the truth for he was never noted for being clean or neat.

Coal-oil Johnny was another character. He obtained his name because he collected and sold five- and ten-gallon coal-oil tins which were plentiful in those days since almost everyone used coal oil. During the time of his collecting and selling activities, Nelson residents noticed a bright light on the side of Elephant Mountain which rises some six thousand feet opposite the city. The light, seen until about ten o'clock at night, was the source of much speculation.

Among the hotels in Nelson when the author arrived was the Tremont, shown above shortly after its completion.

Since there were no roads in the Nelson district for many years after the author's arrival, access to the outside world was by CPR train and sternwheelers such as the magnificent *Nasookin*, opposite page. The bottom photo on the opposite page was found in an old house in 1952 and shows Nelson about 1900.

The mystery was unravelled when Coal-oil Johnny fell into the lake while boarding his boat after buying supplies. He was lucky in that he caught hold of the landing plank and held on until his cries brought assistance. I was called and found him suffering from shock and exposure. I admitted him to hospital and here learned the reason for the mysterious light. It seemed that a spiritualist woman in the United States was directing Coal-oil where to dig for gold and he was using the money from the sale of the coal-oil tins to buy powder and grub. Not long after he was released from hospital Johnny disappeared and so did the light. No one learned if the spiritualist failed or if Johnny just decided to leave. In any event, no successful claims were ever staked on Elephant Mountain.

Another real character but withal a very able man was a Scot from Galway who became known as "The Gunner from Galway." The Gunner was a miner, not of the pick and shovel variety but a promoter and owner of mines. When he first arrived in the Kootenays at the turn of the century he drank considerably and when under the influence sang an unlimited number of verses of a song called "The Gunner from Galway," hence his nickname.

Shortly after his arrival in the Kootenays he began prospecting in the Slocan district for mineral claims. One weekend he became violently intoxicated and was arrested. The magistrate sentenced him to a term in the provincial jail, but since there was no lock-up in the Slocan district he was sent to Nelson. The trip involved a short train journey and the prisoner was put in charge of a rookie policeman. To everyone's astonishment, when the pair reached Nelson the culprit had on the policeman's uniform and delivered the policeman as the prisoner.

Sometime afterward the Gunner went on a bit of a spree in Toronto and was admitted to hospital for treatment. He recovered favorably and one Sunday morning was allowed up in his dressing gown to walk in the corridor. The visiting physicians in those days wore frock coats and silk hats which they removed in the lobby and donned suitable garb for the ward visit. The Gunner spotted one of the doctor's outfits. With his thirst still not under control he commandeered the frock coat and silk hat and slipped out the back stairs. Right before him was a horse-drawn milk delivery wagon with the driver absent. The Gunner, always a resourceful man, mounted the cab and drove into town, where he was later apprehended.

These and many other escapades are truly told of this remarkable man. Upon his return, however, he had changed mightily and I don't think he ever went on a spree again but settled down as a regular mining operator. He was a close friend of the late John McMartin of cobalt fame and, in conjunction with other mining men, operated successfully more than one mining property in the Sheep Creek district of B.C.

The Gunner continued his mining operations for many years and then moved to Manitoba where he became interested in the Flin Flon district. He evidently still prospered for he lived in a suite in the Fort Garry Hotel, where he died. Many friends and acquaintances mourned his passing for despite his eccentricities the Gunner from Galway made an excellent contribution to mining development in Canada.

I particularly remember the Gunner because I operated on his daughter for appendicitis, my first appendectomy in Nelson. The father was naturally anxious about the outcome but all went well and the Gunner was my friend.

Not all cases I handled, however, had such a satisfactory outcome. My medical practice developed rapidly and soon became quite large, not only in the city but in the surrounding countryside. In those days we still made house calls, some for many miles by horseback, railway speeder, sternwheel steamer, horse and buggy and similar means of frontier transportation. Making such calls around Nelson was often a problem since when I arrived there was no road out of town in any direction. Instead there were only rough trails to the many mining properties which were a feature of the district and upon which its prosperity depended. Sternwheelers provided a service up the lake to Ainsworth, Kaslo and other communities, as well as to the Canadian Pacific Railway at Kootenay Landing on the east shore of Kootenay Lake. Below Nelson the CPR had a train some thirty miles along the Kootenay River to Robson where sternwheelers provided a service 256 miles up the Arrow Lakes to Arrowhead. Here a spur railway ran twenty-seven miles north to Revelstoke and the Transcontinental line of the CPR. A trip to the coast took three days under the best of circumstances, a lot longer under adverse conditions.

Because of this isolation, the waterfront was an important part in the life of Nelson's residents. Boathouses and landings stretched for about one mile along the waterfront. In addition, there were two boat liveries and a small shipyard operated by the Walton's who were noted for the dependability of their vessels. There were hundreds of motor boats from six-bunk cabin cruisers to much smaller ones, although sailboats were scarce because of the sudden sharp gusts of wind off the mountains. The most swanky launch was imported from Eastern Canada and owned by a bank manager. It was called the *Laugh-a-Lot* but was nicknamed the *Cent-a-Puff* because it was so costly to run.

The wharf itself was a very popular place, especially on summer evenings. Band concerts, illuminated water parades, races, beach picnics and regattas were regular features. Another popular pastime was greeting sternwheel steamers, the main communication with the outside world. Arrival of the picturesque vessels was always an event, especially the *Nasookin*, the largest sternwheeler to ply the province's inland waterways. She could carry over five hundred passengers and was the pride of Nelson, always met by residents, although I seldom found time to be among them.

Doctors in those days kept office hours morning, afternoon and evening, and usually weekends as well. Many people had little consideration for the doctor and felt that he must come as soon as called, regardless of circumstances.

I remember one night preparing for bed after an extremely busy week. Just then there was an urgent call to come at once and see a patient who lived about twelve miles down the river on the opposite bank. I said it was utterly impossible since there was no train and the speeder was unavailable. The person insisted I must come, and as soon as possible, for the patient was desperately ill and he

A horse race down Nelson's main street on July 1, 1898 and a regatta about 1912. Kootenay Lake was a major source of recreation for local residents both winter and summer.

The photos on the opposite page show Upper Bonnington Falls and an early view of the Silver King Mine, both well remembered by the author—but for different reasons.

was frantic about his condition.

My only alternative was to secure a team of horses and a wagon from the livery stable and drive over a mining trail for about ten miles to just above Bonnington Falls. I knew there was a small ranch there and if Joe, the caretaker, had not been in town for a few days he might be fit to row me across. It was a dangerous crossing in the daytime and more so at night. Only a few days before three men had tried to cross and had been swept over the Falls and were never seen again.

The drive was rough, but uneventful, and while Joe had already gone to bed he was easily aroused. By good fortune he was sober and willing to row me across the river. The boat did not look seaworthy but Joe assured me it was safe enough. He started to row upstream and after nearly a mile struck out into the swift current. The unpleasant sensation as I felt myself drifting rapidly toward those dangerous Bonnington Falls is beyond description.

Joe, fortunately, kept rowing vigorously, and just as I felt we were about to go over he hit the back current on the opposite shore. Arrangements were made that I should signal him when I was ready to return and he left. I later learned that the rowboat in which we had travelled was so waterlogged that it sank when Joe reached the other side. Such courage is unbelievable but this was the spirit of so many pioneers.

When I finally reached my destination I was filled with disgust. Instead of a desperately ill patient I found a middle-aged man obviously suffering from too much strong drink. There was little I could do except give him a sedative and order him to Nelson hospital by train the next morning. The patient made a normal recovery, but it took me some little time to forget that "emergency" case.

But not all emergency calls were frivolous. One Christmas Eve the Superintendent of the Silver King Mine called in my office to wish me the compliments of the season. Hardly had he entered when the telephone rang. The message was terse: "Bad accident at the Silver King. Come at once."

While I dashed home, two blocks away, to change to riding britches, mackinaw and heavy gloves, the Superintendent ordered the best saddle horse from the livery stable. Knowing the seriousness and the necessity for quick action, I pressed the horse unmercifully. The going was easy, although uphill, until I reached snow level about two miles up and from there on progress was much slower as we reached the higher levels with increased snow. I kept urging the poor horse so that when we reached the scene of the accident it was in bad shape. I was not much better for my knees were so cold I could not stand up and had to be assisted to the injured men.

The two men were badly hurt but lucky at that. In those days all mining was done by hand, including drilling holes in the rock face so that the ore could be blasted loose. This drilling was done by a two-man team using a long iron bar and a jackhammer. One man held the bar and turned it after each whack until a hole some twelve inches or more deep was made. After several holes were drilled another team filled them with dynamite and prepared them for a simultaneous explosion. Occasionally, however, not all charges exploded, thus creating an extremely hazardous condition known as a "missed" hole.

The men had drilled into one of these missed charges. Fortunately, the man holding the bar had to be in a squatting position and this saved his life. Had his head been a little farther forward the bar would have gone straight up through his head. Instead his lower jaw was fractured and his face badly lacerated. He was unconscious. The other man received the whole force of the dynamite blast on his face. He was blinded and suffering severe pain. All I could do was to render first aid and phone the hospital to prepare for operations.

When we reached the hospital I operated on the unconscious man first—setting his jaw and cleaning up his other wounds. He recovered and went back to work as a miner. The other chap was not so fortunate. He lost one eye and the other had only about half normal vision. However, with assistance from the Workmen's Compensation Board, he managed to get by.

Altogether it had been a busy Christmas Eve. I got home in time for breakfast Christmas morning, ending another memorable experience during forty-seven years as a doctor in Nelson.

∎

HISTORIC

by PEGGY YOUNG

Reprinted courtesy *The Beaver*

Nootka Sound, on the west coast of Vancouver Island, is a place of extraordinary beauty. Narrow arms of the sea penetrate deep into the land, tree-covered mountains plunge down into the water, and on still days the mirror-smooth sea reflects mountain and forest until it is hard to tell where land ends and sea begins. Sometimes the Pacific fog rolls in, thick and impenetrable; often the clouds hang low along the hills and the rain pelts down for days at a time. The winds can be erratic and blow suddenly and violently from unexpected directions. But in all weathers the Sound is beautiful, and the traveller moving through that labyrinth has the feeling that it might be another world.

It is now two centuries since the white man first saw Nootka Sound. In 1774 a Spanish expedition came up from Mexico to investigate rumours of Russian fur traders in Northern Pacific waters. The *Santiago,* commanded by Juan Josef Pérez Hernández, sailed as far as the Queen Charlotte Islands, but was turned back by adverse weather. Pérez anchored near the mouth of the Sound to trade with the Indians, but made no landing. The following year a second expedition took place with the *Santiago* under Bruno de Hezeta and the *Sonora* under Juan Francisco de la Bodega y Quadra. These explorers cruised along the coast to Vancouver Island but for the time being showed little interest in it.

In 1776 Captain James Cook left England on his third voyage of discovery. The British Admiralty, hoping that Cook would find the legendary North West Passage, supplied him with two ships, the *Discovery* and the *Resolution.* Cook spent a year in the South Seas en route and finally arrived at Nootka, which he called King George's Sound, on March 29, 1778. Here he spent a month at Resolution Cove on Bligh Island, caulking his ships, renewing spars and overhauling rigging and sails. The logbook of the

NOOTKA SOUND

This peaceful inlet on the west coast of Vancouver Island is as impressive today as it was to the Spanish and English explorers two centuries ago. But it was not always peaceful. In 1790 it almost caused war between Spain and England.

Discovery notes: "The bulk of our employment was wooding, watering and brewing spruce beer." The Nootka Indians were friendly and offered valuable sea-otter skins in trade. In April Cook sailed north, still searching for the North West Passage, until he was turned back by ice in the Bering Strait. The following year he was killed in Hawaii.

With the publication of Cook's journals in 1784 the world became aware of the valuable furs which could be obtained at Nootka Sound and sold at great profit in China. Russians, British, and Americans competed for the fur trade, ignoring Spain's traditional rights in the Pacific Ocean. (Spain's claims were based on a papal bull of 1493, dividing the known world between Spain and Portugal.)

The first trading vessels to come to Nootka were under the auspices of the East India Company, which had a virtual monopoly of the fur trade. Captain James Hanna in the *Sea Otter* arrived in 1785, to be followed in 1786 by James Stuart Strange with the *Captain Cook* and the *Experiment*. The crews of Strange's ships, weakened by scurvy, recuperated at Friendly Cove, at the entrance to the Sound, and a young surgeon named John Mackay was left there to winter with the Indians and to prepare for the establishment of a trading post. The profits from Strange's voyage, however, turned out to be too small to warrant further expenditure and the plan for a trading post was dropped. Mackay was rescued a year later in a starving condition by Captain Barkley of the *Imperial Eagle*.

Meanwhile, other trading companies had been organized, with ships registered under foreign flags in order to evade the restrictions of the East India Company. In May 1788 John Meares, a retired lieutenant of the Royal Navy, arrived at Friendly Cove in the *Felice*. He brought with him European and Chinese workmen, and with their aid erected a dwelling house and a shipyard on a piece of land

50

acquired from Chief Maquinna of the Nootka Indians. Here the schooner *North West America* was built and launched. The Sound became a busy place. At the end of the summer Meares' second ship arrived, the *Iphigenia* under Captain Douglas, and two other trading ships, the *Prince of Wales* and the *Princess Royal*. At this time the first American vessels appeared, the *Columbia Rediviva* with Captain John Kendrick, and the *Lady Washington* with Captain Robert Gray.

Word of all this activity finally reached the Spaniards at San Blas in Mexico. The Viceroy decided to build a military post at Nootka to protect Spanish interests, and for this purpose sent Esteban José Martinez northwards in 1789. Upon his arrival, Martinez seized the *Iphigenia* and later the *North West America*, and with great ceremony took possession of Nootka Sound (called by the Spaniards San Lorenzo) and adjacent territories. At Friendly Cove he built a fort and a gun emplacement with sixteen guns. When Captain James Colnett arrived in the *Argonaut*, claiming authority to take possession of the Sound for England, Martinez seized the *Argonaut* and the *Princess Royal* and sent them to San Blas as prizes. The Spaniards did some exploring along the coast, but did not stay to consolidate their position. At the end of October they abandoned the fort and sailed back to Mexico.

The following year reports of the seizure reached England and precipitated what was known as the "Spanish Armament Crisis." The Spanish Ambassador complained of invasion of territorial rights; England demanded complete restoration of property and surrender of Spanish claims to sovereignty. During the crisis Spain reoccupied Nootka and rebuilt the fort of San Miguel. The two countries were on the brink of war and England had mobilized the Navy when Spain gave way. On October 28, 1790, agreement was reached. Reparations were to be made for property destroyed by Spain and Britain was to be allowed rights to within ten miles of Spanish-occupied coasts; the actual boundaries of Spain's occupation were still to be determined. Captain George Vancouver was to be sent to Nootka to establish these boundaries and to carry out the

The photo above is a reproduction of a drawing by John Webber in 1788 showing the launching of the first ship built in what is today B.C. The vessel, the *North West America,* **was built for fur trader Captain John Meares and launched at Nootka Sound on September 20, 1788. The artist was a member of Captain Cook's crew.**

The photos on the opposite page are also reproductions of drawings by John Webber in 1788 when he visited Nootka Sound. At top are Cook's ships *Resolution* **and** *Discovery.* **The center shows an Indian village with its split plank houses and at bottom is the interior of a house.**

At right is the lighthouse at Friendly Cove. It stands on the site of the Spanish fort which was built in 1789 and which almost resulted in war between England and Spain.

ceremony of taking British possession.

In 1792 Vancouver arrived at Nootka with H.M.S. *Discovery*, sloop of war, and the *Chatham*, an armed tender. He was met by Quadra, now commandant of San Blas, and the two men tried unsuccessfully to come to an agreement. Quadra maintained that Spain had no reparations to make, and promised that Nootka would be the northern limit of Spanish territory. Vancouver insisted that since Meares had occupied buildings and land there, Nootka was British property. Both men decided to refer the matter to their governments. A firm friendship had sprung up between them, and together they paid a ceremonial visit to Chief Maquinna at his village of Tahsis, deep in the Sound. In honour of their meeting they gave the name of "Quadra and Vancouver Island" to what is now known as Vancouver Island. In 1795 the Nootka Convention was finally ratified. British and Spanish commissioners met at Nootka for the ceremony of raising the British flag, and the Spaniards withdrew for the last time.

From now on British ships were seen less and less in the Sound as British sailors were withdrawn from merchant ships for naval service in the war with France. In 1803 the crew of the American ship *Boston* was massacred by Maquinna and his Indians, and thereafter the Americans avoided this part of the coast. The fur trade gradually declined, and by about 1825 Nootka Sound had reverted to its former quiet state. Only the Indians remained to carry on their traditional pursuits of hunting and fishing.

The traveller today finds on every side reminders of the early days of exploration. For instance, English and Spanish names on the charts bring history to life. Bligh Island, in the mouth of the Sound, is named after the master of the *Resolution*, the same William Bligh who later was captain of the *Bounty*. Gore Island is called after John Gore, first lieutenant in the *Resolution*; Hanna Channel commemorates James Hanna, master of the *Sea Otter*; and Mackay Passage is named for John Mackay, the young surgeon who spent a year with the Indians at Friendly Cove. Kendrick Arm recalls John Kendrick, master of the *Columbia Rediviva*, and Strange Island is named for James

The photos above and at top left show Friendly Cove as it is today. The stained-glass windows in the church were donated by the Spanish government. Among other communities on Nootka Sound is Zeballos, top right, only recently connected to Vancouver Island's road system. The Indians who live at Friendly Cove, opposite, are direct descendents of those who greeted the early explorers nearly two centuries ago.

Strange of the East India Company. Some of the ships have left their names: Discovery Point, Argonaut Point, Resolution Cove, Princess Royal Point, Boston Point, Princess Channel (named after a frigate sailing with Quadra).

Even more prevalent than English names are those of the Spanish explorers. Many of the islands in Nootka Sound, some of them only a few square yards of rock, bear names given them by the Spaniards: Pantoja Island, Carrasco Narvaez, Verdia, Villaneuve, San Rafael, San Miguel, and many others are all called after explorers of the period. The Spaniards have gone, but the names remain.

At the opening of the twentieth century there were a few white men here and there in the area. A little logging was carried on, a little fishing, a little prospecting for minerals. Suddenly, in 1925, vast schools of pilchards arrived. Canneries and reduction plants sprang up everywhere, and for nearly twenty years the industry prospered. In the early forties the fish decreased in number, and by 1946 they had vanished completely. The mystery of their disappearance is still unsolved.

At the beginning of the thirties gold was discovered at the head of Zeballos Arm. A minor gold rush ensued, and by 1936 over 3,000 claims had been staked. In 1938 six mines were working, each with its own mill. The largest of these, the Privateer, produced gold and silver to the value of $6.5 million. The settlement at Zeballos grew to a town of a thousand inhabitants, with stores, schools, hotels and a Red Cross hospital. Ten years later the boom was over.

With the price of gold set at $35 an ounce it was no longer profitable for the mines to operate. Zeballos shrank to a small village and for some years the only activity in the vicinity was a small amount of logging. Then iron entered the picture. In 1962 International Iron Mines began operating a mine 2,000 feet above the floor of the Zeballos Valley but within a year were forced by lack of profit to close down. In 1964 Zeballos Iron Mines Ltd. reopened the mine and were soon extracting some 1,200 tons of iron concentrates per day for shipment to Japan. After five years the vein ran out and the mine closed down again.

Today there is evidence that Zeballos' gold-mining industry may soon be revived. Exploratory work is being carried out in the New Privateer Mine (the old Privateer under new ownership) and prospectors are working in the surrounding hills. As the price of gold continues to rise, Zeballos looks forward to another period of prosperity.

At Tahsis, where once Chief Maquinna's village stood, there is now a town of some 1,500 people, and a sawmill run by the Tahsis Company, a subsidiary of the Danish East Asiatic Company. Apart from the company's own logging operations, the mill provides a market for the small logging camps which are to be found here and there in the inlets of the Sound. Almost every day there are one or two deep-sea ships at the docks, loading lumber for ports all over the world.

The Tahsis Company operates a logging camp and a pulp mill at Gold River at the head of Muchalat Inlet. Inland nine miles at the junction of the Gold and Heber Rivers the ultra-modern community of Gold River was built for employees of the pulp mill and affiliated logging operations.

At the present time there are approximately 5,000 people living in the Nootka Sound area. Both Tahsis and Zeballos are now linked to the rest of Vancouver Island by road and inevitably will increase in size. But the Sound remains the same, and civilization affects only a part of the whole. When the traveller leaves a settlement behind and rounds a point, there before him is the same scene which has existed unchanged for centuries. The Indians in their canoes saw it first, then the early explorers saw it from their little ships, and now modern man sees it from his modern vessel or his plane. Here and there on the shore is an abandoned building, half obliterated by vegetation. On the hillsides are scars left by the loggers, but the forest grows quickly and will cover them. These are only temporary changes. The mountains still stand as they have always done, towering over the narrow channels. The whale still spouts at the mouth of the Sound, the little black bear still stands on the foreshore, and the eagle still wheels overhead. Nootka Sound is as impressive today as it was to those Spanish and English explorers who first visited it two centuries ago.

∎

ORDEAL ALONG THE

Early in the winter of 1930 a single-engined Junkers aircraft with three men aboard went missing in the unexplored wilderness of northeastern B.C. and the Yukon. The subsequent search and rescue by two men and a single plane was an epic of heroism.

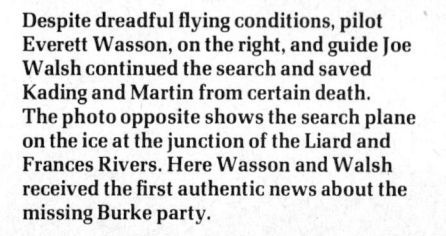

Despite dreadful flying conditions, pilot Everett Wasson, on the right, and guide Joe Walsh continued the search and saved Kading and Martin from certain death. The photo opposite shows the search plane on the ice at the junction of the Liard and Frances Rivers. Here Wasson and Walsh received the first authentic news about the missing Burke party.

LIARD

by F. H. ELLIS

At left is bush pilot Paddy Burke who fought a losing battle with the northern wilderness and, far left, a Junkers aircraft of the type flown by Burke.

At right guide Joe Walsh stands beside the crippled Junkers as he and Everett Wasson found it on the frozen Liard River. The snow covering the plane and surrounding trees effectively camouflaged the missing craft.

The center photo on the opposite page shows Kading, left, and Martin, center, immediately after they had been located on December 7, 1930. Experienced woodsman Joe Walsh made the skis held by Kading right on the spot from small saplings.

Starving, half frozen, hundreds of miles from habitation, the plight of Emil Kading and Bob Martin seemed hopeless. In wilderness silence broken only by trees cracking protest at the bitter cold, they huddled eighteen hours a day in sleeping bags far too light for a Yukon winter. Starvation that had already claimed their companion, Paddy Burke, had reduced them to emaciated scarecrows battling feebly to stave off the icy fingers of death. As cold grey dawn followed cold dark night their grasp on life weakened until they knew that soon the breath of neither would disturb the frigid blanket of winter that nature had spread.

Their ordeal started innocently enough. Robert Martin, a prospector, had chartered a pontoon-equipped Junkers aircraft at Atlin for a trip to a Hudson's Bay Post on the Liard River in the Yukon. With Paddy Burke as pilot and Emil Kading as engineer, the trio left on October 10, 1930. The outward journey was uneventful but shortly after taking off on their way home they ran into an Arctic blizzard. The storm blanketed the pass which led through the 8,000-foot Pelly Mountains and when they encountered snow at 1,000 feet, Burke knew it was time to sit down. He made an emergency landing on the Liard River and the three men huddled overnight to await dawn and better weather.

Next morning snow was still falling heavily but after a meal of beans, bread and coffee, the three unanimously agreed to take off. They well knew that in that mountainous region one storm could follow another for days and even weeks. "I don't know about you fellows, but I have no desire to eat beans for a month," Martin said jokingly, not realizing that shortly he would relish not only beans but any kind of food.

Although the Liard was now running heavy with slush, they took off without incident and headed southeastward on a course that would take them over Teslin, Gladys and Surprise Lakes. However, visibility grew worse every minute and Burke once more headed back to the river. By now snow was falling in an almost solid blanket and they had to skim the treetops to keep the ground in sight. They fully expected each second to be their last but suddenly Kading saw the river and all breathed easier. Again Burke skillfully landed the aircraft but at this point their luck ran out.

As they taxied toward shore a tremor ran through the plane as the floats grazed a submerged object. The three men looked at one another, hoping desperately that there was no damage. Their hopes, unfortunately, were in vain. Ten feet from the bank the plane slowly sank as the pontoons filled with water.

Although the river was only two feet deep, the three realized that they were stranded. They had nothing with which to raise the plane or repair the floats if they could. And it was impossible to haul the plane onto shore because the river bank dropped sheer to the water's edge.

Since they had only a general idea of their location, they decided that the best policy was to make themselves as comfortable as possible and await rescue. Because most of Burke's flying was over virtually uninhabited country, he left standing instructions with his wife to contact the Company's head office in Vancouver if he became overdue.

While the three were certain that she had already done this, they were concerned. Winter was setting in fast, and they simply were not equipped to survive a Yukon winter. With them they had a few cooking utensils, fifty pounds of dried beans, three tins of bully beef, a pound of tea, three pounds of sugar and raisins, three tins of dried vegetables, and two pounds of butter. Other equipment included their sleeping bags—only one of them winter weight—an axe, a rifle with twelve shells, matches, and a hundred feet of rope.

They hoped to supplement their food by shooting game but saw no game or even tracks. After six days and no sign of rescue, they realized that they couldn't wait because their food supply would soon be gone.

The three men held a consultation and Kading suggested they try to float downstream on a raft to reach the Hudson's Bay Post. But they had no nails to build a raft and decided that rope alone would sooner or later be chafed through by the rocks. The idea was abandoned since neither Burke nor Martin could swim and they would have little chance of surviving if the raft disintegrated.

During the summer's flying Burke and Kading had established a food and fuel cache on a lake which they had named Junkers and which they felt was only twenty miles away. Accordingly, they decided to hike overland to their cache. Once at the lake they planned to rest and then push another thirty miles to Wolf Lake, at the headwaters of the Liard River. They knew that a winter Indian campment was established there and they would have no further trouble.

Unfortunately, they didn't know that Junkers Lake was not twenty miles away but over sixty, or that the weather was to be unusually severe with an earlier-than-average winter.

On October 17th they wrote a note outlining their plans and left it in the plane's cabin. Then with hopes high they set out, feeling that they should be able to average ten miles a day. But they quickly learned that this was impossible. The temperature was near zero and the snow already several feet deep. They had no snowshoes, and their ordinary leather boots were the worst possible footwear for such conditions. Worse still, the Liard River hadn't frozen and they were forced to travel along the bank and battle snow already chest deep.

As they groped forward, bushes continuously tripped them and boulders and deadfalls interlaced to form an almost impenetrable barrier. In the bitter cold, with snow falling almost steadily and without adequate food or clothing the three men were soon exhausted. That night they flopped into their sleeping bags, discouraged by the knowledge that they had covered less than half of the intended ten miles.

Day after day they struggled slowly onward, snow conditions deepening and their strength waning by the hour. Some days they covered not even a mile. During one forty-eight-hour period they couldn't move, held to their sleeping bags by a blizzard which howled from the Arctic.

After seven days Burke was completely spent, and since the others were too tired to assist him, they decided to camp where they were. The same day they ate the last of the food and now knew that their sole hope of survival was outside aid. In their desperate straits, Kading, who was the best shot, continually hunted for anything which meant food. However, conditions made it impossible for him to venture far from camp, and there seemed to be neither animal nor bird in the whole frigid wilderness.

They realized that the penetrating cold and lack of food was fast undermining their vitality. To conserve as much energy as possible, they huddled in their sleeping bags eighteen hours out of every twenty-four, cold, hungry, too tired to talk or think, awaiting what seemed an inevitable end. This bitter ordeal lasted twenty-three days, their only food four tiny pine squirrels and one small duck which Kading was able to shoot. Then a miracle happened. They spotted a caribou.

It came within two hundred yards of the camp, and as Kading reached for the rifle, he broke into a cold sweat, fearing that in his weakened condition he would miss. He lined the sights and squeezed the trigger and, as if some Higher Hand had aided him, the animal dropped dead in its tracks.

Unfortunately, Paddy Burke was so weak that nothing but skilled medical attention could save him. Five days after the caribou had been shot he died in his sleeping bag. In the faltering glow from the tiny campfire his helpless friends stood silent, both wondering how long it would be before the Arctic cold and blizzards also claimed them.

Although they had been more robust than Burke, Paddy's death was a bitter blow and their spirits dropped. With the little strength they could muster they fashioned a rough crib of logs and placed Paddy's remains in it, said a brief prayer and covered him with his sleeping bag.

Then they discussed their plight and decided that the only hope of survival was the food cache at Junkers Lake. Before they left, Martin slashed a wide blaze on a tree and scrawled on it a message with a burnt stick. The words read: "Paddy Burke died on November 20, at 6.30 p.m., cause sickness from lack of food, having been 23 days without same. Please pardon our poor efforts as we are in a sinking condition. Expect to leave here Saturday, November 23, for Wolf lake, following the Liard river until Caribou creek. Hope we can make same. Snow very deep and no snowshoes. Bob Martin, Emil Kading."

Writing it was a brave effort because by then both knew that death was in their footsteps. But from somewhere they summoned courage to face the white, harsh wilderness and with as much meat as they could carry, plunged into the snow. They soon discovered that their physical ability was not in keeping with their good intentions. The first three days they covered only five miles and were utterly exhausted. They made a crude camp and prepared to await what fate had in store, their outlook as bleak as the country they were in. Their choice was starving or freezing to death and, like Paddy Burke, they would probably die of both.

At Atlin, meanwhile, Mrs. Burke had notified the head office in Vancouver. A lengthy delay took place before a

The above photo, taken by Robert Martin, shows the Junkers marooned on the Liard River. Kading is on the wing and Burke beside the propeller. The top photo shows the blazed tree bearing the message at the camp where Burke died.

At left is rugged wilderness typical of B.C. and Yukon where the ordeal took place.

search began but finally a plane was sent north from Vancouver. Unfortunately, before reaching the Yukon it crashed while landing on a small lake.

The Company then contacted a pilot named Derbrandt of International Airways. He arrived at Atlin on October 26th and made a number of air sweeps in the vicinity. But his efforts were useless since he scanned areas hundreds of miles from where the Junkers was down. It was no fault of his, for no one knew where the plane had gone missing. But he was soon obliged to abandon even this searching. In the north it is customary for pilots to fly trappers and prospectors into isolated areas and pick them up at a later date. This Derbrandt had done and now he had to retrieve them

Kading and Martin, lower left, after fifty-seven bitter days in the Yukon wilderness, and, lower right, when they had recovered.

Paddy Burke is buried at Atlin in northwestern B.C., the Junkers' oak propeller marking his grave. The tall, needle-like monument to the right honors Fritz Miller, one of the miners who discovered the gold which resulted in the birth of Atlin.

before freeze-up or many would perish.

During this time Sam Clerf, a prospector friend of Martin's, had reached Vancouver on his way to San Francisco to his wife and an infant son whom he had never seen. When he learned that Burke and his companions were missing, Clerf put aside his journey south and chartered a plane at his own expense from Alaska Airways at Seattle.

With pilot Pat Renahan and engineer Frank Hatcher, Clerf headed up the B.C. coast on the first stage of their journey. All was well until they reached Butedale then tragedy struck. They took off on November 4th, heading for Prince Rupert. They were never seen again. Weeks later a single wheel was washed up on the beach of a coastal island.

Here fate had dealt another cruel blow. Both Renahan and Hatcher were old hands at bush flying and Clerf knew the country where the Junkers was down like the back of his hand. Had they been able to carry out a search they might very well have found the lost men.

After the plane from International Airways had to be

withdrawn from the search, Burke's company contacted the Tredwell Yukon Company of Whitehorse, who had a Fairchild aircraft in the north. The pilot was an American, Everett Wasson, and he began the first diligent search for the Junkers.

Wasson's first flight was direct to Burke's original destination, the Liard River Post. But when he arrived ice conditions on the river prevented him from landing. He circled the Hudson's Bay Post and dropped a note to the manager asking if Burke had been there. "Yes," the manager tramped in the snow, and followed with "Burke left here Oct 11 for Teslin. Teslin." The last word was tramped out twice.

Here again fate double-crossed the lost men. The word Teslin was incorrect; it should have been Atlin. However, the Post manager had no idea he was giving the wrong information. Burke's regular procedure always had been to fly back to Atlin along a route which went over the village of Teslin. But the Post manager didn't know that the weather had caused Burke to change his mind.

Wasson then wasted days of vital flying time as he searched hundreds of miles from the vicinity of the Junkers. Winter conditions finally forced him to leave the search while he returned to Whitehorse to have his floats removed and skis fitted. On November 12th he left Whitehorse, this time with Joe Walsh, one of the most experienced guides in the Yukon.

For the first phase of their search they systematically swept the terrain between Atlin and Liard Post. It was an extremely hazardous undertaking. The entire area was a huge, unmapped wilderness, with 8,000-foot mountain peaks thrusting skyward and sub-zero temperatures prevailing. Worse still, fierce storms buffeted the region, making necessary many emergency landings on mountain-ringed lakes lashed by treacherous winds. But the two men ignored all personal dangers and continued their mission.

The first clue came when they landed at a small Indian village at the confluence of the Frances and Liard Rivers. Natives there told of seeing a "big white swan" flying up the river several weeks before. Wasson and Walsh knew at last they were on the right track.

Despite a continuous series of storms they maintained their search, making so many emergency landings to avoid sudden snow flurries that they lost count. From one nameless lake they made ten attempts before the plane shook free from the binding power of the deep, powdered snow. Often they had to laboriously stamp out a makeshift runway with their snowshoes before they could take off.

A standard procedure for Walsh on many a take-off was to run alongside the plane, grasping the side of the open door. This lightened the plane and as the craft picked up speed and the wings exerted their lift, Walsh was dragged off his feet. With the plane airborne he then struggled into the cabin, clumsy snowshoes on his feet, the wind tearing at him with hurricane force. It was a Herculean and almost suicidal task.

On November 24th and December 4th, the airmen made complete return flights from Liard Post to the headwaters of the river. On the return from the last flight they spotted a peculiar shadow on the snow-covered river. Swooping down, they saw the glint of metal and knew that at last the lost Junkers had been found.

By now the river was frozen solid but ice hummocks covered the surface and landing was impossible. They landed on a small lake sixteen miles away and fought through the desolate wilderness to the Junkers. But their hopes sank when they found only a note telling that the crew had left. However, they took heart from the fact that at least they knew where to search.

They wearily hiked back to their Fairchild and flew to Whitehorse to confer with the police on the next course of action. It was thought that Burke and the others might have found refuge with Indians on the Pelly Reserve, not far from Wolf Lake. To test this theory, Wasson and Walsh set off from Whitehorse on December 6th.

As they searched for a suitable pass through the Pelly Mountains they spotted a thin wisp of smoke curling above the tree tops far below. Circling for a better look they saw two men waving feebly from a small clearing. Wasson and Walsh knew that their search had ended.

They swept down to almost tree top level and Walsh threw out a box of food. Then, believing that it had dropped into the deep snow and would be hard to find, the two airmen did a very brave and generous thing. Without a thought for their own safety or welfare Wasson circled still lower, and Walsh heaved out every morsel of their own food supply. They attached a brief note saying they would land at a lake about ten miles away.

After landing, they started out for the two lost men but night overtook them and they camped where they were. Before daylight they were away again but at dawn realized that in their hurry they had overshot their objective. Backtracking, and shouting as they went, they suddenly heard a rifle crack twice. Minutes later they reached the pitiful camp and were greeted by Martin and Kading, now whiskered skeletons almost too weak to stand.

Later as the four men sat around a roaring camp fire, two of them eating good food for the first time in many weeks, Wasson turned to Kading and asked, "Say, Emil, how come you only fired two shots?"

Kading knew that Wasson was referring to the fact that the traditional SOS of the woods is three shots, not two. He turned to Wasson and said, with a tired smile, "Those were our last two bullets."

Two days passed before the emaciated men were strong enough to travel the trail back to the plane. Even when they did set out the trek was a tough ordeal and it took the small party two days to reach the lake. They still weren't safe because the plane's engine had frozen solid and it took many hours with a blowtorch to thaw it. Wasson finally got it started and they reached Whitehorse late in the afternoon. Without adequate clothing or shelter or food, Martin and Kading had survived almost two months of bitter Yukon winter.

Wasson, accompanied by Walsh and Sergeant Leopold of the RCMP, later flew back to the Liard for Paddy's body. With the return of the plane to Whitehorse on December 19th, the first air and rescue search in British Columbia and the Yukon ended. Although they didn't know it at the time, Wasson and Walsh set a record in the annals of northern flying.

In appreciation, the Federal and B.C. Governments awarded Wasson $1,500 and Walsh $500. It was fitting recognition of their brave part in saving two men from certain death. For sheer heroism and tenacity of purpose their search stands unequalled to this day. ∎

THOSE CARIBOO CAMELS

Camels? Used for packing in British Columbia? Yes! And they not only caused mules and horses to stampede but ate anything from a shirt on the line to a bar of soap.

by BRUCE RAMSEY

This photo is believed to be the only one in existence of the ill-fated camels and shows the last of the animals which arrived in 1862. It was taken at Grande Prairie in the northern Okanagan about 1888 behind the Ingram estate. The two men are G. Smith, left, and Adam Heffley.

At right on the opposite page is the Fraser River and a section of the road between Lillooet and Clinton over which the camels plodded in 1862. This road, completed in 1861, was the first in Interior British Columbia.

At far right on the opposite page is the advertisement that appeared in the British Colonist on March 1, 1862, announcing the beginning of the camel venture.

One of the most fascinating episodes in the history of British Columbia is the use of camels on the Cariboo Trail in the early 1860's. That these ships of the desert were used in British Columbia during the Cariboo gold rush sometimes makes the skeptic raise one eyebrow in a sort of wondering manner. But used they were, and often with strange and humorous results.

It all began in the spring of 1860 when an enterprising San Francisco merchant, Otto Esche, went to China and arranged for a consignment of camels to be brought to California to serve as pack animals. His idea was not an original one. As early as 1855 the United States had an army Camel Corps which was used with considerable success in the dry desert country of the southwest. Otto Esche's camels came from Manchuria and Mongolia and were "Bactrians" — ones with two humps.

The problems Esche faced in San Francisco with his animals do not concern us here, but on March 1, 1862, the following advertisement appeared on page two of the *Victoria Colonist*: "To packers. Twenty-five camels for sale. Apply to Henry Walton, general agency office, Commercial Street, near Yates Street."

Commenting on this advertisement, in a story headlined "The Camels are Coming," the *Colonist* said that here was the chance for "Cariboo packers to obtain animals suited to their purpose at a low figure. The advantage possessed by the camels over all other pack animals are too well known to require a newspaper puff, but their greatest recommendation to Cariboo packers appears to lie in their long legs which enable them to breast deep snow drifts, the merest sight of which would disturb the equanimity of the strongest-nerved and best conducted jackass in British Columbia."

And then the paper added: "After the camels have been disposed of and have started for the mines with the first load, we learn that a number of trained whales will be placed on the route between Victoria and the Stikine River carrying freight and inside passengers, a la Jonah, at reduced rates."

So, you can see, when my family and I decided to try to unravel the story of the camels and learn the fate of the animals, we had over one hundred years and more of scorn and sarcasm to put up with. This, however, was only one of the many problems we had to contend with. The greatest obstacle was that we found there were too many loose ends dangling before us. We cannot, for instance, determine the relationship between the advertisement and the story which appeared in the *Colonist* just two weeks later. On March 15 it was announced that Mr. John C. Calbraith of Lillooet had purchased twenty-three dromedaries in San Francisco for $300 each. The fact that the *Colonist* called the camels "dromedaries," or one-humped camels, is of little importance.

The account said they would "be used to pack goods

from Lillooet to Cariboo," and, it continued, "Mr. C. is confident he has secured a bargain and expects them here on the 15th of April."

Exactly a month later, on April 15, 1862, the *Colonist* announced, "The Camels have come!" In the story there is an unmistakable prediction of things which were to come. Here is the story in full as Victorians read it that morning more than a hundred years ago:

"Mr. Calbraith's twenty-three Bactrian camels arrived on the 'Hermann' yesterday. They are singular looking animals and when driven off the steamer frightened the horses at Esquimalt out of their proprietory and a week's appetite. The camels are just now engaged in shedding the winter coat of hair and present a very scalpy appearance. Each has two humps on the back and will pack from 500 to 600 pounds. A practical test of the availability as pack animals in British Columbia will be made in a few days. The strangers, who are guarded by a live Turk, are at the Halfway House."

Who the "live Turk" was — and how long he stayed with the camels — the paper didn't elaborate. I eventually learned that his name was Hadj Ali. He was a romantic figure who had been a driver in the U.S. Camel Corps but whose name had been Americanized to Hijolly. In B.C., unfortunately, he fell on hard times in the form of Chinese gamblers who took everything, including his pants.

A week later, we learn from the pages of the *Victoria Colonist* that Mr. Calbraith got a bonus. On April 23 the paper said that: "Yesterday morning early a baby camel made its appearance for the first time. Two or three more of the same kind are fully due and expected daily." We shall hear a good deal more about this baby camel and its mother before we are through.

On May 2, 1862 a brief announcement said the pack train had arrived in downtown Victoria and was "herded in the lot at the corner of Douglas and Johnson Street."

The paper sent one of its reporters down to have a look, and in the casual newspaper style of the times he wrote this story: "Yesterday morning we strolled to the corner of Douglas and Johnson Street and watched the camels. About twenty persons, on a like errand, were standing about the lot poking fun and sticks at the symmetrically formed and noble looking beasts, and among others we noticed a gaily dressed young stranger who seemed particularly interested in the baby camel and its fond mamma.

"And," continued the scribe, "to evince the lively and affectionate regard which he entertained for the parent and her love for the offspring, the stranger would occasionally drag the latter by the tail some distance from the mother; then he would put his arm around its neck and hug it until it was nearly strangled; next he would beat it with a small cane, and so he kept up his intentions until the poor little animal, annoyed beyond endurance, sought refuge between its mother's feet.

"All these delicate little attentions Her Camelship stood without seeming to notice, save by an occasional low snort or a change of position, until finally her tormentor became still bolder and ventured to place his hand on the animals snout and force her head up and down like the handle of an old fashioned town pump."

And then the action began. The story pointed to the folly of the stranger in these words: "Indiscreet man! He paid dearly for his temerity. It was the last feather which broke the camels back, for rendered furious by the indignities practised upon her, the beast quickly raised her head to a level with her tormentors eye, and with a noise resembling the rush of a full head of steam from a boiler, fired through her nostrils about two gallons of dirty water — pumped up from the secret repository which all respectable camels possess, especially for the strangers benefit and instruction.

"The poor fellow," continued the *Colonist* "surprised, alarmed and quite blinded for a moment by the unexpected visitation, sought refuge in flight, and as quickly as possible placed the fence between himself and the enraged beast, who followed and nearly succeeded in giving him a second dose before he got beyond her reach."

The watching crowd thoroughly enjoyed the show, and the stranger on the other side of the fence, in the words of the reporter, was "looking mean enough to sell out for two bits."

"The stranger drew a delicately perfumed handkerchief from his pocket," the story continued, "and after wiping the water from his face, eyes and shirt bosom, looked around on the roaring crowd of spectators, and making a sickly attempt to look unconcerned, with a woe-stricken grin on his countenance, he remarked, 'Why she spits worsenor a steam-injun' and sneaked off down Johnson Street."

As many newspaper stories did in those days, this little gem from the pages of the *Victoria Colonist* closed with a sort of moral. In this case it was "the gallon of water or two of experience which that young fellow picked up from the poor camel should last him through life."

The camels remained in Victoria until May 4, 1862, at which time they were shipped over to the mainland to begin duty on the Cariboo Trail as pack animals. But before we join them over there, it might be just as well to meet the gentlemen involved in the syndicate which brought the camels to British Columbia.

It would seem likely that Mr. John Calbraith, whose name was associated with bringing the camels in, was acting on behalf of others. For, after the initial story appeared in the *Colonist*, we do not find his name associated with them again. Calbraith was a rancher and packer in the Seton Lake country, and later owned a hotel up in Laketon, now a ghost town on the shores of Dease Lake in the Cassiar district in northern British Columbia.

The chief members of the syndicate were Frank Laumeister, Adam Heffley and Henry Ingram. Others were George Stultz, Gustav Hoffmeister and one identified as "old man Neufelden." It was Frank Laumeister, however, who took all the credit — what there was of it — and all the abuse which was to follow in the months ahead.

As can be seen by the names, most of these in the syndicate were of German extraction. Frank Laumeister was a native of Menslin in Bavaria, and he arrived in Victoria early in 1859, a year after the gold excitement on the Lower Fraser River at Yale began. His first business venture was in a saloon, which stood on the northwest corner of Johnson and Store Streets. The following year he purchased a half interest in the Victoria Brewery, and after his spell with the camels, opened a store in Barkerville. During the gold rush to the Cassiar district in the mid 1870's, he ran a pack train over the Moore Trail from Telegraph Creek to

From Victoria, shown at top in 1863-64, the camels were shipped to New Westminster, at center. Here they were loaded on a barge and towed upstream to Port Douglas by the *Flying Dutchman*, a sternwheel steamer similar to the one at the wharf in the center of the photo. The above sketch of Port Douglas appeared in the *Illustrated London News* on December 17, 1864.

Laketon. This time, however, it was not a camel train.

After a couple of days stay in Victoria, the camels were loaded onto the steamer *Enterprise* and shipped to New Westminster. The *Colonist* had noted, on the arrival of the camels, that they were in charge of a "live Turk" but he must have fallen asleep, for the mother camel and baby escaped into the bush around Victoria.

The pair wandered around for months and months, and on November 24, 1862, six months after the arrival of the camels, the *Colonist* reported: "They were both seen upon the Cadboro Bay Road in good health." Five days later a small headline noted: "Wild Beasts on Vancouver Island."

The account in the newspaper read as follows: "A few mornings since a boy was sent to collect some firewood; but ere long he reappeared with looks aghast and hair standing on end. When he found words to explain the cause of his terror, he declared that he had seen some 'wild beasts' and neither persuasion nor threats could induce him to believe he was mistaken.

"The father of the lad," the story continued, "determined to inculcate by example when he had failed to instil by precept, took a stout cudgel and started with the frightened child to view the objects of his terror. But as soon as his eyes fastened upon the monsters his own courage departed, and with blanched cheek and trembling steps, he hastily regained the shelter of his home.

"To a gentleman living close by, who has resided some years in the Colony, the anxious parent revealed the danger to which he and his youthful heir had been exposed. He was kindly asked what the animals were like, and he described them as 'two wild beasts — bigger nor horses — with humps on their backs'."

And, concluded the story: "For the future we would suggest that the patient mother and her hopeful progeny, be each labelled 'The camel bites not'."

That is the last we hear of Her Camelship and the baby. There is a legend that the roving camels met an Indian hurrying along a lonely trail. The Indian was so frightened by what he saw that he started to run faster — and when he looked behind and saw the camels trotting after him — he

Lillooet in the early 1860's. The photo was taken by a frontier photographer named Gentile whose sign can be seen in the photo of Victoria on page 63. With completion of the Cariboo Wagon Road through the Fraser Canyon in 1863, Yale replaced Lillooet as portal to Cariboo.

The top photo, a sketch from the *Illustrated London News* in 1864, shows miners leaving for Cariboo from a roadhouse near Fountain, a few miles from Lillooet. Since mules and horses bolted at the smell of a camel, the "Dromedary Express" was cursed by all who encountered it.

ran ever faster. When he reached the door of his home, as luck would have it, or rather ill-luck, the lock was jammed. And the camels were right behind. The poor Indian then dropped dead from fright. Only a legend, but there are many in the camel story.

For instance, the original accounts tell that on April 15, 1862, twenty-three camels were unloaded at Esquimalt. Then we have an account of one being born, and two or three more expected daily. Now we come to our first camel mystery.

On Wednesday, May 2, 1862 the New Westminster newspaper, the *British Columbian,* recorded that: "Camels, 21 in number, arrived by the steamer *Enterprise* on Monday and went up to Douglas yesterday on the barge in tow of the *Flying Dutchman.*"

Apparently, nobody bothered to count the baby camels, if any more had been born. It would seem, however, that something happened to two camels in Victoria, not just the mother camel who ran off into the bush. What happened we do not know, but from now on our story deals with twenty-one camels.

The *British Columbian* said: "Their appearance on the wharf caused great wonder and hy-you-waw-waw amongst the Indians who seemed in great perplexity to understand the precise nature of the extraordinary looking animals."

No time was wasted putting the animals to work. On May 17, ten days after the announcement of their arrival on the mainland was made, the *British Columbian* reported that "the camels are employed in packing over the Pemberton Portage and are found to answer admirably."

A week later, the first words of doubt about their worthiness on the trail began to appear. On May 24, the paper said: "The camels are still employed in packing over the Pemberton Portage. Although we believe these animals do not quite come up to the expectations of their owners, yet they answer very well, and we have understood an advance of $600 has been tendered for them. While they carry from 500 to 600 pounds at a load, being double that of a mule, their keep costs less than nothing as they pick up all they require by the wayside — no small consideration when feed is from six to seven cents per pound."

The *Victoria Colonist* reported on May 28, 1862: "... camels have crossed Seton Lake enroute for the Brigade Trail over which they will be packed with provisions for Cariboo. So far they seem to have proved a success."

A week later, nine were reported packing from Seton Lake to Lillooet Flat, making three trips a day and, according to the *British Columbian* for June 4, 1862, they were carrying 400 pounds each with ease, "not withstanding their poor condition." The remainder had gone "up the road" to the mouth of Bridge River where a small community had sprung up following construction of a toll bridge there.

Towards the end of June the first of the great camel trains in British Columbia's history pushed out from Lillooet for the long and dangerous trek to the goldfields of the Cariboo.

The heavily-laden camels could very well have felt at home on the first leg of the journey as they trudged up the Cariboo Trail through the dry benchlands which suddenly ended at the yawning precipitous walls of the canyon of the Upper Fraser. Then they headed over Pavilion Mountain and down to Clinton where they met up with the route followed by the old-time fur traders.

A report which appeared in the *Colonist* for June 30, 1862 states that one of them was killed by falling down a precipice near Pavilion Creek. The story states: "He was pushed over by one of the younger camels that became frightened at some object on the trail." Again, we find some praise for the camels. The *Colonist* noted: "... they are said to answer very well as pack animals." These were, sad to relate, the last words of praise to appear in 1862.

In August they were on Lightning Creek, and here they met Harry Guillod, a young Englishman heading with two companions for the golden creeks of Cariboo. In his diary for August 20, 1862, he wrote: "My 24th birthday, which I forgot all about till it was passed. Was bothered today by camels of which there are about a dozen here who have a neat idea of walking over your tent and eating your shirts."

For another account of camels in this part of the Cariboo, we must turn to a weekly newspaper called *The Province*, which is now the *Vancouver Province*. During 1895 the paper carried a series of reminiscences by an old-timer who signed himself "Cariboo," and in one, published on November 23, 1895, he tells of an encounter between the camels and a dog named Dashaway, owned by Bob Ridley, one of the Cariboo immortals.

"We had camped one evening near Cottonwood," the writer stated. "In addition to our train, Judge Begbie's twelve animals and his two dogs were on the ground. The camels made their appearance and the dogs became as interested in the spectacle as their masters.

"Dashaway was in charge of a number of pack saddles and was faithful to his duty, until one of the 'ships of the desert' ventured to interfere with the sweat clothes. With a bound Dashaway seized the big animal by the nose and away sped the animal roaring. The other camels took up the cry and for some minutes the mountains echoed with the unearthly roars of the stampeding humpbacks."

The writer of these words continued: "I never saw such a commotion in camp, and were it not that Dashaway was recalled, that day would have decided the fate of the camels in Cariboo.

"When horses stampede in a wild and precipitous country it is bad enough — but camels! Good Lord deliver us!"

Another account of the camels appeared February 16, by the same writer. This time, he recalls that Judge Begbie "... was riding his cayuse leisurely along when the little cayuse espied the camel train, and despite the most strenuous efforts on the part of the rider, carried the judge into the jungle, making havoc of his unmentionables. Sir Matthew ever after disfavored camels."

It is unfortunate that we have no date for these two events. The next dated account we find is that contained in the *Victoria Colonist* for October 15, 1862, under the simple heading "The Camels." The account states: "About a dozen of these animals are all that survive. They are turned out to graze at the Forks of Quesnelle River, and are considered the greatest failure of the season."

The following year the camels were back in business. On May 12, 1863 the *Colonist,* in a dispatch from Lillooet, informs us that "the camels have loaded here for the upper country. They are rolling fat. The big one, Barnum, carried 800 pounds of flour; the others 400 to 500."

The correspondent to the Victoria newspaper, who signed himself "Kangaroo," continued that "on the first day they travelled eighteen and the second thirty miles. They beat any transit we have, either ox, wagon, mule or cayoosh ponies. They are now acclimated and will eat anything from a pair of pants to a bar of soap."

The last contemporary item on the camels to be chronicled in newspaper index in the Provincial Archives in Victoria is one for the *Colonist* dated May 29, 1863. The reference refers to an account of a trip over Pavilion Mountain, and is contained in a news item titled "Cariboo Correspondence": ". . . the tinkle of a mule bell warned us that a train was approaching. To our dismay we found on turning a curve in the road that the camels were coming. As we expected our horses were very restive, we were congratulating ourselves on passing so quietly, when one of those animals, a regular old patriarch of ninety, came slowly towards us; our horse gave a snort and away they dashed through the bush, wheeling around to take another look at the laggard that was passing. . . ."

In concluding his report, the writer said: "Mr. Laumeister is the enterprising owner. Each animal packed 430 pounds on the trip just completed to Alexandria."

This is the first mention of the name Frank Laumeister to be associated in contemporary records with the camels. It is also the last time the camels are mentioned in the early newspapers.

What happened to them after that is conjecture. A popular legend has it that Frank Laumeister, who owned the camel train, was forced to remove it from the road as the result of court actions. However, a diligent search through court records of the period show no reference to any actions concerning camels. It is quite likely, and indeed highly probable, that Laumeister was threatened with court actions and probably with physical violence to his person.

Perhaps the real reason why they were taken off the road is contained in a paragraph which appeared in the *Washington Statesman* published at Walla Walla. This item, dated March 12, 1864, says that because of the "stony formation of the country, they became footsore and their owners had to decide their investment was a non-paying one." Apparently the camels were either sold or turned loose and left to roam as they pleased. So, let us try to find out what happened to them.

To learn some of the answers, my family and I set out on a camel hunting expedition that took us all over the province. The first thing we had to establish was the number of camels. As we have already noted, newspaper accounts tell us twenty-three camels arrived at Esquimalt in April, 1862. One was born at the Halfway House, between Victoria and Esquimalt, making twenty-four. Then, the stories say, "two or three more" were expected at any time. So, for the point of argument, let us settle on twenty-seven camels. The "two or three" may not have been born until after they reached the mainland, for we learn from the *British Columbian* that twenty-one camels arrived at New Westminster in May, 1862. Therefore, three vanished in Victoria. We know that the mother and baby did head for the tall timber, and were seen for about six months, and then we hear nothing further. What happened to the other we do not know.

Then, one camel fell over a cliff near Pavilion Creek and was killed. By October, as we learned from the *Colonist*, only about a dozen remained, and they were grazing at the Forks of the Quesnelle River; that is, at Quesnelle Forks.

So, what happened?

Perhaps the answer lies in a story told to us by Mr. Don McLeod, the chief photographer of the *Vancouver Province*. During the last war, Mr. McLeod was accompanying the then M.L.A. for Cariboo, Louis LeBourdais, on a military maneuver near Lac La Hache. In private life, LeBourdais was a telegraph operator on the old Government Telegraph line and he got his start in the business at Lac La Hache.

Louis used to love to visit historic sites, and, on this trip, he took Mr. McLeod to a spot near 117 Mile House, just south of Lac La Hache, and pointed out in a field a mound on the top of which was a weathered headboard. Twenty years passed. Louis LeBourdais had died meanwhile, and one day Mr. McLeod and I were discussing the Cariboo, which we both love. It was then he told me about the mound in the field.

Above is Harry Guillod, the Cariboo-bound miner whose shirt was eaten by the camels. The top photo shows Frank Laumeister, one of the group associated with the camel venture.

It was an amazing story. He said this mound was the grave of either five or eight camels, he couldn't remember which, but thought it was more likely eight. Twenty years before when Louis LeBourdais told him about it, the lettering on the headboard was still legible. It told of how the animals were caught in a sudden blizzard and perished. Don also recalled that two men died in the storm as well, but alas, he could not remember the date.

The tragedy appears to have gone unnoticed by the press. If mention was made of it, we have been unable to find it.

We also heard that in a dry gulch there could be found, probably about the turn of the century, the weatherbeaten bones of some camels. Our informant on this story was taken to the site when she was six years of age, but now she does not recall where it was. She is descended from William Pinchbeck, the first settler in the Williams Lake district, so it was likely that the dry gulch she referred to was in that area.

At least, with Don McLeod's story there was something to work upon. We set out for Lac La Hache to locate the curious grave beside the Cariboo Road.

To help us, Don drew a rough map, apologizing profusely that twenty years had gone by since he had last given the grave a thought. For us, it was like going treasure hunting, using an old pirate map as a guide. As it turned out, Don's map, as far as landmarks were concerned, was surprisingly accurate.

One clue, though, was particularly puzzling. It showed a road branching out from the main Cariboo Road and heading up a hill to what McLeod called an "old changing house." This, he said, was used by the early teamsters as a place to change stagecoach and freight-wagon horses. At the time of his visit to Lac La Hache, it was standing gaunt and empty, with not even a roof on it to protect it from the elements. From here, Don said, we should be able to see the grave.

On our arrival in Lac La Hache, we scanned the lovely green hills for some sign of the old coaching house, but could find none. A little discouraged at not being able to find this important clue, we called in at the post office at Lac La Hache to talk to Mrs. Ogden, the post mistress. She had been in Lac La Hache for forty years, and her husband, a grandson of Peter Skene Ogden, the famous Hudson's Bay Company fur trader of the early days, was born here.

Alas, she had never heard the story. But, she told us, if Louis LeBourdais knew the story and the location, then it was true and the grave was somewhere about. We showed her the map and asked about the changing house.

"That," she said, "was old Isaac Ogden's store. It was pulled down several years ago. But," she added, "the map gives its precise location, and the road which led up from the main Cariboo Road was one used by the drivers to get their freight trains off the main road while changing horses. It is definitely the changing house LeBourdais referred to."

Another clue was a small stream which flows into Lac La Hache. Near the mouth of the creek were several old buildings, Don had told me. I had remembered these buildings from previous visits to Lac La Hache, but now they are gone. The grave was either southwest, or southeast of the farm buildings, maybe a mile away, and set in a field.

The grass was long in the field, and the weather was far from being at its best. It must be recorded, unfortunately, that we were unable to locate the grave. But of one thing I am sure — the grave does exist.

Another clue as to what happened to one of the camels is contained in an article which appeared in the *Province*. In 1895 a contributor, signing himself "Cariboo," recalled his experiences during the gold rush. He tells of an event which took place between 150 Mile House and Quesnelle Forks. Incidentally, this is the area where one of our informants probably saw camel bones when she was a child.

The story deals with a Victoria contractor by the name of John Morris who joined in the rush to the gold-bearing gravels of the Cariboo. East of the 150 Mile he shot what he thought was a grizzly bear, but on close examination he found it wasn't a bear at all, but a camel. Henceforth, John Morris was known as "Grizzly Morris."

At a hotel at Beaver Lake which was operated by François Guy, known as Guy's Place, the writer of the piece in the *Province* found himself one day sitting down

The late Louis LeBourdais at Barkerville in 1929 and, at top, Robert Galbraith, first settler in what is now Fort Steele. In 1870 he stated that the camel meat was delicious, especially fried.

to what he said was a "fine roast that would have had an appetizing effect upon anyone." Subsequently, he was told it was "Grizzly's bear," or camel. Reflecting on this, the writer said: "I have eaten many delicacies in my time (including pork and beans) but for a never to be forgotten dish, give me camel hump. I have often since regretted that the denizens of the Sahara desert have not acquired the art of canning."

One who also ate a piece of Grizzly's bear, or camel, was the infamous gambler James Barry, who was later to die on the gallows in Richfield, just outside Barkerville, for the murder of Charles Morgan Blessing.

Before leaving Grizzly Morris, however, we must not forget one thing about this man. While he was not the world's most successful grizzly bear hunter, when it came to finding gold, few could match Grizzly Morris's achievement. Today, visitors to Barkerville see an historic marker pointing to the site of the famous Grizzly claim. It produced thousands of dollars worth of gold, and the man who discovered it, and after whom it was named, was our great grizzly-camel hunter, John Morris.

There is also a report that Adler and Barry — no relation to the aforementioned James Barry — who were noted restaurant and saloon keepers in the Cariboo, slaughtered a camel at the 150 Mile House and offered the meat for sale. However, it was not popular with their customers for as one writer put it, the miners had a prejudice against camels. It may be that this is the same camel referred to in the *Province* story, but now, after the passing of a hundred years of history, it is impossible to tell, and it is likely we will never know.

If Don McLeod's figures are right, and eight camels are buried at Lac La Hache, we therefore can account for an even dozen. The newspaper report of August 1862 says "about a dozen" remain. So we are pretty close to accounting for all those camels who died in active service on the Cariboo Road more than a hundred years ago. The search for the fate of the others took us to Cache Creek, Kamloops, Westwold, and Fort Steele.

A likely spot for more information, it seemed to us, was Ashcroft Manor, the oldest remaining stopping place on the Cariboo Road. This old home is occupied by Mr. and Mrs. Alan Parker. Mrs. Parker was a Cornwall, granddaughter of one of the Cornwall brothers who built the place back in 1862. When we left this quaint old house by the Cariboo Road we were able to tick one more camel off our list, thus bringing the total to eleven which had to be accounted for.

The Parkers said that one of them had died on the banks of Hat Creek near Cache Creek, and for many years, its bones could be seen lying where it died. According to the story, a stage driver named Walker acquired the animal, and used it, along with a mule, to drag a plough on his ranch. Mr. Walker probably had one of the worst combinations of plough animals imaginable, for of all God's creatures, none are more stubborn, nor unwielding, as a camel and a mule.

From Ashcroft we went over to Kamloops, and to that city's excellent museum. Here in an old record book we learned that a Mr. Ogden had sold some camel meat to the Hudson's Bay Company for forty cents a pound. That meant two down — and ten to go.

Here also we heard an unconfirmed report that one was

Beaver Valley, east of 150 Mile House, where one of the camels was shot when mistaken for a grizzly bear. At top is a memorial erected by the Arizona Highways Commission at Quartzsite, Arizona, to commemorate Hijolly, or Hi Jolly, who arrived in B.C. with the camels in 1862. He died in 1902 after serving as a U.S. Army camel driver and packer for over thirty years.

shot just south of Kamloops by a man who, according to legend, couldn't sleep for a week when he found what his target was.

More news of the camels around Kamloops appeared in the *Washington Historical Quarterly* for October, 1929. An old packer named William S. Lewis related the following story: "A man by the name of Angus McDonald saw a camel grazing not far from the trail. Knowing how to handle the animal from being about the packers in the Cariboo mines, he made it lie down. Then he got on its back and rode down the trail. Just as he was entering the main trail, he saw a freight outfit coming along, and the mules started to stampede. He at once turned his steed into the brush, jumped off, and hid himself to escape censure and possible punishment from the enraged packer."

From Kamloops, we headed over Rogers Pass to Golden, and thence south to Fort Steele to find out what we could about a camel which was reported there in the early days. H. H. Bancroft, the noted American historian, says in his *History of Washington, Idaho and Montana*, that a man named William Henry had a camel which was used to haul supplies into Wild Horse Creek at present-day Fort Steele.

This man is referred to in a newspaper account which appeared in the *Washington Statesman*, published at Walla Walla on March 12, 1864. The story bears the headline "A Pack Camel" and this is what it said: "In that train that left here this week (that is, from Walla Walla) for the Kootenai mines was something new in the shape of a pack animal for this country, an Arabian camel."

The account went on to say that "Mr. William Henry of the Bitterfoot Ferry is the fortunate owner of the animal and obtained it from parties recently from the Cariboo district...."

William Henry was better known as "Blackfoot Bill" and he died the following year — 1865 — as the result of a mining accident. After that it is entirely possible that a Frenchman by the name of Brehaut obtained this particular camel. We find that in 1867, according to Robert L. T. Galbraith, the first settler in Fort Steele, that a French-Canadian prospector brought in a camel from Bonners Ferry.

He kept the beast at Wild Horse for a time, despite the fact that there was considerable hostility against the camel. The reason was, of course, not new — the very sight of a camel stampeded the horses. Brehaut finally turned the camel loose on the west side of the Kootenay River, near Cherry Creek, and the animal lived there for two or three years. It apparently had no difficulty in shifting for itself during the winter months. Eventually it was purchased by Mr. Galbraith.

In 1870 a quarter-breed from Red River, Manitoba, by the name of John V. Campbell, reported the animal living on Perry Creek. He received permission from Mr. Galbraith to kill it for his winter's meat supply. Mr. Galbraith received forty pounds of the camel meat and stated it was most delicious, especially when fried.

So, therefore, we have all but nine accounted for so far.

From Fort Steele our camel hunting expedition turned westward once more and we found ourselves heading for the little farming community of Westwold, between Vernon and Kamloops. At one time this area was known as Grande Prairie, and later Adelphi. It was in this valley that Henry Ingram, one of the syndicate that brought the camels into British Columbia, came to settle. Here members of his family continue to reside, and on the old homestead can be seen Henry Ingram's original cabin.

According to his descendents, Henry Ingram kept three camels on his farm. As farm animals, they were useless, but Ingram kept them around the place as sort of household pets. Every year he used to shear them like sheep, and use the hair to stuff cushions.

One day an Indian came up and asked Ingram if he would trade two of the camels for some horses. It looked like a good deal, so Ingram made the trade. The Indian, however, got the worst of the deal, for the camels wouldn't cooperate. It is likely that the Indian traded them off with another Indian, or he may have shot them. Anyway, nothing more is heard of them.

Until about 1905 the children in Grande Prairie, which we now know as Westwold, used to enjoy going for rides on the back of the surviving camel. And in that year, this old camel, far from his original home on the steppes of Mongolia, leaned against a tree and died. He was the last of the camels, and the only one ever to have his picture taken.

We now have eight to account for, and if we consider the two Ingram horse-traded with the Indian as being written off, then our figure is lowered to six . . . six camels out of a possible twenty-seven which came to British Columbia in 1862.

In dealing with the remaining half dozen camels we are up against a real problem. So far, I have been unable to dig up anything concerning their ultimate fate, but two little stories are of particular interest because they each mention six camels.

The first is a story which has its origin in Hope at the upper end of the Fraser Valley. It is said that in the early days — and I haven't been able to get a closer date than that vague statement — a Frenchman operated a pack train of five or six camels out from Hope over the Dewdney Trail to the Kootenay. Perhaps this Frenchman was the Brehaut we find mentioned in the story at Fort Steele where one was subsequently eaten.

Then there was the story I ran into at Lac La Hache when I was trying to track down the grave of the camels which reportedly perished just south of town. In checking over the story with some of the local residents, I met Lac La Hache's senior resident, Mrs. Rose Williams. She was born in Lac La Hache in 1892 and her maiden name was Hamilton. It is rather interesting to inject here that relations of hers own a ranch at Beaver Lake where one of the camels was mistaken for a grizzly bear and shot by John Morris.

Mrs. Williams told us that when she was four years old — that would be in 1896 — a pack train of about six camels came through Lac La Hache. She does not remember where they were going or which way they were going, but three things stand out in her memory of that event: The first was that these camels smelled something terrible; the second was that the camel driver smelled even worse; the third was that when they came into Lac La Hache, all the other pack animals at the corral stampeded in terror at the sight of the strange beasts.

So with six camels left to account for out of the possible total of twenty-seven, we drew our camel hunting safari in British Columbia to a close. Can anybody supply details on the missing six? ∎

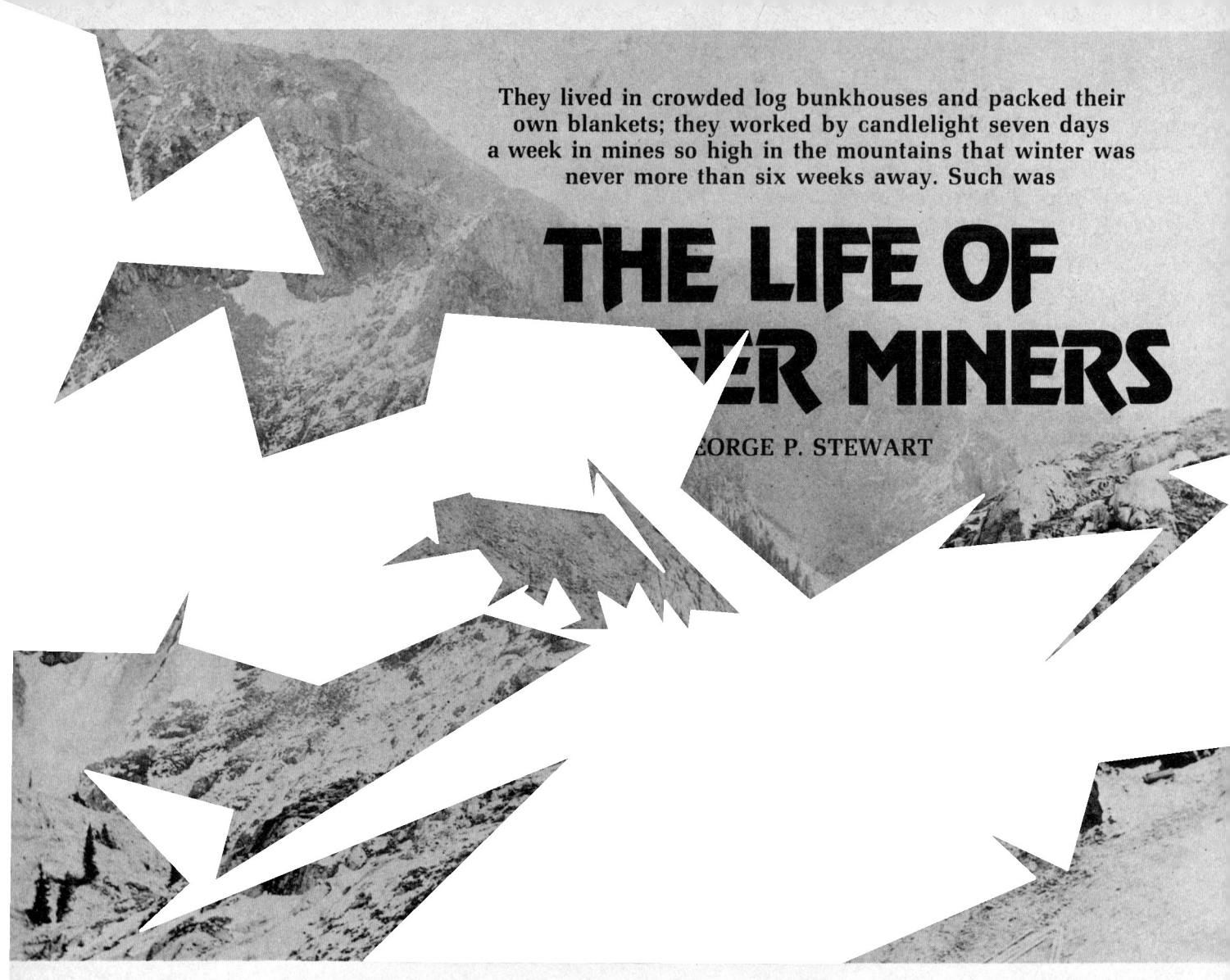

They lived in crowded log bunkhouses and packed their own blankets; they worked by candlelight seven days a week in mines so high in the mountains that winter was never more than six weeks away. Such was

THE LIFE OF PIONEER MINERS

by GEORGE P. STEWART

In most of the mines in the Kootenays today, workers drive to work or are transported by bus. In those areas where mines are remote, the men have excellent accommodation with running water, electric lights, central heating and similar facilities. At the turn of the century, however, conditions were different. Mines were generally in isolated areas and often accessible only by trail or aerial tramway. As a result living conditions were far from first class. In addition, many mines were located high in the mountains in regions of heavy snowfall where men and buildings could be, and were, swept away by avalanches.

Most of the camps were constructed of logs, poorly lit and ventilated, with outside toilets and a washtub for bathing. There was usually one building for cookhouse and dining room, another for bunkhouse and one as a "dry," the place where miners changed their everyday apparel for "diggers," as work clothes were called. Diggers consisted of heavy footwear, overalls, thick shirts, heavy wool underwear and socks. There were no safety items such as hard hats or battery lamps. The miners wore felt hats originally bought for best but grown shabby from wear, and each had a candlestick and candles. This feeble flicker was the only light they had to work by in the ink-black tunnels.

Some mines had good "grub" and some were not so hot, depending on the cook. The food was not fancy but wholesome, consisting of meat, vegetables, dried fruit and lots of pastry. None of the mines supplied bedding so miners packed their own blankets from job to job.

In the bunkhouse the bunks were built along each sidewall and consisted of an upper and lower. Some of these bunks had spiral springs and straw mattresses, while others had only boards and straw. Sometimes the bunks were built three high with the sides boarded up. The occupants crawled into them from the end and for this reason they were given the appropriate name of "muzzle loaders."

A box stove that burned four-foot lengths of wood kept out the winter cold—as long as someone stoked it all night, while coal-oil lamps supplied a dim, yellow glow. For outside light the men relied on a "bug." This was made from a four-pound jam pail or something similar. Small holes were punched in the bottom to provide air and one large hole in the side through which the candle was pushed. A piece of wire provided a carrying handle but if it was intended for horses a hook was soldered on so that it could be attached to a hame strap.

Since there were no machines, work in the mines was done by hand. Getting out the ore involved hand drilling holes in the face, blasting the ore free, then loading it onto ore cars with pick and shovel. Drilling holes was difficult, monotonous work with hammer and drill steel, the latter a steel bar sharpened at one end in the manner of a cross.

In the photo above a packtrain prepares to leave Sandon for the mines about 1891. At right, another winds up the steep mountainside with timbers, cable and supplies.

In the top photo, miners start a tunnel at the Georgian Mine near Rossland in the 1890's. All work was done by hand.

The photo on the opposite page shows a building at the Ibex Mine at Whitewater in October 1896. Like many mines in the Lardeau-Slocan-Sandon country, it was above timberline.

Two methods were used for hand drilling. One was called "single jack." With this method the miner used a four- or five-pound hammer to strike the drill steel which he turned after each blow to keep the hole round. The other method was the "double jack." In this case the hammer weighed some eight pounds and had a longer handle than the single jack. Two men worked as a team. One wielded the double jack and struck the steel, while his partner turned the steel to keep the hole round.

For relaxation after their long hours of work the men had to provide their own entertainment. Mouth organs, violins and other stringed instruments were popular and some of the miners became good musicians and singers. A favorite evening pastime was just sitting smoking or chewing tobacco and swapping yarns. Since horses and mules were a major part of the men's lives, these animals were the topic of many a story—some of them probably even true.

The intelligence acquired by horses was a favorite theme. One teamster swore that his horse was so smart that whenever the ore cars were loaded a bit heavier than usual, the horse reacted by stopping and blowing out its bug. This would give it a longer rest while the bug was re-lit.

Another one concerned a mule in the main haulage tunnel at the Rambler Mine. The skinner spotted the cars under the loading chutes then took the mule down the tunnel and let him stand. When all the cars were filled the skinner went for the mule, only to find it gone. A search revealed nothing, but as he passed under a raise (a tunnel that angles upward at forty-five degrees or more) a couple of small pebbles hit him. The skinner looked up into the raise and, still seeing nothing, he began to climb the ladders. Upon reaching the landing on the second ladder, he found the mule—its bug blown out, quietly hiding from work.

The miners themselves were also favorite subjects for stories. For instance when a miner went on shift he was issued four candles to do him for the day. If a man had a candle left at the end of a shift, he never turned it in but put

At left miners prepare to start a rock-drilling contest at Sandon in September 1904. These contests were a popular event at all sports days. In the photo above a miner digs ore by hand in the upper tunnel of the Cliff Mine at Rossland about 1900. The candles to his left and right on the rock face were the only source of light.

Throughout the West and East Kootenay a host of communities were born to serve the mines and miners. Many flourished then faltered, among them Three Forks, upper left on the opposite page, and Sandon, upper right in 1897. Today, Three Forks has vanished and Sandon consists of a few tumbledown buildings. The opposite photo shows a four-horse team used for hauling ore at Three Forks in 1913. Some mines were so inaccessible that the ore came out by aerial tramway; in others it was wrapped in hides and skidded down narrow mountain trails by horses.

it under his bunk with his belongings. The candles served a secondary purpose in that they were also used to indicate termination of service. When a miner was told there were no candles for him, it meant that he was fired. A story that made the rounds of the bunkhouses was one concerning a Finn who worked at the Richmond Eureka Mine. He went to the wicket for his candles and was told by the shift boss: "No candles for you."

"That's all right," the Finn replied. "I can get lots from under my bunk." The boss thought it such a joke he let the Finn return to work.

Another tale involved a mine where a tunnel was being driven from the surface and another tunnel, started underground in some old workings, drilled upward to meet it. When the tunnels were close to breakthrough, a new miner came to work on the face. He was an Irishman, Mickey Gill, and very superstitious. The boys knew him and also knew that he wasn't aware of the approaching breakthrough. As Mickey hammered away, his steel suddenly jerked from his hand and disappeared into the hole.

Mickey was speechless. Then as he stood staring at the hole, a voice intoned: "Mickey Gill, your day has come."

That was enough for Mickey. He threw down his hammer and beat a hasty retreat to draw his time, certain that the mine was haunted.

During Mickey's time, the men worked seven days a week. After several months of steady labor they headed for the nearest town to break the monotony. Some went for a big drunk, others just for a change from camp life. Those trips also gave rise to many stories—some of them probably true.

One of them involved the Exchange Hotel and Saloon in Sandon. The owner, James A. Thompson, had a bartender named Pat Griffin. On one occasion a poker game was going on upstairs and one player pulled a gun on another. The victim made a dash for the window and jumped out but kept hold of the windowsill. As he hung there Griffin went outside and noticed him. He rushed back into the bar and grabbed Thompson: "My God, Jim, I just saw the tallest man I have ever seen in my life. He was standing with

73

his hands on the sill looking through the upstairs window."

Then there was the story of Billy Myers who owned a pack train at Three Forks, a mining town three miles west of Sandon. Billy owned some mineral claims up in the mountains from Retallick and each spring went up to them. One time as he rounded a bend in the narrow trail he almost rubbed noses with a giant grizzly. The bear attacked at once, knocking the rifle from Billy's hand and hurtling it down the mountainside. Then began a struggle for life.

Both combatants rolled off the narrow trail and tumbled down the steep hill, coming to rest on a patch of snow. Billy was the first to recover. Although dazed and bleeding badly, he managed to get a hand axe from his pack and kill the bear. However, he spent many months in hospital recovering from the mauling.

Another harrowing experience befell Henry Muirhardt, a hotelman in Three Forks, who shared some claims up the North Fork of Carpenter Creek. Because of the altitude of the claims, snow arrived in early autumn and soon built up to avalanche proportions. The partners knew of the danger but one year while doing assessment work necessary to hold their claims, decided to stay two days longer than planned. On the second morning they found almost two feet of new snow. Immediately after breakfast they went to their mine tunnel to see the result of the previous night's blast. They found nothing promising so decided to leave.

Muirhardt said he would pack the tools to the portal of the tunnel while his partner went to the cabin and made preparations for their departure. As Muirhardt packed the last load of equipment to the portal a deafening roar filled the air and the tunnel plunged into darkness, the entrance sealed by a compact wall of snow. Muirhardt grabbed a shovel and started digging, thankful he had not carried the tools to the shed. Hours later he broke through to daylight where a great expanse of snow greeted his eyes. The cabin and his partner had vanished. After some searching Muirhardt knew his task was not only hopeless but also dangerous because of the threat of more avalanches.

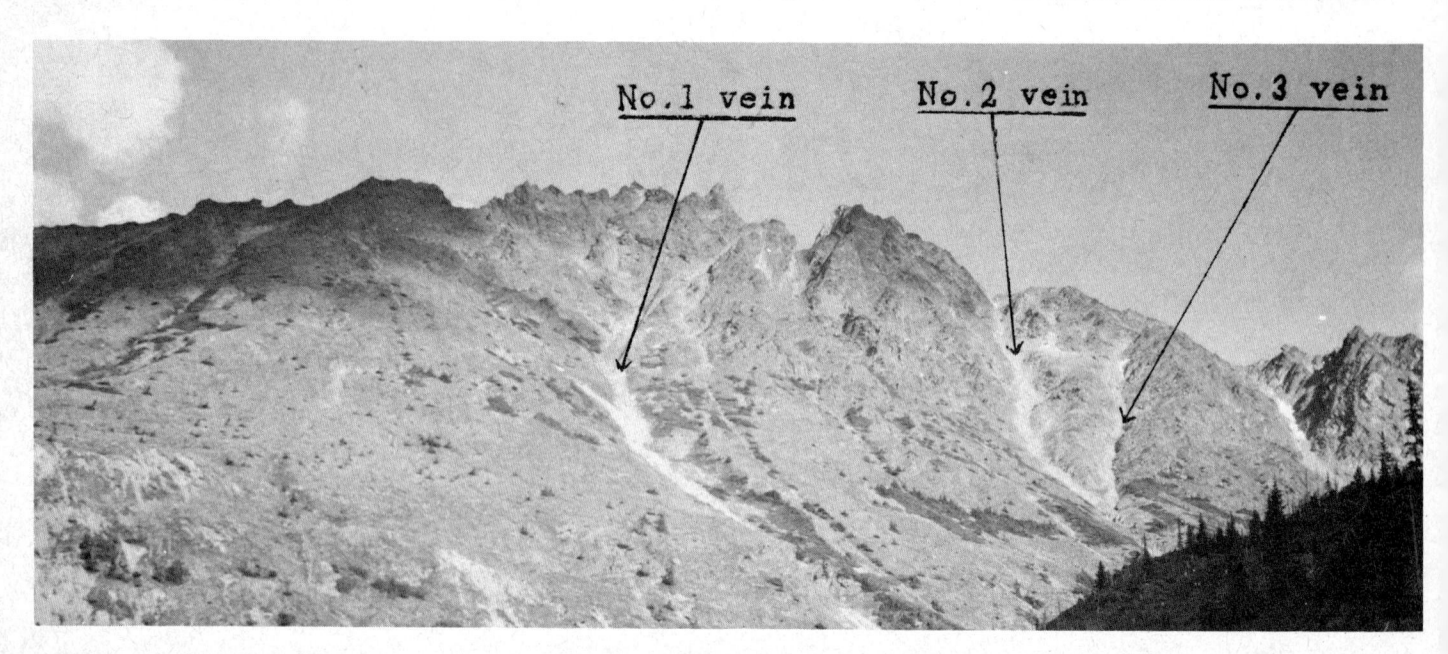

In the Lardeau-Sandon area it was not uncommon for mines to be 6,000 feet or higher in the mountains, resulting in many miners being swept to death by avalanches. The photo above shows the Upper Whitewater camp: log buildings, coal-oil lamps, washtub for a bath and buckets for running water. At right is the bunkhouse of the Oyster-Criterion Mine in the Lardeau country about 1900.

Without food or blankets he started the long trek to town. Before darkness descended he located a dry tree and built a fire. Next morning he resumed his journey and that night staggered into his hotel, more dead than alive. The following summer when the snow melted searchers found his partner in the ruins of the cabin.

A happier story of pioneer days in mining camps involved a down and out old-timer named Tom Mulvey. He used to do chores around the saloons in Sandon, which during the 1890's was the wealthy capital of one of the richest mining regions in B.C.

At one time one of the hotels, the Windsor, was run by Jim Bowes, who liked Tom Mulvey and saw that he didn't lack for clothing and other necessities. Nor did Tom go short at the bar for he was a favorite with the miners. He was, however, the victim of more than a few tricks, and stories about him gave miners many a chuckle when they returned to their camps.

The favorite arose because Mulvey could neither read nor write. Everyone knew it but Tom nevertheless persisted in borrowing books from Jim Bowes to cover up his lack of schooling. One night when Tom asked for another book, Bowes handed him a bible. A few days later he returned it.

"Well, Mulvey, how did you like it?" Bowes asked.

"Oh, it was all right," was the answer, "but it turned out pretty much like the rest. They got married in the end."

The old-time miners are all gone now, many buried in a brush and tree-overgrown cemetery about a mile below Sandon, others throughout the province where their trails led them. Sandon itself is a ghost town, only a few dilapidated buildings indicating a community that was once one of the largest in Interior B.C. Nearly all the mines have closed but high in the mountains traces still remain—abandoned shafts and tunnels, overgrown trails and the ruins of log buildings. It isn't difficult to visualize ghostly figures sitting outside a crumpled log bunkhouse, their pipe smoke blending into the purple twilight as they swap stories to fill in the lonely hours separating them from friends and family.

■

Sleeping quarters were two blankets on bare boards, the stove a five gallon coal-oil can, the engine a strong back and a pair of oars, sockeye salmon brought six cents each, humpbacks one cent—such were conditions faced by

THE EARLY GILLNE'

by WALTER WICKS

Cannery boats on the Skeena River being towed to the fishing grounds. The crew's only protection from the weather was the small tent which the fishermen are erecting.

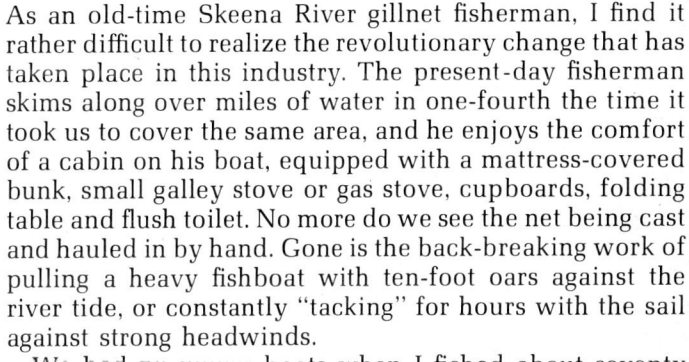

FISHERMEN

As an old-time Skeena River gillnet fisherman, I find it rather difficult to realize the revolutionary change that has taken place in this industry. The present-day fisherman skims along over miles of water in one-fourth the time it took us to cover the same area, and he enjoys the comfort of a cabin on his boat, equipped with a mattress-covered bunk, small galley stove or gas stove, cupboards, folding table and flush toilet. No more do we see the net being cast and hauled in by hand. Gone is the back-breaking work of pulling a heavy fishboat with ten-foot oars against the river tide, or constantly "tacking" for hours with the sail against strong headwinds.

We had no power boats when I fished about seventy years ago; in fact, we hadn't heard of such things as the gas engine. The fish boat was twenty-six feet long with a sharp-cut stern and bow. This type of boat was known as a double-ender and originated with the early development of the salmon industry on the Columbia River.

The boats were open; that is, they had no cabin for shelter and were propelled with a strong back, long oars and a sail. The only weather protection we had was to rig up a small tent, known today as a pup tent, on the foc'sle in the wet weather which seemed to be always with us.

The salmon cannery supplied all boats and fishing gear, paying us six cents per fish for sockeye, eight cents for coho, and fifteen cents for springs, while white springs and dog salmon had to be thrown overboard as the cannery did not want them. (Today the coho, which we sold for eight cents a fish, costs a consumer over $2.50 a pound.) Humpback salmon brought one cent per fish, and when the schools ran heavy, giving the cannery insufficient time to can them, the fishermen were limited to one hundred humps per boat per day. In one day's catch I have seen five thousand salmon heaved overboard because there was not time to can them before spoilage set in. Imagine a fisherman hauling in five hundred humpback salmon in one night's drift and be obliged to heave four hundred of them overboard, retaining only one hundred to deliver to the cannery, and all this work for the fabulous sum of $1 to be divided between two men. This has been my personal experience.

The sockeye season started June 20 and lasted until August 30, followed by a three-week coho salmon season, these last three weeks being filled in by a limited group of fishermen.

During the first three weeks of the season, we would be towed out to the mouth of the Skeena by steam tugboats, there to cast our two hundred fathoms of net and drift out into deep water beyond the river mouth. Each cannery painted its boats one uniform color, and a small uniform flag was flown by each boat. In this manner, the tugboats were better able to recognize their own boats on the fishing grounds. Some canneries had their name displayed on the flags.

After drifting all night with the tide, we would pick up our nets and watch for the steam tug to tow us back to the cannery or to the home cannery fish camp, situated somewhere in the vicinity. We then dropped anchor and pulled out the old, battered coal-oil can we called a stove to prepare a well-earned meal. After a night of rain and wind, that black coffee pot was certainly the answer to a wet and fatigued fisherman. Then, with some sleep, we would be ready for the next night to continue the procedure.

The boats were manned by two men, one casting the net over the stern while the other rowed until the full two hundred fathoms of net was laid out on the water. When it came time to pick up, the man rowing would back the boat toward the net while his partner hauled it in. Often in stormy weather or thick fog, when the tugs would be unable to find us, we would row or sail for shelter to some anchorage. At the age of thirteen, I had pulled a heavily-loaded fishboat for nine hours in the fog.

Our living facilities were rather rough in those old-time boats. The sleeping quarters were simply a couple of blankets on the hard bare boards on which we lay, crouched under the foc'sle head which was not long enough to cover our entire bodies, thus leaving our legs exposed, over which we spread our yellow oilskin raincoats. Our cooking was done on a five-gallon coal-oil can which was cut down to form a crude stove in which we used wood for fuel. Our lavatory? Well, we sat over the boatside. In rough weather we tied ourselves to the mast to avoid being washed overboard.

After three weeks "outside fishing," as we called it, we would follow the salmon into the mouth of the river where fishing became even more back-breaking, as we would then be operating in strong tidal waters. Sand bars, reefs and sunken logs in the river bottom were obstacles which

Port Essington on the Skeena River about 1915, with Frizzell's wharf on the left and Skeena Commercial cannery at right. The fleet of fishing boats between the wharves is being formed to be towed down the river and dropped off at likely fishing areas. Each cannery had its boats painted a distinctive color so that they could be identified more easily at a distance.

At top and center on the opposite page are the Commercial and Balmoral canneries on the Skeena River. The lower photo shows the living accommodation provided by the companies for their workers. Facilities were basic and the closely-packed buildings a potential fire hazard. On the hill is the manager's house, with a commanding view of the area.

often tore our nets to shreds. Then we were forced to return to our home cannery, sometimes a distance of twenty miles. Here we had to haul the net on the rack for repairs, sometimes losing two days fishing. At times, we would drift onto a sand bar and be left high and dry with the full length of the net stretched out on the sand, there to wait for the incoming tide that would refloat us.

From 6 a.m. Saturday to 6 p.m. Sunday was closed to fishing to allow for escapement of salmon. During this weekly closed period, all fishermen would travel back to the cannery to make necessary net or boat repairs and wash the nets in a solution of copper sulphate to remove the fish slime from the web. Then we were ready for a decent night's sleep in a good bunk in the fishermen's cabins.

The canneries at that early period did not supply the fishermen or cannery workers with facilities for bathing which left it up to us to look around for any kind of a barrel or tank to bathe in. We had no union or organization of any kind to fight for better living conditions; we merely accepted conditions as they confronted us.

Thirteen canneries operated in the area, scattered along the river and adjacent coastline. The Fisheries Department supplied the canneries with explosive bombs which were set off on the outer end of the cannery at exactly 6 o'clock each Sunday evening. This was the signal for the opening time for fishermen to set their clocks and their nets.

As the season progressed, we followed the salmon farther upriver and that meant more shallow water, more sandbars and more debris to struggle with. Tide rips — a collision of two tides that creates considerable water turbulence — often caused a number of nets to tangle as they drifted together. At such a time the language used by the fishermen while working feverishly to untangle the web would certainly not be fit for print. However, I recall one occasion when an entanglement proved humorous. An Indian and a Japanese fisherman collided, and each cursed the other in his native tongue. The language they used sounded fierce, and neither stopped to consider that their problem was caused by the natural action of tidal variations rather than by each other.

Another problem we encountered which sometimes caused tragedy was a coastal steamer ramming us at night or severing our net. When a boat returned to the cannery with bow down and stern high, it was a sure indication that it was minus a large section of net. The bones of many fishermen strew the sea bottom at the river mouth because of these coastal vessels cutting nets and even boats in two.

As the salmon travelled upriver to the spawning grounds, the fishing fleet continued to follow until the geographical fishing limits were reached, several miles above the town of Port Essington. But as the fish diminished through the years, the Fisheries Department was forced to confine fishing operations to a limited area of the river, and Port Essington was left "high and dry." Today, this little city that had processed salmon for several decades is a ghost town.

I will always remember her as part of an era now long gone; an era of long wet hours at the oars, miserable working conditions, poor pay, and nights full of hazard. Like all those privileged to look back at events over a half century ago, I often wonder how we stuck it, although at the time it seemed quite normal. ■

The above photo of Cottonwood House is believed to have been taken about 1900. In 1963 when the famous stopping place was 100 years old it was purchased by the B.C. government. Today, it is preserved as Cottonwood House Historic Park, top photo.

The first advertisement for the stopping place appeared in the *Cariboo Sentinel* at Barkerville on May 7, 1866 and noted: "The proprietors having lately fitted up bedrooms and good Beds are now prepared to afford every accommodation for Travellers; the Table is furnished with all the luxuries that can be procured; the Bar is well supplied with the best brands of Liquors and Segars . . ."

Historic Cottonwood House

Dozens of roadhouses once dotted the 400-mile-long Cariboo Wagon Road from Yale to Barkerville. Today, most live only in photographs and newspaper clippings but an exception is Cottonwood House.

by EMELENE THOMAS

In the dignified setting of the library at the University of British Columbia, where they are esteemed as valuable contributions to the history of British Columbia in general, and the Cariboo in particular, is a set of account books. They are from a famous old stopping place known as Cottonwood House at Cottonwood, fifteen miles from Quesnel on the road to Barkerville. A gift to the University from Mr. William Boyd, son of the owner of the hostel, their authenticity assures them an honored place among historical data. These volumes, daybooks and ledgers, are of two sizes and are bound in heavy cardboard of mottled pattern. Their stiff yellowed pages of financial entries and the notes of personal events are a fascinating window into the romantic years when the dust, mire, and snow of the Cariboo Road was churned by countless travellers, man and beast, who passed up and down, up and down, in a never-ending procession, the years when towns now but sadly neglected plots boasted populations in the thousands. They all came to the Cariboo then, old and young, rich and poor: the butcher, the baker, the candlestick-maker; judge and jury, minister and layman, doctor, lawyer, merchant, chief — they stepped through the sturdy doors of the House. Its floors were marked by the tread of strong feet as the wayfarers paused for an hour, a day, or even a month to refresh themselves with a bite, to purchase supplies before continuing on their way, or to sell their often hard-won gold and linger awhile to hear the latest news from the outside world.

The earliest of the books bears the date 1863, for that was the beginning of the second big rush, the hey-day of Cariboo. Throughout all the books, except where some assistant took a hand, the penmanship is the same. From it one can form a mental image of John Boyd, a gentleman of the old school, thorough, precise, meticulous as to neatness and detail. A study of the entries complements the picture, giving a concept of the man's character — competent in business, just to himself and others, kind to his family and charitable to the needy.

John Boyd, above right. Mrs. Boyd arrived as a bride in 1868. She raised ten children and remained at Cottonwood until her death at 89 in 1940, known far and wide as the "Grand Old Woman of Cariboo."

The books are distinguished by the titles Day Book and Cash Book, the latter the more interesting. The Day Books contain the individual accounts and bring to light little personal vanities and indulgences, but the Cash Book is a mirror of the times. On its pages are recorded the sales at the house and store, and memos of important household and local occurrences of the day. Birth and death are there, financial contracts are set down in minutest detail, and small intimate entries round out the scene as the years roll on and the door swings to and fro as the makers of Cariboo history make their entrances and exits.

The names are a roll call of the pioneers of Cariboo: Frisky, Halfbreed Dick, Dutch Charlie and Dutch Peter, Dancing Bill, Newfelder, "Dad" Liverpool Jack, Cameron, Antoine, Ned Toomey, Frenchman, Mah Gee and Ah Wong, Little Billy, Indian Johnny, Pablo, and someone referred to only as Little One. Into the dining-room strides Major Thorpe and his staff, Haggerty and Rankin, Bell, Beedy, Dud Moreland, an old-timer now, for he was one of the first prospectors in the Horsefly country, going in in '59; Mike Fitzgerald, Doctors Chip, Trevor and Bell, Thomas Spence, whose name is perpetuated in Spences Bridge, and hundreds of other people.

Summer is in full strength, and the road is white beneath the August sun, but inside the sturdy log building the air is cool and quiet. On the shelves of the store and stacked on all the available floor space beyond are the staples that make up the bulk of the miners' purchases, with a few fresh vegetables from the ranch. Prices are high, accounted for by the long, slow freight haul and the tolls on the Cariboo Wagon Road. Flour, sugar, bacon, yeast powder, tea, candles, lamp chimneys and wicks, butter at a dollar a pound, beans, barley, soap at $1.25 a bar, and in the meathouse sides of beef and pork. There are tools at one end — picks and shovels, hammers and nails, saws, sledges, axes, and files. On one shelf is ranged an array of nostrums, liniments, ointment, pills of various kinds, painkiller, and Ayer's Cherry Pectoral, an unfailing cure for ailments of chest and throat, and which is still advertised today by modern drugstores. There are clothes, too. Heavy durable shirts, pants, gaiters of canvas, socks, thick boots and warm moccasins.

There is gin, rum, absinthe, Lager beer at $1.25 a bottle. Brandy (both Inferior and Dark), Old Tom at $2.50 a bottle, case brandy at $3.50 per bottle, whisky, porter, milk punches — take your choice, boys!

Provision was also made for cards and dice, for we find entries charging drinks to Monte Game, Monte Bank, and just Game. Down in the book it all goes, and should a customer depart leaving a bill and forgetting perhaps what is due, the page can be turned up, with the date and the reckoning, plain to see.

This is almost entirely a man's world. Except for an entry in 1863 reading "Man and Woman" etc., there is no hint of feminine travellers until 1866, when a Madame Samone makes a brief appearance.

In the earlier books there is frequent mention of tolls being paid. These were collected by a contractor, or his agent, for constructing a section of the Cariboo Wagon Road, and were to compensate him for expenses over the arranged-for amount.

In the store, Mr. Anderson pays out $8 for a garden shovel, and Mah Gee shoulders a pick and goes off with it, dreaming, no doubt, of the gold he will uncover with its aid, while Mr. Boyd sets the amounts down in the ledger and opens the large package of seeds that has just arrived, for it is springtime again. As further proof that gardening time has arrived, he sets off for Quesnelle in quest of a new plough and cabbage plants. The Cariboo Road is so far only a narrow pack trail, and he pulls to the side to make

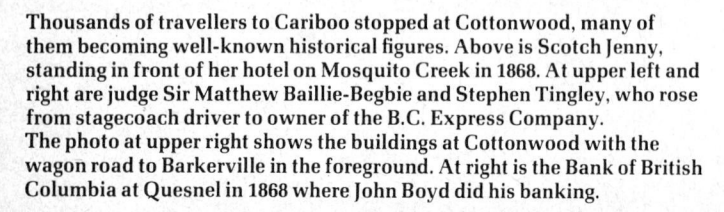

**Thousands of travellers to Cariboo stopped at Cottonwood, many of them becoming well-known historical figures. Above is Scotch Jenny, standing in front of her hotel on Mosquito Creek in 1868. At upper left and right are judge Sir Matthew Baillie-Begbie and Stephen Tingley, who rose from stagecoach driver to owner of the B.C. Express Company.
The photo at upper right shows the buildings at Cottonwood with the wagon road to Barkerville in the foreground. At right is the Bank of British Columbia at Quesnel in 1868 where John Boyd did his banking.**

room for Oppenheimer's train of mules, laden with freight for the goldfields.

Summer and autumn follow in their turn, with the haying calling for extra men. In due course winter is denoted by a purchase of sleighbells and mittens for chilled hands.

The pages turn as the seasons pass, and again it is autumn. The golden leaves of the cottonwoods drift through the quiet air and a film of ice forms on the ponds. The big boom years of '63 and '64 fade into the past, and '65 whirls in on the heels of a snowstorm. Well wrapped to withstand its fury, Mr. Dragon's partner comes up from Quesnelle Mouth. As he reaches the shelter of the stopping place, he shakes the snow from his coat and cap and strips off his heavy mitts. In the dining-room he revels in the warmth as he sits down to a hot meal while waiting for a wagon tongue to be made.

Three days later we are introduced to Antoine Malbouf, trapper and general handyman. He is a rollicking, happy-go-lucky chap who spins a bright thread across the pages as he comes and goes. Early in January is this entry: "Antoine Malbouf Commenced to work at $100 per month and board. Idle time to be deducted."

So Antoine commences work, turning his hand to any job requiring his attention, a plug in his cheek, a drink under his belt, and newly purchased moccasins on his feet. His tenure is of short duration, then off to his trap-line for he is primarily a man of the woods. While he covers the miles with easy strides, Henry McDames, then at Van Winkle, a cluster of rude dwellings farther on, arrives at Cottonwood, where he pays part of his bill for "sundry items at sundry times."

Then here is Antoine again, jolly fellow, needing new clothing and a cash advance. He is accommodated with both, for like all the men of that day, his word is good. The business concluded, he waves goodbye to the familiar buildings and returns to the woods.

A few weeks more and quick heat floods the fields. Tiny pale green leaves uncurl, and turnip and beet seeds are carefully pressed into the fertile soil. The seed-sowing is followed shortly by the setting out of two hundred and fifty young cabbage plants. With the opening of the streams, fresh names appear on the pages of the book: Ah Young, William Patterson (he and his brother took out gold to the value of $10,000 in five weeks mining on Lowhee Creek), Steele, Winn Lunn, and G. B. Wright, who won the contract for construction of the Cariboo Road from Quesnelle to Cottonwood. One hundred white men and two hundred Chinese were employed in the building of that stretch, which at its completion cost $85,000. From his claim below the canyon on Williams Creek comes the famous man of riches and poverty, John "Cariboo" Cameron, who was destined to reap some $350,000 from the creeks yet die a pauper and be buried in a cemetery overlooking his gold-laden claim. "Frenchman with Sheep" follows, and Ah Doo, who is on his way to try his luck on the creeks.

Prices are still high, eggs at $4 a dozen (Mr. M-- buys but half a dozen), flour at $15 a hundred. A new cook, Ah Fatt, is installed in the kitchen, and like all Orientals, has "fliends" who frequently have "bed and breakfast" at his expense.

Antoine is back once more. He breaks a tumbler in his exuberance, settles for the damage, and is off again. In a month's time he reappears for there is a new house to be built, and who so good at bringing out the heavy timbers as Antoine? Ah Doo leaves the creek to work at Cottonwood, and John Cameron is added to the payroll. In this matter there is an interesting sidelight. Whenever a white man is hired a note is always appended re Idle Time, but in the case of Ah Doo, no mention is made of such a contingency. Ah Doo apparently was not one to indulge in idle time!

At the ranch there is much to do, with the animals to be cared for, as well as those left by their owners until such time as they are required. Some of these are stabled; others at a cheaper rate turned out into the fields to graze. Logs for the house are snaked in, and by mid-July Antoine has fashioned 3,300 shakes at $18 per thousand.

As July melts into August, the blueberries in the hills turn sweet and plump. A large picking is bought from an Indian, some to be eaten fresh, the rest preserved or pickled.

Berries in the hills, golden grain in the fields, and long rows of vegetables in the garden. The root crops are so bountiful that the gunny sacks on hand will not suffice, so off to the Wagon Road Mr. Boyd takes his way to secure more.

On November 15 is the first record of a cheque. It is made out on the Bank of British Columbia which, in 1863, had opened a branch at Williams Creek.

Now winter sets in in earnest, customers are few, the cash sales for two days amounting to only $4.50. Antoine, who some time ago returned to his line, brings in seventeen prime marten pelts. With the year drawing to a close, Johnny Hamilton, stagedriver of Beaver Pass, brushes the snow from his clothes before sitting down to a good hot dinner. Afterwards he loads turnips, onions and cabbages on top of the rest of the freight.

And so, with Christmas passing unnoted, 1865 makes room for 1866. Hardly has it gotten into its stride when a newcomer is introduced, Madame Samone, who makes a deal for 1070 pounds of hay at .07 a pound. One wonders who Madame Samone was and what her business, for apart from three billings for hay, we learn nothing about her.

Quickly the days lengthen, even though timbers snap with the cold and the dry snow creaks underfoot. Already supper can be eaten without the lamps being lit. As Ah Fatt stacks the dishes, and the great heater is replenished, a lithe figure on snowshoes with wide spreading pack on broad shoulders, comes swinging over the blue shadowed snow. Antoine is back, calling a cheery greeting as he stands his snowshoes on end in the drift, and pushes open the door, letting in a rush of cold fresh air. With a flourish he tosses the pack on the counter and draws forth glossy beautiful mink and rich soft marten.

A second rush of air heralds another traveller, John Cameron this time. He glances around the well-stocked shelves of groceries, reckoning as he does so, then asks for flour, beef, tea, and matches. As he turns away, crusty loaves of bread catch his eye. Though they are dear — two for seventy-five cents — he buys a couple for a change from the usual bannock. A little gold dust changes hands, then into a chair by the glowing fire he settles to talk for awhile of the prospects for the year.

A soft Chinook soughs through the trees, a hundred tiny streams trickle downhill at the touch of spring, and an early bird calls from the meadow. Picking his way through the soft mud is the butcher, just in time for dinner. He stays for supper, too, and is duly charged in the book for "2 meals with eggs." Eggs, still a luxury item at $4 a dozen, up the cost of a meal, but they are a treat for a hungry man accustomed to only the plainest of fare.

The long-dreamed-of Cariboo Wagon Road from Yale in the Fraser Canyon has been reality for some months now, and the horses can make good time. Barnards Express, the harness of its four-horse team jangling merrily, pulls up with a smart stop, the wheels making deep ruts in the mire. Since snow still lies deep on the upper levels, a sled is hired for the rest of the journey. The freight is transferred while Ah Fatt, who has never heard of union hours, prepares another hot meal. Ah Fatt is a likeable, hospitable chap, with many friends, who stop in on their goings and comings to enjoy with him a round of brandy, followed by another, indicated in the Cash Book by "ditto" marks.

All these gentry seem to go by the prefix Ah: Ah Fatt, Ah Hoy, Ah Sam, Ah Shing, Ah Yett, and so on. Indeed so common is the term that farther on a temporary bookkeeper, a bit of a wag, maybe, refers to Mr. A. H. Lindsay as Ah Lindsay! A. H. is known as a fellow who dearly loves a joke, so probably just chuckles ponderously when he hears of it.

The stage, rolling in on June 2, 1866, is an object of unusual interest and speculation. Down from the coach steps Mr. Andrew of Niles and Co., followed by a bevy of buxom maids. Quickly the word is passed around that these damsels will provide in themselves welcome partners for the men at the dances at the camps. Many a covert look is sent their way as they stand demurely by, long full skirts carefully gathered from the dust, while their escort arranges for transportation to their destination.

Two people there are at Cottonwood who are not concerned with the new arrivals. For weeks now a Mr. Lewis has stayed at the house, helping with the work while an ailing relative — son, father or brother — is cared for by the kindly Boyds. But now the long watch is over. A fresh grave is dug on the hillside, and one more death is recorded in the annals of the Cariboo. And where but in a frontier district will you find such modest remuneration for such taxing services as were rendered the sick man? In the account book lies an entry which speaks for itself of the kindness that was worth more than all the gold in the creeks:

"T. B. Lewis
To attending A. Lewis during his sickness, death, and
 burial $23."

Cash business is always good in summer, when travel is brisk, one day's business in June being given as follows:
"Cash from passengers $7.50
Gained on gold dust $.63
To Heath at Quesnelle   536.00
Today's cash   900.00"

Boyd's partner, Heath, a few days previously had taken to Quesnelle the sum of $603.75, and a fortnight later delivers a further $487.62, so it is readily understood that the financial standing of the house was high.

Four months have passed with no sign of Antoine, but in mid-June here he is on the job once more at $70 a month, and due notice re idle time. While he is busy with hammer and saw, Mr. Boyd travels to Van Winkle by stage, the fare being set at $5, and Thomas Spence, now Government agent, stops in for a cooling drink one hot summer day.

All too soon summer and autumn are memories and winter grips the valley. In the forest Antoine makes the circuit of his trapline, taking from the traps the usual catch of mink and marten. Some beaver skins he has this time, too. The price for these lovely furs is so small (only $29 for four mink and ten marten) that only a man born to follow the trail could be content with such meagre returns.

January 1, 1867, salutes five chaps beginning the New Year right by paying their bills, some in full, the rest as finances permit. These laudable acts are followed by a similar one at the end of the month when money is refunded to someone who had paid too much by mistake.

Taken as a whole 1867 is a dull year, except for trips to Van Winkle and Williams Creek for the purpose of collecting monies due, making new sales and purchasing various necessities.

January 1, 1868, the cash on hand totals $1,021, so apparently the business of the house was satisfactory. This amount is transferred to a new Cash Book, a narrow one necessitating all entries being squeezed into one column. Very few records are kept during the next two years, and those not in Mr. Boyd's handwriting. Though it is a bit difficult to decipher, it is clear enough to conclude that the stopping place is still catering to the needs of the population, supplying them with such items as copper rivets, pick handles, envelopes, ink, door locks, and even hat hooks.

The third volume, dated 1870, is much larger, 14 by 8, an honest-to-goodness account book, all nicely lined, with double columns. This book is a pleasure to the eye, filled with John Boyd's artistic penmanship and neat figures. A journey to Williams Creek, which yielded returns of $375.25, starts off the year's records, followed by one that tells of some unhappy soul, plagued with an aching molar, calling in for Toothache Liniment.

It is a winter of heavy snow. The soft flakes fall steadily, covering everything with a thick blanket, until at the end of the month the barn roof is unable to bear the weight and collapses with a loud rending of timbers.

As February's sun gives heartening promise of winter's back being bent, if not quite broken, a sleigh glides up to the door. From the wrappings that enfold her climbs a woman, thankful to stretch cramped limbs. This is Mrs. Allen, or as she is soon more generally known, Scotch Jenny. She is an immensely fat woman, proprietress of the Pioneer Hotel at Cameronton and later at Mosquito Creek. Poor Jenny, hers was one of the all-too-common tragic ends. As she was driving from Lightning Creek to Barkerville, and looking back over her shoulder, her horse went too close to the bank. In the ensuing struggle Jenny was thrown into the canyon of Williams Creek and killed.

Thus, the story of the country builds up as the Cariboo tides of fortune ebb and flow. In the midst of the shifting scene Cottonwood House stands staunch, a landmark to all, steadily continuing its ordered existence through all times and weathers.

No sooner is it summertime, with all outdoors calling, than the hordes of mosquitoes swarm around. They make the night, and day, too, a torment. Ah Fatt pads in on slippered feet to ask for a fresh supply of Mosquito Bar. A month later as he slips for a moment from his domain to

30

Tuesday October 9th 1877 Continued

        Government of B.C. by
155   Henery Moffat   Dr
   To 273 lb Hay   @ 3   8.19

        Joseph Mason & Daly by
       " Mason   Dr
149 To Supper   1.00
   " 15 lbs Oats   @ 8   1.20

   Cash from Sales   1.50

Wednesday October 10th 1877

        Joseph Mason & Daly by
       " Mason   Dr
   To Bed & Bkft   2.00
149 " 2 Horses fed hay 1 Night 1.50
   " 19 Cattell in Field
   one Night @ 12½ 2.37½
   " 2 Horses in Field 1 Night .25
                 $ 6.12½

        Government of B.C. by
       Henery Moffat   Dr
   To 140 lb Oats

       Cold Spring House   Cr
   By 1½ Doz Tea Spoons @ 9$ 13.50
   " 1 " Table Spoons 3.50 3.50
up to " 377 lb Oats @ 4½ 16.96½
Page 31 " 300 " Flour " 8 24.
   " 910 " hay   .3 27.30

A typical page from the Cash Book which, along with a Day Book, John Boyd kept from 1864 until his death in 1909. By then the books weighed over 100 pounds, and today are an irreplaceable record of daily life in a Cariboo roadhouse.

watch the arrival of the stage, his dark eyes note a lady being handed down, and a child, too! Ha! Two ladies already this year! This is Mrs. Nason, whose husband, in company with Mr. Daly, operates the Antler Restaurant at Williams Creek. An all-night stop is made by these interesting newcomers, the following formal entry being made in the book:

"July 6 Nason — by Lady & Family
To one night's entertainment $3.00"

A nice word, entertainment! Not exclusive in its use, either. Two nights later Mr. Byrne, who sells goods on commission at Williams Creek, is billed for "Entertainment for self and horse."

A cash present to a blind Indian boy is set down and Mr. Spence, a frequent visitor, puts his team of horses on hay while he breaks his journey overnight. Summer is waning, and haying and crop-harvesting speeded up.

Ah Fatt, a thrifty chap who does not believe in frittering his money, draws a full year's wages, buys a coverlid for $6, a clock for $8 and socks the rest away.

As the winter storms begin, cash sales pick up, possibly because of the men coming by on their way to the coast, or others perhaps stocking their larders for the long cold months. Angus McPhail, who has proved himself a capable, reliable assistant, is sent by his employer to Soda Creek and Williams Creek on business. The stopping-place is busy attending to the needs of the travellers, most of whom are charged merely for "bed and breakfast." But for Judge Elwyn the more formal entry, "To Entertainment etc. on trip up and down," is used. Judge Elwyn is not really a judge in the accepted sense of the term but one of the officials known as Stipendiary Magistrates. They also serve as Assistant Gold Commissioners, Assistant Commissioners of Lands, Collectors of Revenue, and Coroners, all for $250 per annum. Judge Elwyn — few call him Thomas — is from Lillooet. He is always a welcome visitor for he can tell interesting stories of his experiences when he was in command of the corps of picked men who made up the Cariboo Gold Escort, formed in 1861 to provide safety for gold sent from Barkerville to Victoria.

December 21, the shortest day of the year, and the skies leaden. There is a seeming lack of Yuletide festivities. Christmas Day is the same as any other, with the arrival of the daily stage and a customer or two in for supplies. Later on the Christmas spirit is evident, but not yet.

The sun, rising to herald New Year's Day of 1871, sees the Cariboo steadying down to a more measured pace. It picks out the figures of Mr. Boyd and Angus McPhail, off to an early start for Williams Creek with a load of hay. The sleigh slips easily over the packed snow, the horses steaming as they pull the bulky load. A quick trip is accomplished, then home to the friendly warmth of the house, and the mild excitement of opening the ledger to begin the record of a new year.

Undeterred by mid-winter snow and cold, Mrs. Boyd, whose presence is indicated for the first time, makes a trip to Quesnelle, leaving the menfolk to shift for themselves. The monotony of the day is broken by a brief call from Dutch George, in for a drink of hot punch and a warm at the stove.

What with lowered freight rates lessening the price of supplies and a recession of the boom tide, charges are down, bed and breakfast now costing only $1.50. Throughout February business remains quiet, with customers scattered. Ah Fong, who has replaced the jolly Ah Fatt in the kitchen, falls ill. Mrs. Boyd takes over until a substitute can be procured, drawing her just wages when she turns the work over to Che Kim.

The warmth of March starts talk of spring even though the land is still snowbound. In the kitchen Che Kim welcomes two friends, and as they are short of cash he pays for their meal. A few days later he gathers his belongings, hangs up the white apron, collects his wages, and bids the house goodbye, the recovered Ah Fong resuming his regular place.

With the advent of April the road begins to break up, causing delay to travellers, and it is almost midnight of the 3rd when Mr. Freeman wheels up with the Barnard's Express. He is cold and hungry, but the comfort of patrons is a matter of pride at Cottonwood, and he is soon sitting down to a hot, cheering meal.

The miners who have been wintering at the coast are drifting back, though this year many of the men who broke their journey at Cottonwood year after year are missing. The big rush to Omineca is on, and, hot on the trail of the reputed new find, they have left the road at Quesnelle, crossing the Fraser at that point to take the trail to Fort St. James. Still there are enough of the old faces to make the spring influx seem familiar, and enough strange ones to supply new interest.

At the beginning of April there was the annual ordering of seeds, at the end there are magazine subscriptions to be made out. One for the *Illustrated London News*, and a second for *Leslie's Lady's Magazine* since Mrs. Boyd likes to keep abreast of the fashions. The subscriptions attended to, Mr. Boyd gives his attention to the terms of a contract between himself and the firm of Gerow and Johnson pertaining to the care of the mail horses by the month while they are stationed at Cottonwood.

With May comes the enjoyment of the almost summer-like weather. The sun shines strongly and the birds chirp and call as they follow the plough. For two days coats are off as everyone basks in the sun's rays. But on the third the skies cloud over, a chill settles down, and the snow falls, and falls, as if winter were still in command. When at last it ceases and blue patches begin to show between the clouds, Mr. Boyd steps out, carefully measures the snow, and returns to report a depth of six inches of the stuff. It does not last long, though, and before many weeks a luxuriant array of wild flowers brightens the wayside: Indian paintbrushes, daisies, columbines, and the never-failing dandelions. Life at the ranch and the stopping-place is a peaceful one this June — shoes to be repaired, ducks bought and turned in with the chickens, all the little transactions that make up the general scheme of things. Judge Ball, driving up from Lytton, pays a short call, a small account with him is settled, and Mr. Landringham sends down a letter to be posted to his wife, postage fifty cents.

Week after week the scattered procession continues: J. H. Turner with his pack of drygoods, Dr. Chip, Dr. Bell, and Mr. Boyd himself, taking the road to Van Winkle in search of extra hands for the harvest.

Though fortunes are made in the Cariboo there are comparatively few who are so fortunate, many just barely get along. But in spite of this, accounts are always paid (in all the years recorded in the books there are only two occurrences where bills are left unsettled) as in the case of ---, who comes in to pay the last $23 still owing. Mr. Boyd knows the man has had a hard time scraping the money together. As a gesture of appreciation he promptly hands back twenty as a present to this conscientious customer.

This year gold dust is valued at $17 an ounce; an accumulated amount is carefully sealed up, and turned over to Mr. Hitchcock, the assayer, to be paid to the manager of the H.B. post at Williams Creek. Next there is another letter from Mr. Landringham to be attended to. It is destined for Omineca, calling for postage of $1.50, a dismayingly high rate, but it can't be helped.

Time moves on, bringing new faces, new names. Among these is Steve Tingley, a name to become well known in British Columbia. From ordinary stagedriver he rises step by step until he finally reaches the top, becoming sole owner of the famous B.C. Express line. Today, however, he is still a driver for Barnard's Express, and with Mr. Barnard himself strides into the stopping place, where a bountiful supper is laid. Fragrant cigars further relax them, then they clamber aboard again and rattle off on the business of the day.

The first days of autumn are slow lazy ones, with the old dog dozing outside the door. A once familiar voice rouses him, and he rises to bark a greeting to an old friend. It is Ah Fatt, who in old days handed out such meaty bones. The former cook, poor fellow, has fallen into a slough of financial troubles. He parts reluctantly with his cherished "patent-lever silver watch No. 20845, maker Wm. Cooper & Co. Liverpool." To augment the money received from the sale of the watch, Mr. Boyd obliges him with a private loan. Ah Fatt beams his thanks as he promises to repay, which he does a few months later when his financial state has bettered.

September, and a bit of sadness. Antoine drops in to say good-bye to the Cariboo. He is going to try his luck elsewhere.

Then comes a milestone in the history of the stopping place. The partnership of Heath and Boyd, always an amicable one, is dissolved, Mr. Heath selling out his interest

Freight wagons at Cottonwood and a Barnard's Express Stagecoach about 1870. Stagecoaches operated on a regular schedule but were frequently delayed by bad road conditions and arrived with their weary and hungry passengers at any hour of the day or night.

for a cash settlement, leaving Mr. Boyd in complete possession.

With the passing of autumn, a Cariboo miner and his "Lady" break their journey out to have dinner and a farewell visit with the Boyds. It is a nice custom, this use of the word "lady" rather than "the wife" or "the missus." Only when a woman is travelling alone is she referred to as "Mrs." Accompanying her husband, the term "John Doe and Lady" is invariably used.

Cold nights, warm, sunny days — Indian summer at its best. But in a trice the weather changes. A cold wind drives grey clouds down from the north, and next morning the first snow of the season falls. Through the snow a train of oxen plod stolidly, heavy heads swinging, urged on by McCullum, the packer. He pushes open the gate while Mr. Anderson herds the slow beasts into the grazing-field. The gate closes and the two men take themselves to the comfort of the house and comfortable beds. Their feeling of well-being is rudely shattered in the morning, however, for during the night the oxen have broken into the cabbage field. They are blissfully munching the heads, trampling on others as they chew. For the loss incurred their owner is assessed $15 and proceeds to drive his charges out with harsh imprecations.

Family events lighten the formal entries, each adding its bit to the story of Cottonwood. Neatly sandwiched between two small business entries is a memo to warm the heart:

"Saturday Oct. 28th 1871.

John C. Boyd Junior two years old this morning, Cash to boy birthday present — $5.00."

November's most important business is the ordering of "a wagon for two horses from Mr. Tompkins to be built at Victoria. Everything complete and of best quality $250, and to be delivered at Soda Creek on Quesnelle free of charge and in good condition." No slipshod work here, one can see!

The wagon will be ready in spring. Meanwhile, winter calls for the sleigh to be got out from the shed, for there is already a good depth of snow. In the cozy house, Mr. Boyd sits down to make out a subscription to the *Victoria Daily Standard*, and another for the *Cariboo Sentinel*.

Each month has some special event to be recorded, the tenth of December being a memorable occasion. The first load of freight from the Hudson's Bay Company at Quesnelle comes through, with freight charges pegged at three and a half cents a pound. The contents of the shipment, and the freight charge, is reckoned at Cottonwood, a long task. Great casks of brandy, each weighing 312 lbs., are counted out, two 125-lb. chests of tea, salt, two kegs of syrup, five bundles of shovels, sixteen boxes of candles, and two bales of blankets. A week later a second load pulls up, supplementing the first with other liquors, canvas, jams, mustard, sugar, and more blankets.

Into the warm house hurries an odd little group, their teeth chattering with the cold. At the head is Ah Whan, shepherding four China women, glad to have respite from the chill of the road, and gladder still to be leaving the rugged and icy mountain country.

Christmas is more fun now, with gifts for a small boy, as well as a cash present. There is a special Christmas dinner, the travellers sharing in the hospitality, and joining in the good wishes for the coming year.

The arrival of 1872 coincides with that of the third load of freight for the H.B.C. post at Barkerville, which is stocking its shelves. Each succeeding load brings some fresh wares: boots and hats, twine and screws, soap, and later on even a supply of oysters. New Year's Day also finds an equine patient in the barn, who is doctored with a bottle of brandy.

A trip to Williams Creek is inevitably one of the early-January activities. As is customary, Mr. Boyd sets off by himself for it is too cold for Johnny. The thriving settlement has acquired a minister at last, and Mr. Boyd attends services there, not forgetting on his return to account for his collection money. Every expenditure must go in, and accordingly an entry for "tickets for a raffle at cards last evening" closely follows the one for the collection money.

The month of February is severe, but by the middle of March the weather has softened considerably, enabling the making of a second trip to the claims at Van Winkle and beyond to the Creek. Each time Mr. Boyd returns from a journey, some special present is stowed away in his bag:

Changing times at Cottonwood. The top photo with its right-hand drive car was taken before World War One. The other photo was taken September 1, 1925. The car is described as a "Skye Blue Oakland Touring." Standing behind it is W. H. Boyd who died in 1959 at 87.

candy from the Creek, a big bag of peanuts from Quesnelle, so that his homecoming is doubly anticipated. A kindly man, church and charitable donations play a regular part in his life, and many a dollar is quietly given in answer to an appeal.

Spring break-up means a resumption of road work, which in turn means a visit from Mr. Spence, who purchases lumber for a wheelbarrow and a pair of "shaker socks." It is pleasant to have him come in, for Mrs. Boyd and John are in Victoria, needing more money, too!

The new wagon, ordered months ago, is duly delivered, all in good order, a source of pride to Mr. Boyd and admiration to Mr. Lindhard, down from Van Winkle on a hot summer day to buy some mules. Buying mules is hard, hot work, and he calls for cooling drinks at intervals.

The stage, rolling in at the end of July, is a welcome sight, even though it arrives at the unseemly hour of two a.m. Among its passengers are John and his mother, home from Victoria at last. Sixty dollars is the passage fare from Yale to Cottonwood, and also to be reckoned is the cost of the boat trip from Victoria to Yale.

Ever the book discloses new names, some to become eminent in the history of the province, others fading into obscurity. Here is a new chap now, Mr. Barnston, a lawyer by profession. He is bound for Richfield where the government office is, the walls of which echo with learned words heard in court cases.

A week from Johnny's third birthday the house is filled with a quiet bustle and excitement, for there is a new arrival, and when all is still once more the big ledger is opened and the event proudly recorded, the birth of a second child at "10 minutes past 12 o'clock, Oct. 22. Son of John and Janet Boyd — the addition to the household is to be named William H."

A leaf of the book turns, and there is the picture of a party — the baby's christening party — with guests from the Creek down for the day. The penmanship, strong and plain, is different from that customarily seen in the book. This is the work of the minister, surely as strange a place for a legal document as one can imagine! It reads:

"Baptized this day William Henry Boyd aged two months, in the presence of Mr. and Mrs. D. H. Ross, Father and Mother John and Janet Boyd, J. W. Shreck, Harry Heesa
   By me Rev. Joseph Hall, Wesleyen Minister, Cariboo."

With two children to keep things humming, the house has good reason to be pleased, and its lamps send forth an even kindlier glow while it stands watching out the old year of 1872 and welcoming in the new. It begins quietly, for winter is at its sternest and indoors a good place to be. Not until February does any real activity begin, with shakes being hauled to the Last Chance Mine, and 2,200 lbs. of butter delivered to Van Winkle. Winter passes quickly, though, and all at once it is time again to sow the timothy seed bought in the autumn from a Mr. Fleming on far-off San Juan Island. A small sorrel horse ready equipped with saddle and bridle is sold to Milton Leamer for the bargain price of ten dollars, and the huge bicycle built in Barkerville in '64 is wheeled out of the shed. It is a heavy queer thing, made almost entirely of iron, with the pedals fastened to the hub of the front wheel, but it has covered many a mile and will yet.

Now that British Columbia has become part of Canada, July 1 is given its due notice. The day is headed Dominion Day in large capitals. As if to match the promotion of the new province there are more little luxuries as summer goes on, including strawberries from Quesnelle and green peas from Ah Sin's vegetable garden. Ah Sin catches salmon, too, selling them at a dollar a piece, big ones that are a delicious change from meat. In the henyard a fine new Spanish rooster, just come in on the stage, is uncrated and let loose, causing quite a stir among the feathered ladies as he struts around.

The heat of August bears down upon the land, and the dust rises thickly as the horses of the Pearson Line trot up the road. At Cottonwood they are pulled up sharply by the driver, a small spry chap with twinkling eyes and sporting a pointed beard. He is Charlie Major, the man who is always pointed out as "the fellow who drove the first four-horse stage through the canyons and later the first Barnard's stage to Soda Creek." It was just luck that brought him the honor of the latter "first," for his regular job was as messenger of Barnard's Express between Barkerville and Quesnelle. On this renowned occasion he happened to be on his way up, and took charge of the stage while Steve Tingley, the appointed driver, went ahead with relays of horses.

All September the sun shines and shines, blessing the stubble fields and the stacked grain. It warms the shoulders of Judge Begbie, a notable man carrying the title Chief Justice of the Mainland of British Columbia, which he upholds well, standing staunchly for justice and enforcement of law, and whose reputation for court judgments is sound.

By October, ice on the ponds and the occasional flurry of snow speak plainly of winter's approach. Long lines of birds pass swiftly overhead, driven on by a keen north wind. At night the coyotes yell insanely, and a lone wolf calls dolorously from the hill. Each week the snow creeps closer until winter shuts down over the land, and the teamsters beat their hands together as they drive up to the house: James Newlan, James Buck, Captain Taylor, Dave Hatherne, Stephen Knox — good men all, their account finishing off the year's work.

By now a decade has passed since Cottonwood House first opened its doors to the travellers of the Cariboo Road. It has seen thousands of faces and heard countless voices speaking in many tongues. It has seen the irresistible flood of fevered fortune-hunters; it has seen poor men become rich and rich men become poor. It has seen lawlessness, and the coming of the law; it has seen sturdy men broken and the weak grow strong. It has seen fat years and lean years; it has seen the Cariboo mature and level off. Yes, it has seen many things, and it will see many more, and will welcome a host of new people. As they come and go their passing will be noted in the books, a record of the days when the first chapters in the history of the Cariboo were written.

And what of Cottonwood House? It will stand substantial and homely during the long decades, an historic landmark, to be pointed out by generations yet to come.

"There, that's it, that's Cottonwood!" a traveller versed in Cariboo lore will exclaim, and from out the shadowy past a faint echo will whisper, "Yes, that's it, that's Cottonwood!" ■

DOG DAYS IN HAZELTON

In the frontier settlement of Hazelton, dogs hauled the winter mail, welcomed the first sternwheeler in spring and enlivened the community in other ways.

by WIGGS O'NEILL

The dog was an invaluable animal in our hinterland in the early days, and Hazelton had its fair share of dogs.

There were all kinds and breeds of dogs, from the big, strong, husky variety to the ordinary Indian cur, or just plain dog, and all sizes imaginable. In winter, they were used extensively as they were trained as sleigh and pack dogs. When the Indians pulled out of town for their trapping grounds in the fall, all their dogs went along, and every dog, no matter how small, had his pack. The larger dogs were used in pulling sleighs and toboggans and making up the dogteams that were relied on so much in winter. During construction of the Grand Trunk Pacific Railway between 1908 and 1912, many fine dogteams were employed by the contractors on the river ice, hauling mail and express, using either Klondike sleighs or toboggans.

The dog was an important animal during the winter months. He was usually fed a kind of rice mulligan, boiled in a large pot on the campfire, into which a goodly quantity of smoked salmon was mixed. At feeding time all had to be fed separately and watched carefully. Each dog would bolt his portion as fast as he could, then try and chase his neighbor away and gobble his food, too, if he wasn't watched. So it was a real chore to feed a dogteam and watch that everyone got his portion.

When springtime came the scene changed, and Hazelton became a real dog town. All the work was over and the Indians didn't do much about feeding them in the "off" season, believing in the policy, "No work, no eat." There were hundreds around town, doing all the thieving they could. They also helped us welcome the first sternwheeler to arrive when spring navigation opened.

Usually this event was in May and an exciting day it was. Since Hazelton is 180 miles up the Skeena River, which froze in winter and cut off navigation, all supplies were brought in the previous autumn. By spring stocks of everything were nearly exhausted and the rum in the hotels almost gone or watered profusely.

As a consequence, the arrival of the first sternwheeler was a rousing event. The Indian kids ran around shouting, "Steam Boatum Gilhowlie" (Steam boat of the woods). Even the dogs got excited and lined up along the river bank. Everybody, both Indian and white, joined them at the landing and when the Captain blew his whistle at the big cottonwood tree on the point, everyone cheered. The dogs, not to be outdone, sat on their hindends, opened their mouths to the sky and howled their heads off. So the first boat to arrive got a real noisy greeting.

Since Hazelton was truly a dog town, it wasn't surprising that there were many stories about dogs. I suppose some of them weren't even too far fetched. One I remember was considered true.

The Omineca Hotel, located at one of the main corners of the town and owned by Mr. Jack Sealy, had the reputation of serving the best rum in town, really free from Skeena River water. On the other hand, Jack operated the crummiest dining room one could imagine. The food was terrible and the surroundings far from tempting. The tables were covered with oil cloth of many shades, a mecca for thousands of flies which were often taken for currants. Hanging in front of the hotel was a big steel triangle used as a dinner gong. When mealtime came around Sing, the Chinese cook, beat the triangle. The dogs seemed to know when mealtime was due and gathered around in swarms. When Sing hit the gong they sat on their haunches and howled in a wonderful chorus.

One Christmas a well-loaded local citizen was standing out front when the gong went and the howls started. He bobbed his head up and down a few times, glared at the dogs and roared: "What's the matter with you guys? You don't have to eat the damn grub!"

At left is the main street of Hazelton about 1908. The Omineca Hotel is at right center.

At lower left is the sternwheel steamer *Port Simpson* arriving at Hazelton in 1909. The first vessel upstream in spring received a tumultuous welcome from local residents and a mournful serenade from dozens of dogs.

During the five months or longer when winter made the Skeena River unnavigable, the only means of bringing in mail and essential supplies to Hazelton was by dogteam, some 150 miles from the coast. The photo below shows the mail on its way in 1910.

Mrs. Jowett in 1900 at her Foggy Day claim. She was 94 when the photo opposite was taken, the same year that she experienced her first airplane ride and insisted on being flown over her claims.

The photo on the opposite page shows Lardeau country typical of that where Mrs. Jowett had her claims. Despite the rugged mountain topography characteristic of the region, she inspected the claims on horseback every year until she was in her late eighties.

Alice Elizabeth Jowett ...grand old lady of Lardeau

She was a vital, robust woman - at home on the roughest mountain trails or in the dining room of the hotel she operated for fifty years.

by ELSIE G. TURNBULL

She was a fabulous person, Alice Elizabeth Jowett — a first-class cook, hotel proprietress, prospector, and a woman of courage and daring. Her colorful life spanned a century, more than half of which she spent in the Lardeau, a land of minerals, mountains, and lakes full of fish. She loved the adventurous life in the wilds and gloried in her ability to handle horses and to hike over the roughest mountain trails. A robust, vital woman, she never feared hard work. Even when she passed ninety she was active, and while her thatch of hair had turned white, her restless eyes remained a vivid blue and never lost their penetrating gaze. As she approached the century mark she admitted to feeling "less spry" but her mind was keen and her memory retained its clarity.

On a night of storm in 1853 she was born Alice Elizabeth Smith in the English village of Bradford, Yorkshire. Here she learned the confectionery business and in 1878 married Thomas E. Jowett. Left widowed with four young children, she decided to try her fortune in Canada and in 1889 boarded a sailing vessel for the long journey around Cape Horn. Upon reaching Vancouver she set up a bake shop on Cordova Street where for seven years she turned out pies and cakes, bread and buns. Then, with an urge for change, she sold her store and moved to Trout Lake City. With only an Indian woman for help she operated a hotel in a log cabin, cooking excellent meals for the miners flocking to the mineral-rich Lardeau area.

Trout Lake is a long narrow body of water lying in a deep cleft between the glacier-topped mountains of the Lardeau and Duncan Ranges. It is caught in a valley thirty miles above the head of Kootenay Lake and twenty miles from the northeast arm of Upper Arrow Lake, far from civilization and difficult of access. During the 1890's venturesome prospectors were combing the high, scarred peaks and finding rich pockets of gold and silver. So extensive was the mineralization that two towns soon appeared — Ferguson up in the hills and Trout Lake City at the head of the lake. They boasted populations reaching the thousand mark and hotels sprang up to cater to miners and incoming prospectors. Among them was the Windsor, owned by McLennan, Black & Co. and run by Dave McLennan in 1897. It was a large three-storey frame building with dormer windows and it stood on the lake shore across the road from Mrs. Jowett's log cabin hostelry. She soon found her quarters too cramped so purchased the Windsor.

Under her management the Windsor Hotel became a noted institution. Luxuriously furnished in the style of the day, its fittings included a bar and a billiard room. Its dining room gleamed with silver flatware and white tablecloths, while Alice Jowett's roast beef and Yorkshire pudding gladdened the hearts of all its guests. Those guests came from far-away places — New York, Dublin, Gotenberg, Johannesburg, Coolgardie in West Australia, and all the towns in British Columbia. Some of the visitors were famous people, including W. C. Van Horne, president of the CPR. Many a miner holidayed at the hotel, giving as home address the mine where he worked. Consequently, the old register abounds in colorful place names: Free Coinage, Bad Shot, Rawhide Trail, Circle City, Rabbit Creek, Horseshoe, Nickle Plate. On January of every year added comments were supplied by celebrating miners describing their friends: "Sinner, Barber, Butcher, Hobo, Methodist, Dusty Simon, Rubber Neck, Stiff, Dead Bum, Coyote Ketcher, Hasher, Swamper, Masher."

Once established in the Lardeau, Mrs. Jowett soon caught the prospecting fever and began to hike into the hills on a search for claims. Riding horseback she explored a ridge at the headwaters of Ottawa and Eight-Mile Creeks near the summit of Silver Cup Mountain. Here she located the Foggy Day, the Arralu, the You and I, the Alpine and the Hercules, prospects which she leased for working. Mining became a passion and she attended conventions in Nelson and Spokane, while visiting engineers and geologists were assured a warm welcome at the Windsor. Every year she made an inspection trip to her claims until she was in her late eighties. At the age of ninety-two she insisted on flying over her properties to see them from the air.

The Lardeau country has long since passed its boom period. The best mines were finished by the 1930's and guests at the Windsor Hotel grew fewer. During all the years of decline Mrs. Jowett refused to lower her standards. Her spotless tablecloths and good silver still greeted the occasional traveller and she typified a spirit of optimism and hope which refused to let the Lardeau die.

Age finally crept up on Mrs. Jowett, forcing her to sell the Windsor in 1945. She had operated it for fifty years. She remained in the Lardeau for several years and then entered Rest Haven convalescent home in Kelowna. There on November 5, 1953, she celebrated her 100th birthday with a big party and a cake bearing 100 candles. One more birthday remained for her, then the end came in the spring of 1955. Funeral services were held in Vancouver but her ashes were carried by her family to be scattered in the alpine basin she had frequented so often in life.

Today, the Windsor Hotel is still open to travellers. In the bedrooms the high square oak headboards belong to the 1890 style of furniture but the mattresses are spring-filled. Carved dressers and mirrors are those which served guests at the turn of the century but electric lights and basins with running water cater to a modern taste. In the lobby are the hotel's old registers and account journals where one can read of those long-ago visitors. It is easy to imagine how pleasant the Windsor must have seemed to miners away from the rough life of camp or to travellers who had just braved the arduous journey to Trout Lake City. ∎

Mrs. Jowett in front of the Windsor Hotel on June 22, 1947 with members of the Revelstoke Board of Trade. The top photo shows her at 65 on a trip to her claims in the mountains above Trout Lake City. At center is the Windsor Hotel which she operated for fifty years.

APOSTLE IN THE ROCKIES

In September 1845 Father Jean De Smet, the first missionary to reach the Kootenay Indians, placed a large "Cross of Peace" in a pass north of here as he struggled on foot through the Rockies seeking the Blackfeet tribe. Born in Belgium in 1801, this Jesuit priest laboured for 35 years among Indians from the Missouri River to the Pacific.

PROVINCE OF BRITISH COLUMBIA 1966

STOP OF INTEREST

This plaque, honoring Father Jean De Smet, is on Highway 95 just south of Canal Flats. The pioneer missionary came to North America in 1821 and joined the Society of Jesus, the Jesuits. He was ordained in 1827 and sent to Oregon in 1840. The next year he established a mission among the Flathead Indians and served the West for over thirty years, travelling some 250,000 miles on foot and by boat, canoe and horseback. Several times he risked his life acting as mediator between Indians and whites, on one occasion visiting Sitting Bull's camp in the Bighorn Valley, even though the Indians had threatened to kill the first white man who entered.

He visited Fort Vancouver in 1842 and Fort Edmonton in 1845, and on one of his trips in the West noted the presence of a massive lead and silver outcrop on the shores of Kootenay Lake. This ore body eventually led to development of the Kootenay's famous Blue Bell Mine. At another point in his travels through the Rocky Mountains, the Father's party entered the Crows Nest Pass where he reported seeing fossils and coal seams. These seams were later brought into production as the noted Fernie coalfields.

The trails of this devout and zealous priest crisscrossed and covered the American West. With boundless enthusiasm he preached his faith to the natives, who eagerly waited for the coming of their beloved "black robes," as they called the pioneer Jesuit priests.

THE COMING OF THE STEEL

It was nicknamed the "Overall and Tobacco Railroad" because old-timers maintained that the company made more from selling these items than it did from the construction contract. Nevertheless, the Grand Trunk Pacific resulted in the birth of communities such as Prince George, Vanderhoof, Smithers, Terrace and Prince Rupert.

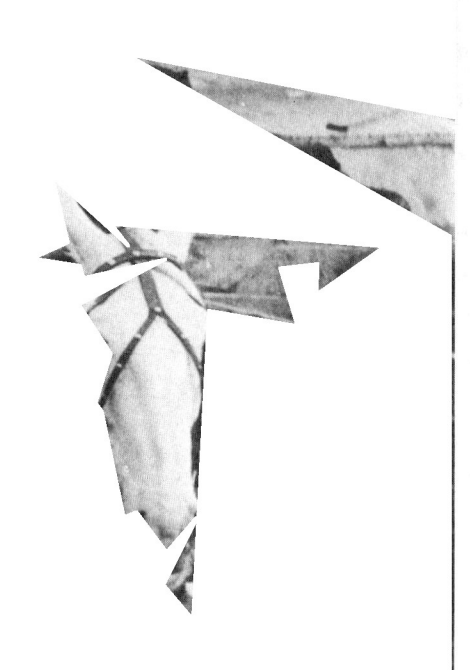

by BLAINE BOYD

It was spring, 1906. The big land boom was on in Central British Columbia with construction underway on the Grand Trunk Pacific Railway that would provide a direct link with Winnipeg, Edmonton, and the new port of Prince Rupert on B.C.'s north coast. Every town was plastered with posters urging people to make themselves rich by investing in new townsites and farms, and if a person as much as stopped to read a poster, the salesmen descended. They just happened to know about a town lot that would make you wealthy in a few years, or if you liked country life, would sell you 160 acres of the world's finest farm land.

My brother, Pat, and I decided that country life was for us and headed for Prince Rupert to take advantage of the new frontier. We were young, enthusiastic, confident—and, of course, inexperienced. Prince Rupert proved to be a city being carved from rock and overflowing with hundreds of people from all over the world, attracted by the brash advertising of the townsite speculators and looking for land that would make them wealthy.

We soon learned that there was no farm land around Prince Rupert, but were told that Hazelton, some 180 miles up the Skeena River, was the place to go. Here we would find miles of the finest land on earth just for the filing. So Hazelton became our destination. The Grand Trunk Railway was completed about 100 miles east from Prince Rupert to a point on the Skeena called Kitselas Rapids.

The photo above shows men grading near Fort George in 1912 and, at left, men and equipment near Burns Lake in 1909. Construction of the Grand Trunk Pacific was sometimes spread over a hundred miles of right-of-way, with most of the work done by horses and hand.

Above the rapids a sternwheeler connected to Hazelton. We took the train to Kitselas but on our arrival discovered that from the end of steel to the start of sternwheeler service was a five-mile stretch over which we had to walk, carrying our 100 pounds of luggage.

The Indians would carry it for $5 apiece but money was scarce with us and we decided that what Indians could do we could do. Ever since then I have had a great respect for the Indians. With a huge brass-bound trunk on their back and a big suitcase in each hand they took off up the trail as casually as if they were pushing a baby buggy in the park. We struggled and sweated with our 100 pounds that appeared light by comparison and finally made it.

On the way we got acquainted with a couple of men who were going to take the boat. Since they had no heavy luggage, they offered to take ours if we wanted to walk to Hazelton. Well, Hazelton was about sixty miles away, two days walk we figured, and since the boat fare was about $30 we could make good wages by walking.

When we reached the boat landing we left our bundles with the two men and started up the railroad track to Hazelton. We quickly learned that walking railway ties is a real art. The ties are too close to be a comfortable step apart, but then two ties are too much for a single step. Usually it comes down to taking two or three extra short steps and then one extra long one. The result is a somewhat comic hippityhop gait.

Pat's shoes proved a little too big for him; consequently, his feet slid around in them. By the time we had walked twenty miles his feet were a mass of blisters. He took his shoes off and slung them around his neck and wrapped his feet up in a couple of burlap sacks that we had picked up along the track. My one regret about the trip is that I did not get a picture of Pat hiking in his gunny-sack shoes.

While we were clumping along a big husky foreigner caught up with us. He had an employment ticket to Hazelton but his job was ten miles down the river from the town. For some reason he decided to walk the fifty miles up the river to his job rather than ride to Hazelton and walk the ten miles back. He gave us his ticket and we decided that

The sternwheel steamer *Port Simpson* **churns up the Skeena River in 1911 with the Coast Mountains forming an impressive background. From 1891** until completion of the Grand Trunk Pacific, sternwheelers regularly plied 180 miles upstream from tidewater to Hazelton.

Pat would use it because of his sore feet and I would buy a ticket on the next boat. When we reached the landing we found several people waiting for the sternwheeler that had been at Kitselas when we left. We had apparently walked faster than she sailed, and all wondered what the problem was. In about an hour we could see her coming up river and we suddenly realized the difficulties of river navigation.

The Skeena River was in full flood. Just below the landing was a turbulent stretch that in normal times would have been a riffle. The steamer snorted up and hit the riffle at full speed. About half way up her progress slowed to nil and, puffing in protest, she slowly drifted back downstream. Below the riffle she halted and black smoke rolled from her funnel as a new head of steam was built up. With the paddles churning furiously and flames shooting from her smokestack, the old girl tore into the riffle again. At first it seemed she would make it, but progress became slower and slower and she was washed downstream again. But the pilot learned something about the current and he hung a monkey wrench or something on the safety valve. The next time he tore triumphantly to the top of the riffle, teetered a moment and plopped into the slower water and to our landing.

Pat presented his ticket and for $2.50 I got a ride the rest of the way to Hazelton. The trip on the sternwheeler was interesting. All along the river there were cords of dry wood and as needed the boat stopped and all hands loaded fuel. The vessel had a tremendous appetite. The fireman, who worked a two-hour shift, stripped to the waist and stood in a pit in front of the firebox. He picked up a stick of four-foot cordwood, opened the fire door with the end of the stick, threw it in, and banged shut the door. He reached for another stick and repeated the operation. Probably during a normal flow of water he had a breathing spell but that day there was no rest until he went off shift. The heat from the firebox made his body a pinkish red and the sweat literally ran off his naked torso. I have never seen what I considered a hotter or more monotonous job.

We reached Hazelton without trouble and soon had our tent pitched on the edge of town. We stayed in Hazelton a week but learned that the good land had been corralled by the big land companies for speculation and they were not as yet willing to sell it. Later on a wild-land tax helped to turn the land over to the bona-fide settlers but for quite awhile most of the good land was tied up by speculators. There is no doubt this action held back development of the country.

At Hazelton we also learned why laws are made and how they are evaded. A class of society known as the "B" girls—and no frontier town is without them—either became too thick or too bold and were banished from the town. Thereafter no B-girl could operate within a three mile limit of Hazelton. Well, the girls went the three miles out of town and set up their own place and called it Three Mile. Since their trade was largely with the construction men who craved companionship, they managed to part a lot of them from a payroll which had previously been spent in Hazelton. As a result Three Mile flourished. I understand that it is now known by the more dignified name of New Hazelton.

Hazelton, like so many northern towns at that time, was infested with dogs. In winter dogs were at a premium for sled animals but in the summer a great number of them which were not used for pack dogs were turned loose on the town to shift for themselves. Half starved and half wild they looked to be a menace and were. Luckily they were well grounded in the belief that man was a superior animal who must be obeyed, or I think that in their starving state they would actually have attacked people.

We heard that at Telkwa, seventy-eight miles up the Bulkley River from Hazelton, there was plenty of good farm land so we headed in that direction. There was a wagon road of sorts along the railway right-of-way on which supplies for construction crews came by freight teams and a horse-drawn stage to Telkwa but rumor had it that the stage was rougher than a wild bronco. This news gave us a good excuse to save some more money by walking to our destination. Three days later we reached Telkwa and set up our tent just across the river from the town.

In our search for land we encountered the same problem as at Hazelton. It was all tied up by promoters. There was, however, plenty up the line at Decker Lake. The story about easy land was now growing stale and we could see that it would be expensive to get started with transportation so high and the cost of supplies so great. We sat down to count our money, time and enthusiasm. The supply of each was growing smaller day by day. Then fate took a hand.

One evening we were up town watching a baseball practise, and since we loved playing we horned in. We were not big leaguers by any means but we had played some semi-pro ball and the manager watching us became very interested. Were we going to stay in town? He could get us some pretty good jobs if we wanted to stay. We inquired cautiously and learned that Telkwa was baseball crazy. I was offered a job tallying lumber in a little mill whose owner was an avid baseball fan. The pay was a little above average and I could have the afternoon off to practise. Pat also was given a soft job by an old one-legged farmer and a former ball player. There were two or three others in the town who also had suspiciously soft jobs, one of them a Northwest League pitcher. Of course, the team was strictly amateur. No one actually was paid to play ball, even though that was what we did.

A series of games was arranged with Hazelton, the only comparable town within reach, and when the players arrived, excitement was great. Large bets were made on the game, with a character called Roadhouse Charlie making his usual bet of $1,500. That was Roadhouse's regular bet. Although he practically never won, he still considered $1,500 a lucky bet. Our first game didn't help his luck any, since Hazelton beat us six to one.

Despite the loss a big dinner was prepared for us that night in Black Jack MacDonald's hotel. The dinner started in a gloomy atmosphere, but with a bottle of whisky between every two men, a bottle of beer at each plate, and the waiter bringing on spiced wine, the gloom didn't last. I was seated on the right of toastmaster Smith, who was not only an enthusiastic fan, but had a reputation for holding his liquor well. By my side was a potted plant, and after about the third drink when Smith got up to call on another speaker, I dumped my drink on the potted plant. Smith sat down, saw my empty glass, drained his own, and filled both again. This performance continued through the evening. Eventually the toastmaster was rather the worse for wear, while I stood up well. Always thereafter, Charlie looked at me with great respect, but I never did learn what happened to the unfortunate potted plant. The party did have one good result. After such strenuous training, we won the next game six to five.

In the summer the dirt roads dried up and became almost passable, so much so that one truck came into town. It was the first automobile most of us had seen, bright red with solid tires. The driver sold the baseball management the idea of hauling the team to Hazelton for the return series. The plan was to start Friday, reach town in time to practise, and be in good shape for the Saturday game. We started out proudly, but it rained a little. By nightfall the twenty passengers had managed to push the truck about forty miles to a small roadhouse where we were fed, but only about half of us got any sleep. Next day we got into Hazelton just in time to start the game. Again we split the series, but that was our last big splurge.

My job checking lumber became so monotonous that I asked for a job on the log drive. I had once helped drive a few logs on a placid stream in Washington but this job proved different. The river was swifter and colder. Each morning, early, we were out. The first thing we did was wade into the stream to our waist "to take the chill off." Since the river had fallen, most of our logs had grounded and were high on the gravel bars. We rolled and "sagged" them into the deep water and started them on their way again. (Sagging is a term that originated in an old river town in Michigan called Saginaw. To "sag" a log, two, four, or as many men as necessary get opposite each other with their cant hooks and literally drag or carry it to the water until it floats.)

The first day our boat took a lot of water, and my bed roll got soaked and was never entirely dry during the job. The next drive I ran a boat, but by the time I got through, most of the glamour was gone from the white-water river driving.

My brother, Pat, decided to return to his family in Washington, but I decided to go on to Decker Lake. Before we left, we went to a fair in Telkwa, at which the

The above photo, taken in 1913, shows the first stores and other business places in Smithers, including, at right, Ed Orchard's canvas roadhouse. The top photo is of Prince Rupert in 1906. The photos on the opposite page are, at upper left, the first buildings in McBride and, at bottom, the community of New Hazelton in 1911. The other photo shows smuggled whiskey found by police at Tete Jaune Cache in 1912.

main attraction was the horse show. The teamsters of the four- and six-horse teams practically lived with their teams. They were beautiful draft animals, curried until they shone like polish, their harness decorated with ribbons and gaily colored celluloid spreaders and rings. The show ring filled with these teams performing for the prizes and answering to the least sound of their drivers' voices or pressure of the lines was a sight that I vividly remember to this day. The Grand Trunk Railroad could hardly have been built without them. Now their day is done, but I am glad that I saw them.

A problem which caused much trouble — and sometimes laughs — was the liquor situation. In the beginning only a few of the roadhouses or hotels along the right-of-way had licenses to sell. When construction started, a ten-mile-wide strip along the line was proclaimed a dry area. Since it was no crime for the licensed houses to sell liquor, or for a person to have it in his possession, this loophole opened up quite a field for the bootlegger.

Construction men are notoriously thirsty, and soon there were many roadhouses along the right-of-way with illegal stocks of liquor. At first there was a $300 fine for bootlegging, but some of the places were making so much money that they paid the fine and never even closed. Then the penalty was increased from $300 for the first offense to six months in jail for the second. Traffic still didn't stop, so the penalty became six months for the first offense. Then liquor became hard to find.

After I left Telkwa, I met an older man who persuaded me to enter into a roadhouse venture with him west of Decker Lake. We pooled our slim resources, established credit and headed westward again.

My partner was a man about six feet, four inches tall who was nicknamed "Slim." I was six feet and skinny, and I was also known as "Slim." The potential for confusion was obvious but the problem was solved by one of our supply men.

"We can't have two Slims in this outfit. You will be Slivers," he said, pointing to me. The name took, and our supplies were shipped to Slim and Slivers, Decker Lake.

To save money we walked the 100 miles to Decker Lake. Along the way we discovered that facilities in the roadhouses were somewhat basic. Since a white woman was seldom seen above Telkwa, all the bunks were in one room, often upstairs so travellers could get the benefit of heat that came from the big iron stoves below. If a woman did happen to appear, blankets were hung around a bunk in a corner of the room and that was her private apartment.

We had to wait a day at Decker Lake for our supplies and tools to come, and when we went to get them some were missing. Upon questioning everyone around we learned that two fellows with a sled had loaded them and left.

Now stealing supplies on the frontier, and in late fall at that, was an unpardonable sin. A man's life might depend on his bundle. Ordinarily a person could leave any kind of package, box or parcel for weeks and no one would touch it. I took out after the sled tracks, rifle with me. I was very young and very angry.

I followed the tracks about four miles and came to a log cabin. The sled was outside, and although the door was shut I heard a slight noise inside. I knocked, and no one answered. I knocked again with the end of my rifle and said, "Open up, I know you are there!"

The door flew open and showed two hard looking faces, one of them beside the door with a heavy iron poker in his hand. My bundle lay on the floor as if they were just going to open it. I told them to throw it outside, and after a little hesitation and a look at my rifle, they did!

We stayed at Decker Lake a few days and made what we called a "One-Armed John." It was a simple but effective method of transporting supplies — a single sled runner and handles to hold it erect. One man could hold the handles and shove, and one man with a rope in front could pull.

We decided to build our roadhouse at a point called Shovel Creek, some forty miles westward. There was about a foot of snow by now and we followed an old trail along Decker Lake. The trail went straight up the hills and straight down the other side, so we found ourselves having to split up our 400-pound load to get to the top and to snub it with a rope going down.

By the time we got to Burns Lake it was getting cold and a woodcutter there said the trail was much worse alongside the lake. We decided to camp and wait for the lake to freeze, since the ice had already formed and we thought in a week's time it would hold us. Just as we were about to leave, the rail construction crew blew up a long rock cliff which bordered the lake and cracked the ice the entire width of the lake. We decided to wait another few days, but our woodcutter friend told us that two fellows were going to try to beat us to Shovel Creek. We decided to try the ice anyway.

All went fine until we hit the broken stretch. Then we found the pieces were too small and not yet frozen enough to hold us and the One-Armed John. We lengthened our rope to its full fifty feet and I ran ahead until I found a large piece of ice. Then, pulling frantically, I would bring Slim and the sled across and the second they hit the piece I would take off again. We had about half a mile of that and the only reason we did not wind up at the lake bottom is the special providence that takes care of fools and drunks.

At the head of the lake we found that the other party was ahead of us. However, they had dogs and two runner sleds and were making poor time over the rough terrain. We took after them and soon could hear them. Since they wouldn't reach Shovel Creek that night and were breaking trail for us, we trailed along behind. They camped about three or four miles from the creek with us just behind them. In the morning before they even had their breakfast we passed their camp.

"Where you bound?" they asked, as if they didn't know.

Feeling safe by our good start we said, "Shovel Creek," and kept going. They turned around and went back.

Picking our location, we felled a few trees to show occupation and then looked for shelter. Luckily we found an old log cabin nearby. The roof was only about five feet high so we dug the dirt floor about eighteen inches deeper and put the dirt on the roof and banked up around the walls. It was well we did for the thermometer dropped to fifty-two degrees below that winter.

We decided to build three log cabins, each sixteen by twenty-four feet. Although we had our location right in timber we had to haul a lot of the logs and do it by hand. It was tedious work but we slugged away and after a few days I knew how the slaves felt while they were building the pyramids.

I found out my partner was no hiker so it was up to me to go to Decker Lake for our supplies. It was thirteen miles to Burns Lake, then twenty-seven more on the ice of Burns and Decker Lakes to the Decker Lake Supply Station. I made it to the Station in one day empty, and back in two loaded. As long as the ice was clear I could pull wonderful loads on the sled. One time I pulled close to 500 pounds, although I learned I had to be very careful where I stopped. Once I met a trapper and stopped in about three inches of snow, then when I started again had to call him back to help me break my sled loose.

The entire winter was one of hard work, with all days the same and even Sunday just another work day. We cut logs, hauled them in and rolled them onto the house and fashioned them to fit. The frozen timber was hard to cut and handle but it was unbelievable the size of log two husky men could haul on the frozen snow. In places we threw water on the trail until it was a sheet of ice.

In February we learned that because of the light snow the contractors were not moving in. This worried us since we would have no source of revenue. To break the monotony and cheer ourselves up we made a trip up Shovel Creek hoping to find some deer, but there were none. We did find a beautiful location for a ranch, but when we got home and looked at the map it had already been purchased. I think that really gave me the excuse for quitting my homestead hunt. Also I had decided that homesteading at that time was a very rugged proposition and no place to bring the bride I hoped to have next year.

I think what really made me decide to quit was the time I bought the onions. One trip I had a light load on my return from Decker Lake and I found a man who had a sack of onions. Of course they were frozen, but as long as they were kept frozen, would last indefinitely. Fresh vegetables and canned foods for us were out of the question for when packing forty miles only dried food is taken. But fresh onions! And I was loaded light! So I bought twenty pounds.

At left men work on a rock cut near Jasper in 1912. The two top photos show the author with his "One-armed John" on Burns Lake, and the Shovel Creek roadhouse. As can be seen, facilities were undoubtedly basic. The above photo shows a construction camp with the bunkhouses which the author immediately disliked. Each held about 100 men and were not noted for comfort.

The two above photos, taken in 1913, illustrate the type of communities which sprang up to serve construction workers. The one above is at Mile 145 from the Alberta border and the middle one is Tete Jaune Cache, head of navigation on the Fraser River. Both vanished when construction ended. The top photo shows a Grand Trunk Pacific train leaving Prince Rupert for Winnipeg in 1915.

I stopped at the upper end of the lake for the night as usual, and in the morning went on to Shovel Creek. Thinking to surprise my partner, I opened my pack with a flourish and then stared in disgust. The first day my body heat had thawed the onions. They had frozen solid again in the night. The next day they thawed again, and now were a mushy mass of peelings and roots. They were entirely inedible and I had packed them forty miles on my back!

After that episode my partner went outside and negotiated. When he came back we were out of business, with our bills paid and $100 in cash to show for our winter's work. So once more we hooked up our One-Armed John and took the trail back to Decker Lake, which we found to be booming. Axemen were needed for work on a log hotel so I hired out at once. Broadaxe-men were paid $1 per day more so Slim tried that. His work was so ragged that the boss did not approve, but Slim told him he had been drunk for a week and would be all right the next day. After a day's practice he got along well enough to hold his job.

I discovered that one of the worst hazards was the outdoor toilet. By the seat of each was a stout club and I often wondered what it was for. On one night visit during a cold spell I sat down as usual and promptly popped up, feeling as if I had been speared. Then I realized what the club was for. However, I won't explain farther since people who have used outside privies in winter will understand and those who haven't probably wouldn't appreciate the details.

About that time quite a lot of excitement was caused by Foley, Welch & Stewart freighting in a steam shovel and two twenty-ton dinky locomotives for a long stretch of road along Decker Lake. These were all taken apart and hauled in on sleds during the winter because when the snow came and the roads were packed, a horse could pull a ton. By contrast, in the summer at times the teams had trouble hauling 1,000 pounds to the horse.

I found out that my partner was an old locomotive engineer. In fact an informant told me he had been an engineer on a fast freight in the south but because of an accident and other troubles, had pulled out and headed north. He was typical of the type of men who followed construction work at that time. One of my bunk mates had studied art in a large academy in New York and amused himself drawing caricatures of the people around. Another, a cook, had been chef in one of the leading hotels in Toronto. I believed it, for his sauces were unbelievable. He said he once worked in a food factory for six months to secure a closely guarded meat sauce. The last I saw of him he was drunk and on a muck stick (shovel). Men who had made two or three fortunes and blown them in; men who still had fortunes, but were working from force of habit; professional men — doctors, lawyers — even a college professor — all came into the melting pot. Mostly drink or misfortune was responsible. Never, I believe, could there again be found a collection of the good, bad, wise, foolish, talented and stupid as were in construction camps at the turn of the century.

When the hotel at Decker Lake was finished I looked for another job. I had once fired a mill boiler for a short time so I decided that since Slim had a job on the dinky locomotive, I would try for firing the shovel. I approached Dick Johnson, superintendent of construction, who had made a couple of fortunes and sent them across the green cloth.

"How about a job firing the shovel?" I asked.

"I got four firemen and only need two," he answered gruffly.

"Then how about a pump?" I asked. I knew nothing of pumps but had heard they were simple.

"Don't need any," he said.

Then letting the tail go with the hide I asked, "How are you fixed for dinky skinners?"

Old Dick looked at me. He must have sensed that I didn't know one end of the machine from the other. "I need four and have eight, but you stick around and help set up the shovel and maybe I can find something for you."

I stuck around and helped set up the shovel. When they wanted blocking I was Johnny-on-the-spot with a chunk. When they needed know-how I was off looking for another chunk. But I was willing.

One day Dick told Slim, "I am going to give you one of the dinkies so you take your partner and set it up." We put it together, stealing everything off the other machine to fix up Slim's. After we had it set up I found out where the cab was and by the time we ran it up and down the short stretch of track to break it in I knew where the throttle was.

Then Dick told me, "I guess I'll give you the other dinky. Set it up." We did and it was a dandy. Somewhere we found a whistle (I think it must have come from a merry-go-round) to replace the one we had stolen. We cut the jam nut on the safety valve and raised the pressure from 110 pounds to 165 pounds and did other things for which we could have spent many years behind bars. But supplies took at least three weeks to arrive and we knew that if we didn't improvise we would get nothing done.

Once we got started it didn't take Slim and I long to decide we didn't like bunkhouses. Generally they were made of logs with pretty low roofs to house up to 100 men. Most of them had what were called shotgun bunks. Those were on tiers of three high and placed close beside each other. The only way to get in was to crawl in the bottom like going into a tunnel. Some places they gave you enough straw to cover the bottom of the bunks and sometimes they charged 25 cents for it. The men in the top bunks next to the big iron stoves roasted all night, and those on the bottom bunks in the corners slept pretty cold. The men who wanted to sleep started in early, for when 100 men began to snore, gurgle, have nightmares, and shout in their sleep it took a tired man to keep sleeping.

So we bought a tent and put up a poplar log wall which was not exactly windproof. We got a small air-tight heater but that did not keep us warm when the weather dropped to thirty-five degrees below. Each trip to Decker Lake we would get a new Hudson's Bay blanket. At the peak of our buying spree we figured we had eighty-four pounds of bedding. In the morning we awoke feeling tired from carrying forty pounds of bedding all night.

When spring came the days got long and the green came by surges. I was homesick and left, securing passage on an outgoing six-horse freight wagon. The driver proceeded to get a bottle and drink himself stupid in the bottom of the wagon. For two days I drove a six-up which knew more than I did, but we made Hazelton and from there I rode the steel back to Prince Rupert and caught a boat south.

Often I have wanted to go back to the old places I knew over a half-century ago, but always something has prevented it. Maybe this is the year. ∎

THE HOMESTEADERS

They built their houses, cleared their land and planted their crops. But their oats and wheat and barley generally burned up during the hot, dry days of summer. One by one they left until all were gone.

by FERDI WENGER

Once this abandoned sleigh hauled the homesteaders' wood to Kamloops and the binder cut their grain. But like the Cold Creek community hall, at top, they are now lonely symbols of unfulfilled hopes.

Something was going on in the old log house that still stood on an abandoned homestead known as the Lawton place. There was a crash inside and my horse shied nervously. Then came an angry bellow and a black calf shot through the doorway, followed by three more. I had to laugh.

So they were the latest inhabitants of the log house left by a family who had homesteaded this land, tried to make it support them, but failed and moved elsewhere. I climbed off my horse to give him a breather and me a chance to roll a cigarette. Then, sitting on a half-burned log, I let my mind dwell on the stories I had heard about the homesteaders.

There were many of them. In fact, this region—located about ten miles northeast of Kamloops—is called "The Homesteads" by local ranchers. The house in front of me was typical of their homes. It was still in fairly good shape with even the roof intact. Its builder certainly had been a proud member of the carpenter trade for the logs were fitted smoothly and the corners chopped to perfection.

To one side was the chicken house, a small square building about ten by ten feet and equally well built. The logs were tight and closely fitted at the corners. Even some of the mud packed between the logs to fill the cracks had survived the storms of almost sixty years. Only the roof was gone. It was lying some twenty feet to one side, a mess of dusty sods, rusty wire, and rotten rails.

Running snake-like up a slight grade were the remains of the high deer-proof garden fence. Built of thin jackpine rails, it had at one time been close to seven feet high, put together in zig-zag fashion to save wire and nails. Only the uprights were visible now among the new fir and pine saplings and the rugged berry bushes which had taken over the once cultivated land.

Many times I have searched the ruins of the homesteads, trying to learn something about the people who lived there, their hopes and aims, and why they pulled out. Judging from the things remaining, they must have left in a hurry. Perhaps, though, most of them were so disgusted with the fruitless efforts of their labor that they didn't want to take anything along which would remind them of the years and years put in on their land.

Whatever their reasons for leaving, they had a common purpose for coming: to grow wheat or oats or barley on the dry ground. They all built a set of corrals, planted a garden for vegetables and fruit such as rhubarb, currants and crab apples for winter canning. They all picked tons and tons of rocks and piled them along the boundaries of their land. They all experienced the same problem—crops that grew to the milk stage and then usually burned up through the latter part of July. One by one they left.

Although their fields have now reverted to native grasses, the rock piles are still there and serve as perfect homes for whole colonies of groundhogs. Still there, too, are the berry bushes and the log fences, although rotted now and crumbled into a tinder-dry pile of woods.

In the front and back yards are many reminders of family life: a wheelbarrow, a big hole in it and the wheel long lost somewhere; a galvanized wash tub; old picture frames; a broken doll buggy; and always a pile of jars and bottles once filled with berries of all kinds—saskatoons, blueberries, Oregon grapes, wild strawberries and raspberries.

In one of the store rooms I discovered beehives and the

extractor for the honey. A pile of used jam tins on a shelf were still full of sweet clover honey. In a barn were a set of steel harrows; a set of harness, the leather rotting and mouldy; a double tree; and a chewed-up horse collar, now a nest for pack rats. On one stall hung a sidesaddle in good shape and a pair of spurs, their style indicating English origin.

In a toolshed I found hoes, a four-tined fork, a dull double-bladed axe, a draw knife for peeling logs, a broken crosscut-saw, and a broadaxe for hewing logs.

Scattered all around the different buildings were old cast-iron stoves, wagon wheels, frying pans, coffee pots, tea kettles and an old set of tires. There was a sleigh with a seat fashioned out of slabs. Upstairs in all houses were deer hides by the dozen with elk and deer horns nailed along the log walls.

Then, of course, there were always the bookshelves. In the corners magazines were stacked, only pieces of dirty paper now, chewed and chewed again by squirrels and packrats. But once in a while the year of publication was legible. Among others, there was a *Field and Stream* from 1931 and *National Geographic Magazine* dated August 1929. In one place I even found a beautiful set of the *Harvard Classics,* twenty-three volumes of them!

All these things revealed that once there were hopes and happiness; now there are only ruins and piles of junk, sad reminders of dreams unfulfilled.

One day while talking to Dave Corbould, a successful rancher in the area, I learned the background of the abandoned buildings and fields. Dave told me the story of the Homesteads, known officially as Cold Creek Community, while sitting in the tool shed on a rainy July day. It was a fitting place to tell it, full of the same things the homesteaders had left behind but smelling strongly of the more modern stuff: gasoline, diesel oil and grease.

At the turn of the century the area was divided into three major leases. They were held at the time by big outfits—the Burns Ranch, Hull Ranch and the Fruitland Ranch. The bunchgrass was still plentiful and provided excellent feed for their steers and other livestock.

Kamloops, above, during the 1890's, was the supply point for the settlers and a market for the produce they hoped to grow. But not only in the Kamloops area were pioneer dreams shattered. The empty farm house, the horse-drawn plough and the abandoned wagon on the opposite page are relics of the southern Interior and Cariboo-Chilcotin, other regions where many attempts at farming were a failure.

Then, the district was thrown open for homesteading. It wasn't long before the first hardy men and women came along, their possessions on a string of packhorses. One of the first men to try his luck on the barren soil was Charlie Leroy. Soon to follow were Walter Bott and men named Grundy, Simson, Lawton, and Shepherd who all came from England. More people heard about the free land, until at one time thirty-five families lived in the community. Among them was Wes Day from Ontario, Nenan from Ireland, the Lees from China, and many others, including Charlie Bacon, Ed Williams, Robert Taylor, E. Fleet, Ernie Meyers, F. S. Lawrence, Sam Body, Walter Right, and Jack Anderson who had one of the first cars of the district.

This vehicle drew some sarcastic and perhaps envious jokes. Charlie Urchit, a Yugoslavian, was at the time local correspondent for the *Kamloops Daily Sentinel*. He once noted: "Mrs. P. R. Phillips and daughter Lilly of White Rock have been visiting here. As they are dependent upon . . . Jack Anderson's car to get back to town, it is likely that they will be here for some time yet. . . ."

Most of these men had never farmed in their lives and their mistakes were many and costly. But they were courageous and determined. By 1918 many of them had built their homes and rocked their fields, planted gardens and built roads. They also began to realize that the land itself could not feed them and their families. Grain hardly ever ripened and by harvest time was just so much straw. The alfalfa patch on the steep hillside was never big enough to support their cattle. They had to find other work.

Most of them cut firewood in the long winters and hauled it with team and sleigh to Kamloops, a two-day trip at best. Others worked for neighboring ranches, or found winter jobs elsewhere. In all, farming proved a hard and uncertain life.

To make the burden more bearable and ease the loneliness, on November 10, 1923, a few of the more progressive men and women, like the Lees, Urchits, and Grundys, met at Charlie Leroy's home to discuss the possibilities for social improvement. They decided to build a hall which could also serve as a school for their ever growing crop of children.

The settlers organized the Cold Creek Community and built a log hall at the entrance to the valley. It was opened with a dance on December 10, 1924.

But it never felt children's feet or heard a teacher's voice. One by one the settlers grew discouraged at the fruitless effort of trying to make a living under the hot sun and in the dry fields. Most sold out to surrounding ranchers and left.

The Cold Creek community hall still stands, unused and deserted, a matter of time before it, too, crumples. Today, the homesteaders are remembered only by the names of their places. "The Lawton place is grazed out," or "go check the fence in the Simson place," a rancher might say to one of his men. Once again the whole area is only part of a few bigger outfits, the same as it was over seventy years ago.

Once in a while a rider might take shelter in one of the abandoned cabins to wait out a storm or to have lunch. Calves now play in and around them, but that is the only activity. No lamps light up at night for reading and no children kneel in prayer. The homesteads are today abandoned reminders of dreams that didn't come true.

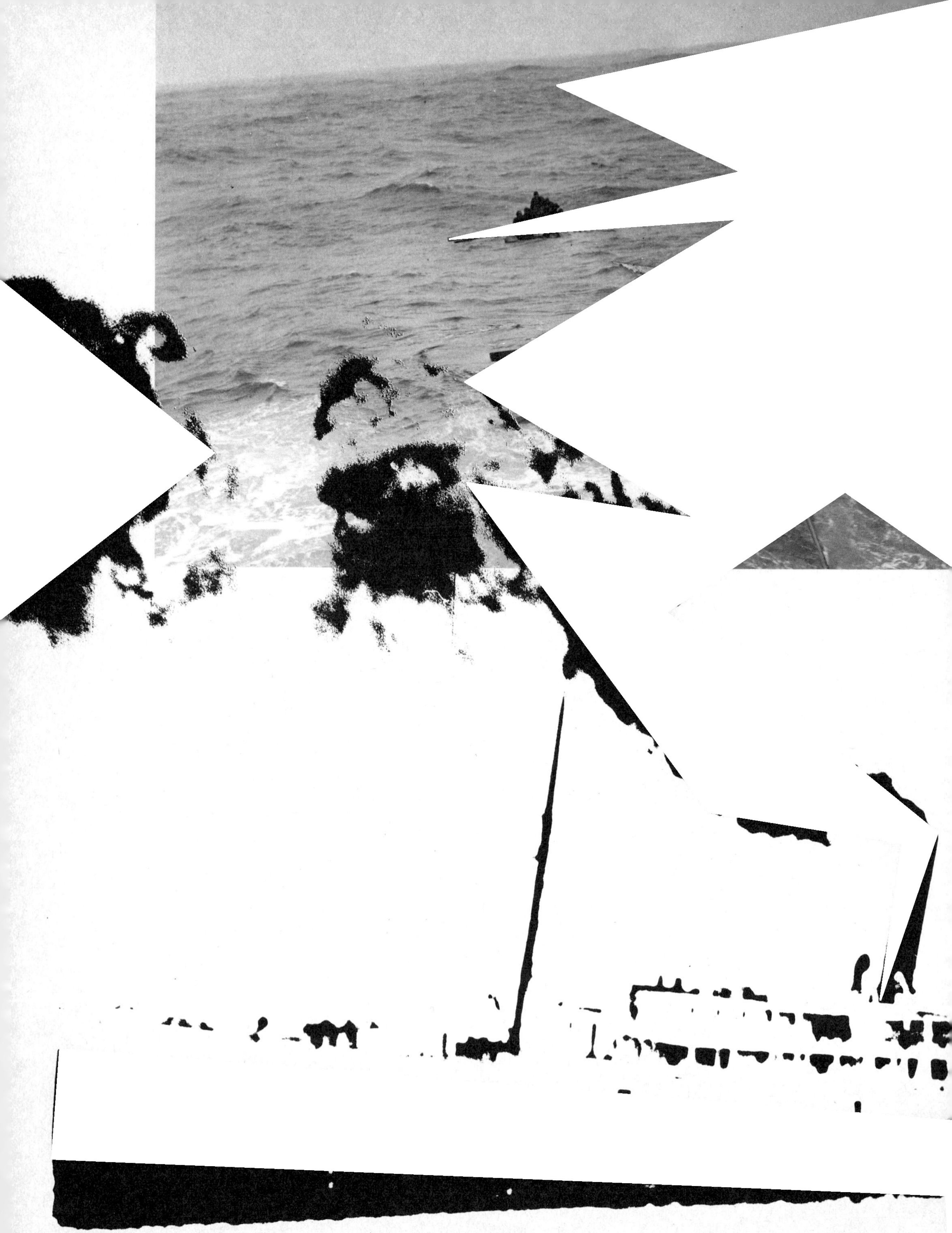

Cape Beale – graveyard of the Pacific

Blown off course by gale winds, the *Valencia* slammed into the rocks off Cape Beale. While rescuers watched helplessly, she foundered with the loss of 136 men, women and children.

by W. J. BETTS

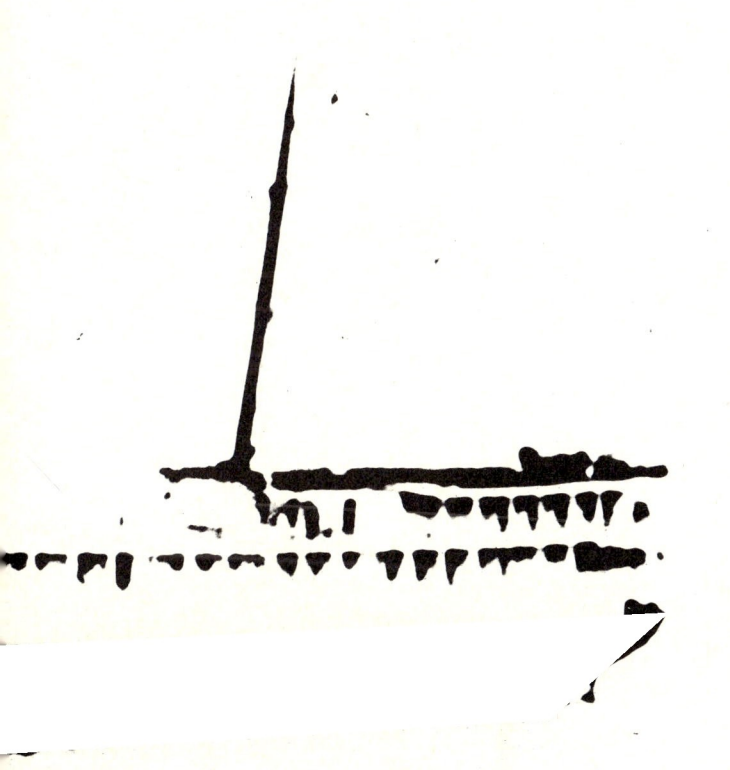

On the rock-strewn west coast of Vancouver Island Cape Beale thrusts into the Pacific Ocean thirty miles from the Pacific entrance to Juan de Fuca Strait. With rocky headland jutting into the cold blue ocean, green sweep of evergreens climbing the mountainsides and cloud-flecked sky overhead, the Cape can be as peaceful as a marine painting. But there are times when the scene isn't so peaceful. Cape Beale, actually, should be studded with hundreds of crosses to mark its victims.

As early as the seventeenth century when the Spanish explored the region, navigators dreaded the treacherous area. When the English and the Americans came—Captains George Vancouver, John Meares, Robert Gray and other pioneer skippers—they, too, learned how dangerous this section could be. The west coast of Vancouver Island, in fact, gradually became known as one of the most dangerous places in the world for shipping. In four decades between 1867 and 1906, the jagged, cliff-strewn region claimed fifty-six vessels with a death toll of 711. Seventeen of these ships—and 399 lives—were lost in the forty-mile section between Port Renfrew and Bamfield, with Cape Beale being the most deadly. In just one month, January 1906, its rocks claimed three ships and 169 lives.

A combination of factors makes this section so deadly. The entrance to the Strait of Juan de Fuca is narrow, only some thirteen miles, with Vancouver Island and Washington forming a rocky barrier on either side. A ship's captain must find this "hole" in the rocks even though driven before a gale or shrouded in thick fog or caught in the strong currents that characterize the area. Winter is the worst time, when storms blot out landmarks and carry vessels miles off course. Such was the fate of the *Valencia* which shattered on the rocks at Cape Beale with the loss of 136 men, women, and children.

She had been running before gale force winds all the way from San Francisco and, on January 22, 1906, was groping for the entrance to Juan de Fuca Strait. Since heavy wind, rising seas and foggy conditions made navigation difficult, all day Captain O. M. Johnson had been proceeding at half speed. He cursed the weather. He was behind schedule and would be late docking at Seattle. But as the murky winter skies changed from dark grey to pitch black, he had more immediate things to worry about.

According to his reckoning, the *Valencia* was somewhere off the northern coast of Washington, still south of Cape Flattery, entrance to the Strait of Juan de Fuca. At intervals the helmsman pulled the whistle lanyard. The low, mournful wail blasted the darkness for a moment and then was lost on the stormy seas. As long as there was no echo, they were safe. Even so, he called for soundings and felt comforted as the leadsman called out thirty fathoms from his station on the bow.

His hands gripping the bridge rail, the Captain listened for the fog horn at Cape Flattery's lighthouse. But for some reason the foghorn was not working properly, was not loud enough to be heard at sea. Captain Johnson, however, had no way of knowing about this defect. Nor did he know that the southerly gale force winds and storm induced current had already carried his ship past the entrance.

At 11:45 p.m. she drove onto the rocks at Cape Beale. After the grinding crash the only sound was the howling wind and waves bashing the stricken vessel. Captain Johnson grabbed the signal tube and whistled to chief engineer K. F. Carrich. "Reverse, full speed!"

Carrich, already at the controls when the Captain called, swiftly reversed the engine. The vessel backed off the rocks. Then another rending crash. She stopped dead in the water. Carrich saw the engine room bulkhead crash inward and a wall of water cascade into the ship. Stokers and firemen raced for the ladder, seconds ahead of the rising waters.

Carrich paused before climbing the ladder, looking at the flooding engine room. He knew what would happen if sea water hit the boilers with a full head of steam on. He plunged into the engine room and turned the relief valve. As the pop-off blasted the air he scrambled after his men.

On deck everything was confusion. The lights had failed when the engine room flooded and the deck was as dark as a cave. Carrich was unable to tell whether the *Valencia* was aground on rocks or the mainland. Passengers and crew ran aimlessly about the deck. Women were weeping and crying hysterically for their children or husbands. Little children, lost from their parents, wept.

Captain Johnson gave orders to abandon ship. The crew seemed unable to launch the boats. About ten minutes after the *Valencia* struck, a new shifting and lurching shuddered through the ship. Captain Johnson knew his ship's back had broken under the strain.

Then three huge waves threw her back on an even keel. She rested, as though wedged between rocks. But every wave, foaming in from the open sea, smashed over her decks. As passengers ran from their cabins some were swept into the seas to drown in the surging surf. Others clung to the rigging or climbed to the safety of the hurricane deck.

Two lifeboats launched from the weather side were almost immediately smashed against the side of the ship. Then lifeboats on the lee side were readied. Four crewmen and a number of passengers, with purser J. J. O'Farrell in charge, boarded one of them. As it was being lowered a davit fouled. The stern plunged into the water while the bow hung in the air, throwing the occupants into the raging seas. Before lines could be thrown, all were gone. One survivor, G. Willets, later remarked: "Everyone was swept away in an instant. For a second or two I caught a glimpse of an agonized face, and then another and yet another as they were washed by me. It was awful."

The photo opposite shows the rock- and island-strewn waters of Barkley Sound near Cape Beale. Above is Cape Beale Lighthouse. In the same month of the *Valencia* disaster, the rocky foreshore claimed two other ships and an additional thirty-three lives.

The huge waves breaking over the *Valencia* were gradually pounding her to pieces. Survivors clung to the rigging and deckhouse all through the long night — cold, hungry and exhausted.

When grey dawn brought light to the angry seas they could see the beach only some 300 yards away. Captain Johnson knew if he could get a line ashore a breeches buoy could be rigged over which the survivors could reach safety.

A crewman volunteered to swim ashore with a line. He reached the shore but was confronted with a rocky cliff. He decided to climb to the top where a suitable anchor could be found for the breeches buoy line. Those on board the *Valencia* watched with dread and hope as the man slowly climbed the face of the cliff. About half way to the top he slipped and fell to his death.

John Segalos (some reports gave his name as Cogalas, while the official crew list called him F. Seajala) then volunteered to swim ashore with a line. Half way to the beach he became entangled in the line and was pulled back more dead than alive.

Finally, after two more attempts to launch a lifeboat, one managed to get clear. Before it reached the beach, however, it capsized and only six men out of twenty survived. It was these men who managed to climb the steep cliff to seek help.

Another lifeboat was launched with six crew members and was able to reach Cape Beale lighthouse.

Lighthouse keeper Paterson flashed news of the wreck to Captain Gaudin, Agent of Marine at Victoria: "Steamer wrecked between here and Clo-oose; about one hundred drowned; nine reached telegraph hut. Will wire more particulars as soon as possible."

As soon as word reached the outside world, rescue ships proceeded to the scene. Among them were the *Lorne, City of Topeka, Salvor* and the whaler *Orian*.

Meanwhile, the plight of those on the *Valencia* was appalling. G. Willets, one of the last to escape the doomed vessel, recounted his experiences. "We all clung to the rigging and deckhouse until morning (Tuesday). One of the most pitiable incidents was a little boy about five years old. His father, mother and two little sisters put off in one of the boats. The boat capsized and all were drowned. The little fellow waded around the deck, crying for his parents. The last I saw of him he was clinging in the rigging.

"By Wednesday morning the ship was rapidly going to pieces. Every swell carried away a portion of the ship. The deck rose and fell with every breaker and it was impossible to stay on deck without clinging to a support. The ship was sunk about the level of the hurricane deck.

"In the (same) morning another sad calamity occurred. About fifteen or twenty persons, among them one or two women, had taken refuge in the foretop mast. They appeared to be in the safest place as it was removed from the wash of the waves, although flying spray dashed far over their heads. Suddenly and without warning the mast tottered and then there were shrieks from those in it, and the next moment it fell with a crash, carrying its load of human freight to a terrible death. I don't think there was a single one saved."

When all lifeboats had been launched, some to reach shore, others to be dashed to bits in the heavy seas, the Captain ordered liferafts launched. But the women passengers who still survived refused to leave the ship. They could now see rescue ships on the horizon. Certainly, they surmised, it would be only a matter of time before they were rescued. One rescue ship, the *Queen*, steamed in closer to the *Valencia*. A cheer went up from the men and women desperately huddling on the wreck.

But the captain of the *Queen*, as well as those in command of the other ships, was afraid to bring his ship too close to the rocks for fear of wrecking his own vessel. He waited for the *Valencia's* crew to launch boats or rafts so that they could pick up the survivors clear of the rocks. Captain Johnson begged women passengers to leave on one of the two remaining liferafts. All refused. Among them was Mrs. Mary Musgrove. "I'm going to stay by the *Valencia*," she told Walter Raymond, a steward for the officer's mess, who had helped launch the liferaft.

Twelve of the eighteen men rescued from the *Valencia's* raft and one of the rescue ships, the whaler *Orian*, near the scene of the wreck. The rocky shore thwarted attempts from both land and sea to save those marooned on the grounded *Valencia*.

As Raymond paused before plunging into the boiling seas, Mary Musgrove asked, "Are you going, Walter?" He nodded. Mary smiled and started singing "Nearer My God to Thee."

Raymond steadied himself on the rail of the quivering ship and then leaped far out into the water toward the tossing raft. "As I went down, down, down, the words of that song kept ringing in my ears," he later recounted. "I had never sung or spoken to God in my life. It is strange what thoughts a man will have at such times. I thought: 'I'm nearer to Him now than I ever was before, God pity me'."

It seemed to Raymond that his lungs would burst before he surfaced and then he popped up. For a long moment he just floated, inhaling drafts of spray-salted air. Then he frantically searched for the raft. It was about fifty feet away.

For the first time since the *Valencia* had struck the rocks he gave up. He was numb from the bitter cold water, and felt that he could not swim to the raft. Why not just drown and get it over with? Then a huge wave swept him high and literally hurled him through the air. He landed squarely on top of the men on the raft. They grabbed him. Raymond knew no more until he was hauled aboard the *City of Topeka* later that day.

In the meantime, a telegraph lineman named Logan had arrived from Cape Beale at the scene of the wreck. He was joined by two others, D. Martin and W. P. Daykin, who had come overland from the telegraph hut. The three arrived just in time to watch the death of the *Valencia*.

They saw the ship lying on the rocks just off the jutting cliff. Survivors, huddled on the deckhouse, saw the men and shouted for joy. At last someone had arrived to rescue them. But silence fell when they realized that the men on the shore were powerless to help. They clung to the rigging, quiet now, waiting for the constantly pounding waves to send them to their death.

At noon, after endless hours of clinging to the stricken ship, the end came. The three men on shore watched as a huge roller swept in from the Pacific. It crushed everything left on the steamship. When the wave passed only the stump of a mast and some spars were above water. None of those still aboard survived. In all, 136 men, women, and children drowned.

One of the six survivors who reached shore in the first lifeboat, F. F. Bunker, bitterly accused the officers of the *Valencia* of negligence. Bunker had good reason to feel bitter. He had lost his wife and two children when their lifeboat capsized. He later said that there was an evident lack of discipline among the officers. This statement was corroborated by some of the other passengers.

But crew members testified that at no time did they see any acts of negligence; that Captain Johnson acted in the highest traditions of the sea, calming hysterical passengers, attempting to save as many as possible. In the end he went down with his ship.

The awful tragedy of the *Valencia* stirred two nations to act. Both the United States and Canada established life saving stations, one at Neah Bay and another on Vancouver Island. Better lights, foghorns and other navigational aids were erected. Today, Cape Beale and the rocky shores of the southwest coast of Vancouver Island are as rugged as always, but as much as possible, navigation dangers have been removed.

SOUTHERN CROSSROADS

A valley north and south, a sandspit east and west—this was the crossroad of the centuries. Down the Valley on Indian trails came the laden horses of the Fur Brigade from 1824 to 1848. Later, miners and settlers streamed northward. Across the sandspit ran the busy Dewdney Trail to the eastern goldfields. Routes of the past are highways of today.

DEPARTMENT OF RECREATION & CONSERVATION

STOP OF INTEREST

This plaque is on Anarchist Mountain on the Southern Trans-Provincial Highway some three miles east of Osoyoos. The mountain received its unusual name from an early Irish settler. He held radical political views, was labelled an anarchist and fired from his job with the government. He had land on top of the parched-looking mountain which turned out to be poor for cattle – then the predominant industry — but fine for wheat.

The community in the background across the sandspit is Osoyoos, pronounced O-soo-yus. It is an orchard and tourist center with a population of some 1,200. The following history is from Chess Lyons' book *Mileposts in Ogopogo Land*:

"Osoyoos, the first place in the Okanagan Valley to be visited by a white man, strangely enough was the last to become developed and settled. It was in 1811 that David Stuart of the Pacific Fur Company made his way up the Columbia River, past 'Big Okanagan Lake' and on to Kamloops. From that time until 1860 this strategic point was shown on early maps as a fur traders' campsite. Then Fort Okanagan, 100 miles to the south, where bleak winters were spent 'buried in snow, sipping molasses, smoking tobacco and masticating horseflesh,' was largely abandoned in favour of new forts at Osoyoos and Keremeos. General Sherman in his war with the Nez Perces often camped here with his U.S. Cavalry.

"Next came the period of the large cattle ranches. Over 20,000 acres of grassy sidehills around Osoyoos were owned by Judge J.C. Haynes who ran herd on 3,000 'dogies.' By 1890 the mountain sides of this and the Keremeos Valley were dotted with an estimated 20,000 head. A few years later a flurry of mining activity helped focus attention on the district but it was not until 1906 when a model orchard was planted that the district was found to be ideally suited for soft fruits.

" 'The earliest fruit in Canada' is the claim made by the Osoyoos district. It is difficult to believe a difference of only four degrees in average annual temperature between the north and south extremities of the valley and a twenty-seven-day longer growing period would make such a change in the time of ripening. Peaches, cherries, apricots, cantaloupes, grapes, watermelons and most types of squash are favorite crops. Grape growing in particular is expanding rapidly to supply wineries."

John Bunyan Ray..

Wells Gray is one of B.C.'s most beautiful provincial parks. Here is the man who first settled in this region of mountains and rivers, and as long ago as 1912 felt that it should be preserved as a public recreation area.

The Ray farm in Wells Gray Park, with John Ray's original cabin in the foreground and his house in the background. The photos on the opposite page show Ray at Azure Lake and taking a boat into Clearwater Lake over the trail and bridge he built.

116

Wilderness Pioneer

by NIGEL POOLEY

Wells Gray Park is a million-acre region of lakes, rivers, and forest in the Cariboo Mountains some eighty-five miles north of Kamloops. It is named after a former B.C. cabinet minister, A. Wells Gray, but an equally appropriate name would have been John Bunyan Ray. He was a hardy trapper and woodsman who first saw the area in 1912 and was always in favor of having it preserved as a public recreation area. In the course of time it became a park, and while it wasn't named after Ray, this concerned him not a bit. He was basically a "loner," and like all people who keep to themselves, he cared little what the rest of the world did or said.

Even in the farming community of Upper Clearwater where the homesteaders were acquainted with John Ray, he was regarded with a slight aura of disbelief. He did nothing to dispell this impression. When he "came out" at Christmas with his marten catch or in spring with his beaver, he swept through the community with the urgency of a man who has discovered oil and is determined to keep the secret.

For years from the 1920's to the 1940's people talked about a man who had a farm and was raising a family somewhere near Clearwater Lake—in much the same way as one might discuss the probability of a Yeti living in the mountains behind Lillooet. Few people on the North Thompson River or around Kamloops had ever met John Ray but everyone could tell about him.

John Bunyan Ray was an American who was born in North Carolina about 1885. His parents set out for Portland, Oregon two years later in a covered wagon. Whether travelling in a covered wagon at the age of two made him restless or whether he inherited a legitimate yearning for pioneering from his father is not known. At any rate, in his mid-twenties he left the family sawmill business near Portland and headed north to the wilds of British Columbia.

In 1910 he landed at Horsefly Lake in the Cariboo and took to trapping muskrats. He fared poorly that first winter, but the following summer he got a job building houses for the local branch of the Shuswap Indians at three dollars a day. While he was on this job an epidemic of measles broke out among the Indians and John found himself

117

The home-made chimney on the Ray house and Mrs. Ray with Nancy and Douglas. At right is Dawson Falls, one of many spectacular waterfalls in Wells Gray Park. The photos above it show the Ray house and his grave in the Park. The cross was stolen in the spring of 1973.

building coffins instead of houses. They were mostly children's coffins and after he had finished the twentieth, Ray made some health recommendations to Chief Sam. It was the Indians' practice, as soon as a child developed measles, to carry him or her before the Crucifix in the little Catholic church. Ray suggested that the children be kept in bed in a darkened room and that if this were done they would most likely recover.

Chief Sam passed this new remedy to his people and it was so effective that when the epidemic ended only two more children had died. The Indians attributed the improvement to John Ray's advice. As a reward, Chief Sam gave Ray permission to trap and hunt for the rest of his life on their traditional hunting ground in the Clearwater and Azure Lakes country.

That winter John loaded a hand sleigh with 200 pounds of provisions and gear and dragged it into the Clearwater country by way of Mahood Lake. It took courage for a man of his limited experience to penetrate this solitary land but he was well rewarded. Thereafter over the years he built up eighty-three miles of trap line on the shores of Clearwater and Azure Lakes, up Hobson River and Angus Horne Creek, and over by PilPil Mountain. One winter he took out $2,700 in furs by Christmas, a lot of money in those days, and in spring added to his total by trapping beaver which were plentiful.

He became dedicated to the Clearwater country and applied for land to start a farm. Besides his modest farming activities, he took hunting parties out after moose and caribou in the fall and hauled clinker-built boats into Clearwater Lake over twenty-three miles of trail for the benefit of fishermen as well as hunters. His program of developing the area for its recreation had unlimited possibilities. The region had mineral water springs, (good for pregnant women, he claimed) and lakes, rivers, and mountains by the mile. In addition there was excellent accessible big game and excellent fishing—all these things hidden in an area practically unknown to the rest of North America. But Ray failed to make a name for himself as a big-game guide, partly because mail service once a month or less kept him out of touch with customers, and partly because his cabins were too rough for most big-game hunters. It was all right for John to do things the hard way—going around in bare feet and having dirt floors in his cabins—but not everyone shared his views. The dirt floors discouraged pack rats from building nests but they also discouraged the hunters who liked things dry and comfortable just as much as the rats. Added to this the 1930's were a poor time to get going in the big-game guiding business. Most hunters at that time were purely out for the meat and didn't regard hiring guides as a practical way of finding it.

Ray's biggest success was as a family man and a pioneer. When I stayed with him in 1938 he had a self-sustaining farm unit and a completely self-possessed wife from nearby Blackpool on the North Thompson. Perhaps because she had been raised in the country, she thought nothing of heading into the complete wilderness to raise a family. But I think there was more to it than that—she had what it took. Nancy, their first child, was born in Kamloops Hospital in the middle of winter. When Mrs. Ray returned home she covered the last fourteen miles on horseback in twenty-five below weather, her daughter strapped papoose style on her back.

The farm consisted of fifteen acres of pasture and half an acre of vegetables and grain. The rest was unimproved land except for a seventy-acre natural hay meadow. They had twenty-five sheep, which supplied wool for most of their clothing; three pigs, and fifteen goats which later provided most of their food. For a permanent income for himself and family in his old age, John invested more than $2,000 in fencing to keep beaver in a private beaver swamp. He bought this fence much as one would buy an annuity, and he was even experimenting with wild rice to feed the beaver.

He carried in on the backs of pack horses, besides the clinker-built boat, one set of discs, a mower, a hay rake, the $2,000 worth of paige-wire fencing for the beaver, a three-hundred-pound iron stove and I forget what else. All this practically single handed.

In his later years he was much concerned with the decadence of his fellow North Americans. "You know, Bob," he said to me one day. "When I was a boy they taught us to put pencils behind our ears and to let the other fellow do the work. And now you see the result. Why I have seen fellows come up here who couldn't even pick up an axe without crippling themselves. I am going to raise my kids to work and not to expect the other fellow to do it all."

He would doubtless be horrified if he knew how many people driving past his farm today had never seen an axe, except in a hardware store. His idea of a real milksop was someone who couldn't disappear into the woods with nothing but an axe and some salt and live comfortably for a couple of weeks.

When he finally reached the end of the trail he was, typically enough, all alone, having sent his family "out" for the winter. In December 1947, during a spell of bitter weather, he fell dead in the snow from a heart attack.

Although it is too late to call the area "Ray's Park," many visitors will be interested to know that it was the home of a man who sought solitude. A mountain in the park is named Ray's Peak after him, and this is appropriate, because like a mountain, John Bunyan Ray was a rugged type—a man who lived the hard way, and liked it. ∎

119

STERNWHEEL DAYS ON THE PEACE RIVER

by HAROLD FRYER

During the century-long era from 1858 to 1957, sternwheel steamers plied virtually all of British Columbia's major lakes and rivers, including the Peace River from the Rocky Mountains downstream over 500 miles to Fort Vermilion in Northern Alberta.

The *Peace River*, above, was the second sternwheeler on the Peace. For ten years the 110-foot-long vessel plied over 500 miles of the river.

Bishop Emile Grouard, above right, ordered the first sternwheeler on the river. She was the *St. Charles*, her primary purpose to help the Bishop in his mission work.

Largest of the Peace River sternwheelers was the *D. A. Thomas*, top right. The other photo on the opposite page shows settlers waiting at the Fort Vermilion sternwheel landing in 1920.

In B.C.'s thriving Peace River community of Fort St. John is a fifty-five-foot-long replica of a sternwheel steamer, a Centennial project that serves as tourist attraction and picture museum. The vessel is the *D. A. Thomas*, the largest and the last of the sternwheelers which plied over 500 miles of the Peace River from Fort Vermilion in Alberta to Hudson Hope just fifteen miles from the Bennett Dam.

The Upper Peace River paddlewheel era was not long — about thirty years — but it played an important role as the country changed from a fur-traders' domain into one of the world's prime agricultural regions. To hundreds of pioneer settlers, the sternwheelers meant mail, supplies and the assurance that they were not entirely isolated in a frontier land.

The first white men to travel the waters of the Peace were Alexander Mackenzie and his voyageurs during their epic canoe journey to the Pacific Ocean in 1792-93. Later came the York boats of the Hudson's Bay Company, bringing trade goods to posts which included Fort McLeod, founded in 1805, and Fort St. John, established in 1806.

During fur-trade days, the Peace River country was a magnificent area of wilderness covering some 25,000 square miles. It is rolling plateau country, deeply incised by rivers and streams, especially at its western boundary, the Rocky Mountains. Here its main waterway, the Peace River, flows in a valley about 1,000 feet deep. But as the Peace continues its northeastward journey to its junction with the Slave River, the banks gradually drop away until at Fort Vermilion — some 550 miles from the Rockies — they are under one hundred feet high.

The country that rolls away from the river varies from heavily wooded to areas so open they reminded the fur traders of the Western prairie and were given names such as "La Grande Prairie." Massive herds of buffalo grazed over the plains of grass and peavine, while poplar woods and miles of Saskatoon bushes that grew ten feet tall provided cover for countless elk, bear, moose and other wildlife. Since berries and meat were the ingredients of pemmican,

The Hudson's Bay Company trading post of Fort St. John on the Peace River in 1906. The top photo shows settlers arriving at Grande Prairie in 1910 to seek land; the center one, scows on the Peace River. These scows were the main method of transporting freight before the arrival of the sternwheelers. As can be seen in the photo, each scow was laboriously pulled upstream by men on a tow line.

for decades the Peace River country was a prime source of this fur-trade staple.

The Peace River country was still the domain of the fur traders when the first sternwheeler appeared in 1903, although by then miners and trappers had joined the traders and the first wave of settlers were poised to enter the land. The sternwheeler was the *St. Charles*, built for Bishop Grouard at the Catholic Mission at Dunvegan, a fur-trading post established in 1805. She was only a teakettle of a steamboat, but when her whistle broke the silence of the eons of the Peace, she heralded a new age.

In the book *Paddlewheels on the Frontier* is this description of Bishop Grouard and his small paddlewheeler:

"The vessel reflected the vitality of Bishop Grouard, probably the best known of all the northern priests and one of Canada's great frontiersmen. For nearly seventy years from 1862 he served the Indians and Eskimos, travelling tens of thousands of miles by foot and snowshoe, dogteam and canoe. His travels took him past the site of future Dawson City to the Bering Sea decades before the Klondike rush. When settlers started moving into the magnificent Peace River country in 1907 he had already served the region over forty years. His small sternwheeler operated 525 miles upstream from rapids called Vermilion Chutes to Hudson Hope, a few miles below the Peace River Canyon, carrying supplies for the mission at Fort St. John plus goods for the N.W.M.P. and the H.B.C."

By the summer of 1905, the *St. Charles* had competition on the river when the Hudson's Bay Company launched a sternwheeler of its own, the *Peace River*. She was built at Fort Vermilion in the northern part of Alberta's Peace River country the previous winter, a 110-foot-long vessel that could carry a modest forty tons of freight. She plied the Peace for the next ten years, a familiar vessel to trappers, prospectors, traders and the settlers who arrived in increasing numbers.

An excellent description of the *Peace River* is contained in a booklet called *North With Peace River Jim*, written in 1910 by L. V. Kelly. Mr. Kelly, a reporter for the *Calgary Herald*, was one of a group of journalists, financiers, professors, businessmen, and members of parliament taken on a tour of Alberta's Peace River country in 1910 by James Kennedy Cornwall, the member of Alberta's provincial legislature for the area. On August 6, 1910, the group reached Peace River Crossing where they boarded the *Peace River* for a journey north to Fort Vermilion. Of the sternwheeler, Mr. Kelly wrote:

"Lying up against the far bank, when we arrived, was the little white Hudson's Bay steamer *Peace River*, 'coaling up' with cordwood, slid down a 200 foot chute to the river bank and packed on board by the half-breed hands.

"At 2 o'clock the boat was back. A purser assigned us to our cabins and there were white sheets on the berths. Everything was as trim and neat as a steamer on the Great Lakes, and the table manners were observed with great care, the passengers being allotted seats and tables, the captain taking the head and the purser the foot of the first table. There was a real service provided, cooking of a sort, and the course service was handled by a boy, who was better in many ways than the real waiters in some of the restaurants of the west.

"As the boat pulled out, the citizens, and entire population of Peace River Crossing, gathered on the bank and gave us god-speed and good wishes. We responded with three cheers and a tiger. Three half-breeds with loaded rifles knelt on the bank and fired the royal salute, with rifle muzzles pointed skyward and the butts on the ground. Again we cheered and again the salute crackled out, then the steamer swung wide and took the big turn, and the current and the sternwheel paddles soon took us from the sight of the beautiful Peace River Crossing.

"And then we headed down stream at a rate of about 12 miles an hour for Fort Vermilion, 310 miles north. The river, ranging in width from 600 yards to a half mile at some points, silently bore us around the great sweeps and the beautiful islands, past the towering banks. The hunting brigade was out in full force with binoculars and spyglasses, scouring the steep slopes for bear, because the boatmen said bear were pretty frequently seen, and in fact they still had the big head of one black bear they had killed at Fort St. John on the up trip through the instrumentality of the marksmanship of Engineer Sutherland."

The booklet also contains an excellent description of Vermilion Chutes, the only rapids on some 700 miles of the Peace River from where it breaks through the Rockies to its junction with the Slave: "The rapids roared and crowded on the points; piles of splintered and massive logs bore mute testimony of the power of the water when it came up, and exerted itself to the full.

"... great ten-foot caverns yawned blackly forth from the mighty shelves of rocks, worn deep by the wash of hundreds of years of floods; the flat, water-smoothed slabs widened until some were almost a half acre in extent, but still the river thundered along until with a twist and a whirl and a sullen snarl it threw itself on the smooth ledges and against the massive boulders in the last 25-foot jump over the falls. The river, over a mile wide here, sprang in a wavering line of flashing water and leaping foam down to the boiling cauldron where the whole element hesitated and swerved and came back before it finally decided to obey the laws of gravitation and go down the grade with the rest of the now fairly quiet water that preceded it."

The rapids were an effective barrier to the sternwheelers, although one eventually was to go up and another come down this formidable obstacle.

The stories which Kelly and other journalists on the Cornwall expedition wrote about their journey brought considerable publicity for the Peace River country. As a result, more and more settlers arrived and the *Peace River* became too small to handle the H.B.C.'s freight. In 1915 the Company replaced her with the *Athabasca River*, a vessel that could carry 100 tons.

She was built in 1912 to ply the Athabasca-Slave River but was brought to the Peace River in the winter of 1914-15. This transfer was a thorough test of her ruggedness since she was winched up the mile-long Vermilion Chutes. But sternwheelers were remarkably adaptable and she took this unusual journey as part of the day's work.

Another, but less hazardous, obstacle she encountered was shallow water, especially where the Peace breaks through the Rocky Mountains. "Between Fort St. John and Hudson Hope the river got very low at times and we would run onto sand bars," recalls Z. L. Hull, a member of her crew in 1915. "Sometimes these bars reached clear across the channel and the boat would have to be hauled over them. This was done with a system of poles, blocks and tackle called a 'grasshopper'."

"A grasshopper can actually pull a thousand ton boat off a sandbar," said Captain John D. Cadenhead, who sailed the Peace River for many years. "The idea was borrowed from the Mississippi River and the name comes from the look and action. Either one or two poles with an iron point to prevent slipping are put on one or both sides of the bow to the bottom of the river. Then with an arrangement of blocks and tackle and the vessel's steam winch, the sternwheeler can be lifted about a foot. While the bow is thus suspended, full steam is thrown onto the paddlewheel and the boat lurches ahead then falls with a splash. The operation is repeated as many times as necessary to get over a bar, with the action of the sternwheeler resembling a giant grasshopper."

The *Athabasca River* churned up and down the Peace for five years until she was retired in 1919. By then a new vessel had appeared. She was the *D. A. Thomas*, a magnificent twin-stacker, 167 feet long by 40 feet wide, built on the banks of the Peace in the winter of 1915-16 by Vancouver boat builder George Askew. Her owner was Baron Rhondda, a Welsh coal millionaire.

Rhondda intended to develop an immense coal field near Hudson Hope and also hoped to discover oil in the Peace River country. So confident was he of success that he had oil tanks fitted to the *D. A. Thomas*. Unfortunately, Lord Rhondda's hopes for the big ship never materialized. He plunged some $250,000 into his Peace River Development Company, but just as he began opening up the Hudson Hope coal deposits, World War One came along. Coal sales were soon cancelled and all other activities suspended. Had he not been interrupted, it is quite possible that he would have discovered the immense gas and oil fields uncovered in the Peace River district in 1948 and 1952. Ironically, the *D. A. Thomas* burned neither coal nor oil, but got along on copious quantities of four-foot-long cordwood.

With development curtailed, the *D. A. Thomas* proved too big to be practical for the Peace River and Lord Rhondda sold her to the Lamson Hubbard Trading Company. This Company operated her until the fall of 1922 when a shortage of both passengers and freight made further operations unprofitable. She lay idle for two years until 1924 when the H.B.C. took her over.

While the *D. A. Thomas* proved too big and a hard-luck vessel besides, she was impressive nevertheless. Perhaps Georgina Murray Keddel described her as eloquently as anyone when in the October 3, 1963 issue of the *Alaska Highway News* she wrote:

"The *Thomas* was a beautiful ship, the biggest riverboat afloat.... She was built at a cost of $119,000 and could carry more than 100 passengers and more than 200 tons of freight. Her galley was properly fitted out, her dining saloon commodious. Silver and linen covered the tables and the staterooms were comfortable and spotless. Empty she drew two feet of water; loaded, five feet. She could,

The *Athabasca River*, opposite page, plied the Upper Peace for five years. Below is the Peace River Canyon, the formidable head of navigation where the river breaks through the Rocky Mountains.

and occasionally did, make the 250-mile run from Peace River town to Hudson Hope in seventeen hours. She was a mail ship and didn't tarry. But usually the journey took several days...."

Or several weeks, according to Gordon Sculthorpe, longtime resident of Fort St. John who sailed on the *D. A. Thomas* during her last summer on the Peace.

"She was quite a boat," he recalled. "The cabins were placed along each side of the boat and down the center was a huge room which included the drawing room with the dining room near the stern. The Hudson's Bay Company monogram was on the silverware and woven into linen. There was plenty of glass between lounge and deck, and the interior was bright and cheerful with leather furniture, card tables, carpets and rich dark shining wood. Brass spittoons and potted palms completed the decor.

"Docking her was quite an event and usually most everyone living at each stop would come down to the river to watch the big show. Her only trouble was she was too big for the Peace and was lucky to make two round trips a season as she was always getting hung up on sand bars."

Captain John Cadenhead, for three seasons her pilot, recalled the time in 1927 when she failed to complete even one trip. A new pilot had taken over and he probably wasn't as familiar with the river as he should have been. While Captain Myers slept, he piled the big boat on some rocks. The shock brought Captain Myers on the run. The crew tried to plug the gaping hole with a tarpaulin but were unsuccessful and the skipper headed the vessel for shallow water. He didn't make it. Fifty feet from shore the big sternwheeler foundered.

"They tried to raise her," Captain Cadenhead remembered, "but finally after wasting more than a month, they had to send for George Askew, the builder. Askew floated her all right, but by then the whole shipping season was lost. The next year the *Thomas* had a new skipper for the captain always got the blame whether it was his fault or not."

Captain Cadenhead also recalls that a paid ticket wasn't always a guarantee of a leisurely boat ride. Although the

Because of Vermilion Chutes, center, the community of Fort Vermilion, shown above in 1912, was the northerly terminus of navigation on the Upper Peace. The last sternwheel to beat the waters of the Peace River was on the motor vessel *Alcan*, top photo. Built in 1943, her sole purpose was to help with the construction of the Alaska Highway suspension bridge over the Peace River near Fort St. John.

126

Hudson's Bay hired contractors to cut and stack cordwood at various points, when the river was high and the *D. A. Thomas* under full load she burned wood in such prodigious quantities that she didn't always reach the next wood pile before running out. Then all ablebodied men — passengers included — were requested to set to with axes and crosscut saws to replenish the fuel supply.

There was, however, one compensation for the big sternwheeler was famous for its spendid cuisine. And since the captain kept a rifle in the pilothouse and wildlife was plentiful along the river, the menu often included bear roast or moose or venison steaks.

In 1926, during his last season with the *D. A. Thomas*, Captain Cadenhead was at the wheel when the big steamer matched her engines against the powerful current of the Peace River Canyon. The entire population of Hudson Hope turned out to watch. "Twice," said Cadenhead, "the ship was halted by the boiling waters and we had to run her right in against the rock walls to get her going again." Just a mile short of her goal, with the river roaring by and cliffs rising 1,000 feet on either side, the vessel could go no farther. There was nothing to do but maneuver her slowly around and head back.

It is possible that the sternwheeler — though too big and too expensive to operate on the Peace — may have been kept in service a while longer had it not been for an incident in 1929. In July of that year a large party of the Edmonton Board of Trade chartered her for a pleasure and business cruise. But while they waited at Dunvegan for her to return from a trip upstream, the big steamboat piled onto a sand bar near Fort St. John and left the unhappy businessmen stranded. It was the last straw, although it did not as yet signal the end of the steam navigation on the Peace River. The *D. A. Thomas* would undertake one last memorable voyage.

While the *D. A. Thomas*, *Peace River* and other sternwheelers plied the Peace, there were several smaller vessels also on the river, although their dimensions and other statistics have been lost or rest in some forgotten archive. Most belonged to sawmill companies: the Diamond P's *Grenfall* and Peterson's *Pine Pass*, both used to move logs and lumber around Peace River town. There was the *Northland Echo* and the *Lady Macworth*, the latter a diminutive sister ship to the *D. A. Thomas*.

In addition to sternwheelers, the H.B.C. operated a fleet of motorships on the Peace from 1920 to 1952. The first was the *Weenusk*. She was built in Vancouver by George Askew and shipped via Edmonton over the newly completed Northern Alberta Railroad to her launching spot at the town of Peace River. From 1920 until 1940 her throbbing diesels pushed her up and down river, two barges lashed alongside, carrying both passengers and freight.

In 1930 she was joined by another Askew-built motor vessel, the *Buffalo Lake*. Both of these were replaced in 1940 by an all-steel tug, the *Weenusk II*. Under Captain Cadenhead she efficiently hauled two barges along the river until 1951, when she was replaced by the last of the H.B.C. boats on the Peace, the powerful diesel tug *Watson Lake*. When she in turn was taken out of service in September 1952, it spelled the end to 160 years of Hudson's Bay fur trade on the Peace River.

Taking the *Watson Lake* out of service, however, seemed rather anticlimactic to pioneer residents along the river. For them most of the glamor of river travel vanished in a cloud of smoke in 1930 when the H.B.C. decided to terminate steam transportation. That summer they transferred the *D. A. Thomas* to the Athabasca-Slave River route via the treacherous Vermilion Chutes, a passage that had never been attempted. Fur Trade Commissioner C. H. French of the H.B.C. described that event in the December 1930 issue of *The Beaver*:

"The river (just below Fort Vermilion) is perhaps two miles wide and drops thirty feet in a distance of one mile.

"The drop is nothing provided there is plenty of water, but the rapids are above a mass of rocks, over which it foams and boils until it reaches the ledge of rock known as the chutes. Here it dives down a steep incline ending in a large comber.

"The upper rapids were passed without difficulty and the chutes we found to be just wide enough to allow the ship to pass.

"When the steamer had entered at exactly the right spot in exactly the right position, she reached the very crest, then grounded. The hull held back the water, immediately raising it sufficiently to allow her to slip over this smooth worn rock far enough for her bow to drop and her stern to rise in such a position that she must go through or be a total wreck. The big combing wave weighing many tons dropped on her bow and the real final test was at hand. . . . The steamer's bow raised up and at the same time her stern went down, causing her wheel to strike heavily on the chute rocks and rip about half of it away. . . ."

"We hung there a lifetime," recalled Gordon Sculthorpe, one of eight crew members on board, "though I suppose it couldn't have been longer than a minute or two. The *Thomas* was over 160 feet long, with lines something like a shallow saucer. The fall straightened her right out and then some. You could actually see the inverted heave in her hull as she hung there trembling."

The main concern was that the unnatural bend in her hull would break the steam pipes, with disastrous results. However, it was then that her paddlewheel ripped free and she swept down the rapids. Once through, Captain Cowley backed her to the shore and after temporary repairs continued some 300 miles to Fort Fitzgerald.

It was the big sternwheeler's last voyage. Although Captain Cadenhead was not on her for the final run, he was well acquainted with her fate. "At Fort Fitzgerald," he said, "there's a big eddy about a mile across. I've landed boats there many times and know it's quite a trick to pull in there against the current. Well, sir, they didn't make it. They stuck her in the mud above the dock and there she stayed."

When Captain Cadenhead visited Fort Fitzgerald seven years later there wasn't much left of the *D. A. Thomas* but "a bunch of ribs sticking out of the mud and the kids were using the wheelhouse to play in." It was a harsh fate for a hard-luck ship for which there had been such high expectations.

Still, she is luckier than some. At least she lives in replica at the corner of Mackenzie Avenue and the Alaska Highway in Fort St. John. True, the replica can never portray the full magnificence of the original. But with a little imagination anyone looking at her should be able to envision just a little of the romance of a by-gone age when big sternwheelers plied the waters of the mighty Peace. ∎

THE BARD

OF BARKERVILLE

James Anderson never found the gold that lured him to the Cariboo in 1863, but the poems he wrote are a historical treasure with their record of the life led by the "Poor but Honest Miner."

by R. M. THORBURN

"The rough but honest miner, who toils by night and day,
Seeking for the yellow gold, hid among the clay—
His head may grow gray, and his face fu' o' care,
Hunting after gold, with its 'castles in the air'."

So wrote James Anderson, a poet-miner who left his native Scotland in 1863 to spend eight fruitless years on the Cariboo goldfields. He wrote songs and verses for the entertainment of his fellow miners at the frequent concerts held in Barkerville's little community hall and, since his eagle eye and rhythmic ear missed little of the town's goings-on, his poetry reflects with sympathetic accuracy the pleasures and pathos of the miner's life.

Anderson portrays the real Barkerville. Most of the millions of words that have been written about the old gold town have focussed on the bizarre, the spectacular, or the grotesque. Articles about Bill "Dutch" Dietz, "Ten Foot" Davis and the legendary "Cariboo" Cameron are ten-a-penny; eyewitness accounts of the disastrous fire of '68, and quotations from the tragic little headstones on the hillside cemetery are readily to hand.

But what of the day-to-day life of Barkerville in the 1860's? Anderson, in a slim volume of verse entitled *Sawney's Letters*, gives an account of the existence led by "the rough but honest miner," and describes his pastimes, fears, hopes and aspirations. Writes Gordon R. Elliott in his book, *Quesnel, Commercial Center of the Cariboo Gold Rush*: "The poetry of James Anderson can restore a great deal to us. The poems reflect a picture of the town both economically and socially while he lived there." The fact that Anderson's comments on Barkerville life and times have not been more widely circulated is due, no doubt, to his use of broad Scots dialect.

Anderson's musings on contemporary life were originally published as single poems in the *Cariboo Sentinel*, Barkerville's newspaper of the time. In 1895 they were later collected and published through the good offices of the Gold Commissioner, John Bowron. Most of the poems purport to be letters in verse to a friend, "Sawney," back in Scotland, giving him the news from the goldfields.

It is, in fact, doubtful if Sawney ever existed. More probably the "letters" were for local consumption, as critical commentaries of Barkerville life. Much of the comment is bitter and barbed, and one cannot altogether ignore the bias that Anderson's Calvinistic Scottish upbringing would bring to it. Nevertheless, *Sawney's Letters* are of value in that they are virtually the only on-the-spot writings of one who actually worked in the gold mines and shared the ups and downs of the less successful miners.

Anderson, in describing for us his own struggles as a prospector, gives a vivid picture of what must have been the common lot of those who did not "strike it rich." On his arrival at Barkerville, he risked his savings in the purchase of a claim from Cariboo Cameron, or Cameron Jock o'Canada, as he calls him. Cameron seems to have dealt honestly with the novice miner, since Anderson tells us that the claim put money in his pocket within three weeks. (In writing of Cameron, incidentally, Anderson reveals a facet of Cariboo's character that seems to have escaped his many biographers; that he had "a gae strong liking for the women.")

Anderson's modest prosperity was short-lived. As the gold fever gripped him he bought up other claims that proved to be white elephants. All the claims had names, and with one in particular, the Ayrshire Lass, he fell expensively in love, and:

"I tried my best to catch her tin,
But, ah, the jade, she took me in;
For four long months I ran her drift,
Then, wearied o't, gi'ed her in gift."

Again and again he returned to his original claim to recoup his losses. Again and again his profits were dissipated in reckless prospecting.

And so he finally descended—as no doubt did many of his fellows for the same reason—to the humble rank of mine laborer in the employ of luckier, or wiser, men. He worked from morning till night among "face-boards, water, slum and mud," to keep the wolf from the door. For this soul-destroying labor he was paid ten dollars a day—not too much when, as he tells us, a pound of sugar cost a dollar, the same weight of butter three dollars, and a letter from home by what he calls sarcastically "Barnard's Cariboo Delay" a dollar and a half. (Oatmeal, flour and vegetables were, apparently, equally expensive, and milk not to be had at all.)

Yet, for all his bitter disillusionment, Anderson seems never to have lost his capacity to stand up to life, grim as it might be. Through the dark grey of his poetry runs a silver thread of cheerfulness, and a determination to pass this desperate optimism to his fellows. His bitter-sweet verses,

At left is the main street of Barkerville in September 1868. Here in the summer was printed a selection of Anderson's verses. A few days after the photo was taken, fire destroyed the community.

appearing regularly in the local newspaper, forced the cold, hungry, mountain-fever wracked miners to smile at their own plight, and at the often-ridiculous posturings of those who had "struck it rich."

Social life in the Barkerville of Anderson's era was rigidly divided into two groups—those who had and those who had not. The hierarchy, or "top ten" as he describes them, were those who had amassed wealth. Wealth and rank were inseparable:

"Gold, gold! We worship gold. What signifies the man?" A rich strike was the entry ticket to a Barkerville "peerage," without regard for other circumstances. The fortunate few basked in the smiles of the saloon keepers and the dancing girls, while those whose pockets were empty were shown the door without ceremony.

But it was a dangerous and unstable "aristocracy," and Anderson and his friends often had the last cynical laugh. The high rate of spending, coupled with the uncertainty of a claim's continuing to yield pay dirt, saw frequent changes in the social hierarchy. This state of affairs seems to have afforded Anderson a certain grim satisfaction when he wrote:

"Whene'er he entered a saloon you'd
see the barkeep smile,
His Lordship's humble servant he,
without a thought o'guile;
A twelvemonth passed and all is gone,
both friends and brandy bottle,
And now the poor soul's left alone,
wi' nought to wet his throttle."

Others besides the hypocritical saloon keepers aroused Anderson's contempt. Mine-salters and claim-jumpers he considered to be despicable cheats. The salter put a few nuggets in a claim to get a high price for it from the greenhorn prospector, while the jumper moved in on any mine that had no legal protection. In telling of these pests, Anderson consoles himself as, no doubt, did the many other victims of such tricksters, with the observation that they would eventually be jumped by their ally, the Devil.

Even more contemptible, he tells us, were the hordes of

nattily-dressed professional gamblers who sat like poisonous spiders in the saloons, intent on relieving the "rough but honest miner" of his hard-earned gold. They are described as:

"... a set of men up here,
Who never work through a' the year;
A kind of serpents, crawling snakes,
That fleece the miner o' his stakes."

But, though he chides the miners obliquely for their reckless gambling, he does so gently, writing more in sorrow than in anger. He holds the Barkerville clergy of the period squarely to blame for the widespread drinking and gambling, and for turning blind eyes to the low moral standards prevailing. There is, he states, "neither kirk nor Sunday here, though there is many a sinner."

Barkerville, it appears, had three churches at the time Anderson lived there. They were, however, closed down each fall so that their preachers might enjoy the creature comforts of the coast during the cold winter months. With an abrupt change of tone, Anderson pays handsome tribute to one Christian meeting-place that catered to the miners' spiritual needs during winter. It was not a proper church, but simply a small building called "the Cambrian Hall," in which a handful of men gathered to worship. It is a thousand pities Anderson has not recorded the name of its preacher.

Women being an integral part of social living anywhere, *Sawney's Letters* inevitably touch on the subject of the contribution of the fair sex to life in Barkerville. Records from other sources prove beyond doubt that many fine, courageous women took up residence in the town, but this does not seem to have impressed Anderson sufficiently to cause him to deal kindly with the weaker sex. He chooses, instead, to dwell on the less savory females who would undoubtedly be attracted to an easy money town such as Barkerville.

Of such women he writes, with some venom:
"There are some women on this creek,
So modest, and so mild and meek!
The deep red blush aye paints their cheek;
They never swear but when they speak.
Each one's a mistress, too, you'll find,
To make good folk think that she's joined
In honest wedlock unto one.
She's YOURS—or ANY OTHER MAN'S."

Even allowing for Anderson's narrow religious background, there must have been some cause for his making such shocking accusations, and Barkerville's prominently-placed "Sporting House" is perhaps confirmation of his accuracy of opinion.

His only other reference to Barkerville women in *Sawney's Letters* is to the "Hurdy-gurdy" girls, and certainly he does not question their morality. The Hurdy-gurdies were a troupe of dancing girls imported from San Francisco to Barkerville to provide professional dancing partners for the miners in the saloons of the gold town. These young ladies sold their dances in the saloons nightly, and also helped, on a commission basis, to persuade the miners to drink what was loosely called champagne. Since the girls were German by origin, conversation with them must have been difficult—but then, the miners did not go to the saloons for conversation!

Despite the peculiarity of their professional calling, and the rough handling they underwent by the enthusiastic miners, Anderson appears to have developed not only a healthy respect for their morality, but also an affectionate regard for their charms.

"Bonnie are the hurdies, O!
The German hurdie-gurdies, O!
The sweetest hours that ere I spent,
Was dancing wi' the hurdies, O!"

Thus wrote Anderson to Sawney, adding regretfully that the girls resisted all amorous approaches, "the dollar" being their only love.

Anderson's writings on the Hurdy-gurdies, incidentally, give a different impression as to the length of their stay in Barkerville from that given by most other commentators on the gold town scene. There seems to be a popular misconception that the dancers stayed in Barkerville for several years, but in a letter to Sawney dated March 1866, Anderson writes:

"Last summer we had lassies frae Germany—the hurdies, O!" and, a few lines later, he remarks:

The Hotel de France in Barkerville, with the Express Office at left. Here lonely miners waited for news of family or loved ones in countries around the world.
The top photo on the opposite page shows Yale in 1867 or 1868. Sternwheelers provided a connection to New Westminster or Victoria while Barnard's Express, lower photo, operated a stagecoach service to Barkerville, some 400 miles and a minimum five days travel to the north, provided that road conditions were favorable.

"They left the creeks wi' lots o' gold,
danced from our lads so clever, O' "

Thus the German girls could not have remained in Barkerville for more than nine months, and probably stayed for even less time.

Anderson's poetry, as typified by his two references to Barkerville's women, is a curious mixture of bitterness and tenderness, but never is he more tender than when describing the hardships and heartaches of his fellow-miner. Besides *Sawney's Letters* he wrote several other poems, and one of these, entitled "Waiting for the Mail," is perhaps the most touching of his works.

First, the mounting excitement as word of the mail's approach:

"A teamster from the Beaver Pass—
'What news o' the Express?'
'Twas there last night, if I saw right;
and here today, I guess.' "

Then, the arrival:

"A few hours more—a great uproar
—th' Express is come at last!
An Eastern mail, see by the bale, as
Sullivan goes past."

Next, the eager, anxious crowd waiting at the postmaster's office to "buy" letters addressed to them, (there were no postage stamps at this time), and cursing his delay at opening the delivery window of his office:

"And now, an eager, anxious crowd,
await the letter sale,
Postmaster curs'd, their wrath is nurs'd, while waiting for the mail."

Finally: "Hurrah! The window's up!"
and the pathetic plight of those for whom the long wait has been in vain:

"And many come, and many go, in sorrow or delight,
While some will say theirs met delay, whose friends forgot to write;
An anxious heart that stands apart,
expectant of a letter,
With hopeful mind, but fears to find some loved one still

his debtor.
A sweetheart wed, a dear friend dead,
or closer tie is broken:
Ah! Many an ache the heart may take by words, tho' never spoken."

Drinking, gambling, praying, dancing, dying—Anderson touched on all facets of Barkerville life in the eight years of his stay on the goldfields. Of a versatile turn of mind, he was also responsible for the foundation of an amateur dramatic association, and wrote much of the material that was performed at the Theatre that first opened its doors, according to him, on New Year's Eve, 1867. He tells us also that the Theatre was rebuilt by voluntary labor; "Built by kind labor volunteered by all," and re-opened on January 16, 1869, with a performance of "Still Waters Run Deep."

Eventually, however, Anderson seems to have lost heart. In 1871 he decided to leave the goldfields forever and return to Scotland. His feelings are expressed in his last poem, "Farewell!," which appeared in the November 25, 1871 edition of the *Cariboo Sentinel*:

"Cold Cariboo, farewell!
I write it with a sad and heavy heart;
You've treated me so roughly that I feel,
'Tis hard to part.
'Twas all I asked of thee,
One handful of thy plenteous golden grain,
Had'st thou but yielded, I'd have sung "Farewell!"
And home again.
But, time on time, defeat!
Ah, cold and cruel, callous Cariboo!
Have eight years' honest persevering toil
No more of you?
Ah well, then since 'tis so—
Since Fate hath will'd I should no longer here—
I, e'en submit, while disappointment starts
The hidden tear.
But still I'll picture thee
As some dear loved one in the days gone by,
And think what might have been, till dreaming brings
The soothing sigh.

The photo at right shows Barkerville's Library and Post Office in 1871, the year Anderson left. Standing in the doorway is John Bowron, who became Gold Commissioner and after whom Bowron Park is named. Above is St. Saviour's Church, a famous Barkerville landmark built in 1869 and still used for services.

The two photos on the opposite page were taken in 1868 and show some of the men Anderson referred to as "the rough but honest miner." The lower photo is the Forest Rose claim which yielded $480,000 in gold. For Anderson, however, the creeks did not surrender even "one handful of thy bounteous golden grain."

SAWNEY'S LETTERS,

— OR —

CARIBOO RHYMES.

By James Anderson

FROM 1864 TO 1868.

LETTER NO. I.
[WRITTEN FEBRUARY, 1864.]

DEAR SAWNEY,—I sit doon to write
A screed to you by candle light,
An answer to your friendly letter,
I ne'er had ane that pleased me better.
Your letter cam by the Express,
Eight shillin's carriage—naethin' less.
You'll think this awfu'—'tis, nae doot—
(A dram's twa shillin's here-aboot);
I'm sure if Tamie Ha'—the buddy
Was here wi' his three legged cuddy
He hauls abent him wi a tether,
He'd beat the Express, faith a'thegithe—
To speak o't in the truest way
'Tis Barnard's Cariboo Delay.

You'd maybe like to ken what pay
Miners get here for ilka day.
Jist twa pound sterling, sure as death—
It should be four—atween us baith.
For gin ye count the cost o' livin'
There's naething lett to gang and come on;
And should you bide the winter here
The shoppy-buddies 'll grab your gear.
And little work ane finds to do
A' the lang dreary winter thro'.

Sawney—had ye your tatties here,
And neeps and carrots—dinna speer
What price—tho' I could tell ye weel,
Ye might think me a leein' chiel;
Nae, lad, ye ken I never lee.
Ye a believe that fa's frae me;
Neeps, tatties, carrots—by the pun'
Jist twa and a penny—try for fun
How muckle twad be for a ton.
Ait meal four shillin's, flour is twa,
And milk's no to be had ava.
For at this season o' the year
There's naething for a coo up here
To chaw her cud on,—sae ye see
Ye are far better aff than me,—
For while you're sittin warm at hame,
And suppin' parritch drooned in cranme,
The deil a drap o' milk hae I
But gobble our my parritch dry;
Of course, I can get butter here,
Twal shillin' a pund—it's far oure dear.
Aye—a' thing sells at a lang price.
Tea, coffee, sugar, bacon, rice,
Four shillin's a pound, and something mair.
And e'en the weights are raither bare—
Sae much for prices.

Noo for claims,
And first a word about their names;
Some folk were sae oppressed wi' wit
The ca'd their claim by name "Coo——,"
And tho' they struck the dirt by name
They ne'er struck pay dirt in their claim.
Some ithers made a gae fine joke
And christen'd their bit ground 'Dead Broke,'
While some. to fix their fate at once.
Ca'd their location 'The Last Chance.'

There's 'Tinker,' 'Grizzly'—losh, what names,
There's 'Prince o' Wales'—the best o' claims,
There's 'Beauregard' and 'Never Sweat.'
And scores o' ithers I forget.
The 'Richfield' and the 'Montreal,'
They say they struck the pay last fall.
But will the strik' it gin the spring,
Aye, Sawney, that's anither thing;
But by an' bye they'll ken, nae doot,
If they can pump their water oot,
Some strik' the bed-rock pitchin' in,
And some the bed-rock canna win,
But ne'er a color can they see
Until they saut it first a wee;
And syne they tell to ilka man
They struck twa dollars to the pan.
You'll see'd into the Victoria Press
As twenty dollars—naething less.
Aye, Sawney, here a wee bit story,
Gin ance it travels to Victory,
Is magnified a hundred fold.
The bed-rock here, doon there is gold;
Some folks would manufacture lees
To mak' a bawbee on a cheese.
Shame on the man who salts a claim.
A man he is—but just in name—
NO MANHOOD'S IN HIM, HE'S A CHEAT,
A SMOOTH, DISSEMBLING HYPOCRITE,
WHO, IF HE COULD BUT GAIN HIS END,
WOULD E'EN DECEIVE HIS DEAREST FRIEND.

There is a set o' men up here
Wha never work thro' a' the year,
A kind o' serpents, craulin' snakes,
That fleece the miner o' his stakes;
They're Gamblers—honest men some say,
Tho' its quite fair to cheat in play
IF IT'S NO KENT O'—I ne'er met
An honest man a Gambler yet!
O, were I Judge in Cariboo
I'd see the laws were carr'd thro',
I'd hae the cairds o' every pack
Tied up into a gunny sack,
Wi' a' the gamblers chained thegither
And banish'd frae the creek forever.
But, Sawney, there's anither clan,
There's nane o' them I'd ca' a man,
They ca' them "jumpers"—it's my belief
That jumper is Chinook for thief;—
The jump folks claims and jump their lots,
They jump the very pans pots;
But wait a wee—for a' this evil—
Their friend 'll jump them.
He's the deevil.

And sae ye think o' comin' here,
And leavin' all your guids and gear,
Your wife and bairns, and hame, eh, Sawney,
If ye wad listen to advic—
And sae ye will if ye be wise
Jist bide at home and work awa',
Ye mauna think we 'houk up gold,
As ye the tatties frae the mould.
Gude faith, y'ell maybe houk a twa'l mo't
An' never ev'n get a glisk o't!
An' then what comes o' us puir deevils,

We get as thin and lean as weevils;
O' wark we canna get a stroke,
We're what they ca' out here 'dead broke,'
Which means we hinna e'en a groat
To line our stomach or our coat,
Sae doon the country we may gang,
And this the burden o' our sang:
To ilka ane that comes alang,
Freend be advised and turn aboot,
For Cariboo is noo ' played out!'

Noo, Sawney, I'll blaw oot the light,
I'll finish this some ither night,
I'll cast my coat and brecks, that's a',
And sleep until the daylight daw.

DEAR SAWNEY,—I noo tak the time
To feenish oot my thread o' rhyme,
But as my bobbin's getting bare
I'll no can spin ye muckle mair,
An' sae ye're guid auld mither's dead,
This aye keeps runnin' in my head.
Eh, weel I mind the awful lickin'
She gae us twa for pusie stickin'!
Noo even whan I think o' that,
What gar'd her flyte sae 'boot a cat?
An' it had worried oor she rabbit,
An' feckled a' the young an's grabbit;
But when ye're mither fand this oot
She ca'd the cat a clarty brute,
An' as she skelped us sae cruel
She fill'd our stomachs fu' o' gruel.?
Aye, Sawney, lad, auld folks maun dee,
An' young uns may—so let us be
Twa doonright honest, trustin' men,
Syne we'll be ready noo or then.
An' ye hae got anither bairn,
Another stone to haip the cairn
Aye, aye, for ilka ane that dees.
There's ane and maybe mair that sees.
Sae dander-headed Smiddy Jock
Is rivetted wi' Maggie Lock!
I canna think hoo she could mairy
Sic a blethrin' harum-scairy;
Some folks dislike what ithers like,
An' some see guid in the warst tyke,
Sae Maggie may see this in Johnnie,
But, certies me, he is no bonny!
Ye ken I liked this lass fu' weel,
An' thocht mysel' a happy chiel.
Ah, I should ne'er hae trusted Mag,
She's like her mither Eve—the hag—
Wha fell in love, lang time ago,
Wi' that auld blacksmith doon below;
Believin' a his words were true,
She put the aiple in her mou',
An' whan auld Aidam she had gotten,
They ate it, but they foond it rotten!
They lost the guid, and got the evil,
A' thro' oor mither's bein' sae ceevil!
Ye ken that like produces like,
That bees are bred in a bee's byke,
Sae evil doon frae Aidam ran
A thro' the veins o' every man,
An' woman, too—SAE MAGGIE LOCKE
FORGAT HER JEAMES AND SPLICED WI' JOCK!

A reproduction of the first edition of *Sawney's Letters*, printed at Barkerville in the summer of 1868. One of the rarest of early B.C. imprints, it consists of a single sheet folded in four. It was printed in the office of the community's famous newspaper, the *Cariboo Sentinel*, on the first press ever brought into British Columbia.

In the photo opposite, spruce trees grow among the graves in Barkerville's cemetery, the "wee hill claim" where many of the miners known to James Anderson found their last claim.

"Farewell! a fond farewell
To all thy friendships, kindly Cariboo!
No other land hath hearts more warm than thine,
Nor friends more true."

The same issue of the paper contained the following news item: "Mr. Anderson has been a resident of Cariboo for the last eight years, during which time he has won the esteem of many friends, and we are certain has made no enemies. Fortune, we are sorry to say, has not smiled on him; and weary of wooing her embraces in the search for gold, he now returns to his old Scottish home, where a fond wife and family have long been mourning his absence. He was one of the original members of the Amateur Dramatic Association, and by his vocal talents rendered much assistance at their performances, his songs always much admired."

In Scotland, Anderson settled on one of his father's properties near Dollar in Clackmannan. He later moved to Cupar in Fife and eventually to England. He died in 1923 at the age of eighty-five.

Fortune in the goldfields had evaded his grasp, and his stay in Barkerville had brought little but heartache and disillusionment. He can be called lucky only inasmuch as he escaped the mountain fever, (or "tumtum," as he called it), that claimed the lives of so many of his contemporaries and laid them in the "wee hill claim," as he described Barkerville's cemetery.

Yet, if Anderson owed nothing to Barkerville, the gold town most certainly owes much to him. It owes him a searching, but sensitive, pen portrait of the Barkerville scene, with, standing large and lusty and lonely in its centre, "the rough but honest miner":

"His weather-beaten face, and his sair-worn hands,
Tell-tales to all o' the hardships he stands;
Toiling and sorrowing, on thro' life he goes,
Each morning sees some work begun,
each evening sees it close.
Though fortune may not smile upon his labors here,
There is a world above, where his prospects will be clear." ∎

THOMAS ELLIS
Okanagan Pioneer

He started a ranch that became the Okanagan's largest, planted the Valley's first orchard, built its first Protestant Church and helped found Penticton.

by ERIC D. SISMEY

The Ellis homestead in 1877. The building to the right of the house was the Okanagan's first store and post office.

For fifteen years the Dewdney Trail, opposite, was the route used by Tom Ellis to bring in equipment and supplies. A trip from Penticton to Hope with a packtrain such as the one below took a week—if conditions were good.

On the opposite page are Mr. and Mrs. Ellis in 1905. When Mrs. Ellis went to the Okanagan it was so isolated that once she didn't see another white woman for nine months.

When Thomas Ellis staked a claim to 320 acres of land between Okanagan and Skaha Lakes in 1866, he was the first white man to settle at what is now the city of Penticton. He had arrived in Victoria from England the previous year but after a month on the coast joined a group of three other men on a trip from Hope over the Dewdney Trail to Judge Haynes' ranch on Osoyoos Lake. Hampered by fallen trees and wet snow, they were eleven days travelling the 170 miles.

A few days after arriving at Osoyoos, Ellis accompanied Judge Haynes on a trip to the head of Okanagan Lake so that "... I may see the country before I fix on a place to settle." He wasn't too impressed, noting in his diary: "... I got a good look at the place, but did not like the look of it, though everybody says it is a good place to winter cattle."

For the next year he explored the Similkameen, Southern Okanagan and Kettle River Valley, but as he became familiar with the area, he modified his opinion of Okanagan Lake. He had realized that there was almost unlimited forage on the bunchgrass covered hills bordering the valley, that the meadows along the river, while swampy in early summer, were ideal winter pastures and that the flatlands between the foothills and the river would be well suited for hay after the heavy growth of balsam poplar was removed. And, further, the land could be irrigated from a nearby creek.

In 1866 he filed for 320 acres, then started clearing land, fencing and building a shelter for himself. To accomplish many of these things he first had to build the tools. His first cart was home made, with rounds of logs for wheels. His draft animals were oxen until he could afford to import work horses from the United States. His house was log, finished with whipsawn lumber and roofed with hand-split shakes.

Early in 1872, after a comfortable house, plus stables, sheds, store and trading post were finished, Mr. Ellis decided to visit his old home in Ireland. While there he married Wilhemina Wade and after a few weeks returned to the Okanagan over the Dewdney Trail.

For the first fifteen years all supplies and merchandise for the Ellis ranch were packed from Hope over the Dewdney Trail. The Ellis pack train, from twenty to thirty horses, made the round trip once or twice a year. At that time all ranch help were Indians from the Penticton Reserve and there are still Indians at Penticton who remember their fathers and grandfathers riding range, putting up hay, and accompanying the Ellis pack train.

In the way of foodstuff, little was purchased by the Ellis homestead. In common with other large ranches, it was nearly self-sufficient. Ice from nearby sloughs was cut in winter and stored. Meat, poultry, dairy products, fish, vegetables of every sort, and fruit from the home orchard were always in the larder. Then after 1872 flour from home-grown wheat was milled at the Barrington-Price mill at Keremeos.

The pattern of freighting supplies and merchandise continued until April 1886 when Captain T. D. Shorts, after building several not-too-successful small steamships, convinced Tom Ellis that freighting from Okanagan Landing at the head of the lake was cheaper than running pack trains. Consequently, in September 1890, the twinscrew, seventy-foot steamer *Penticton*, owned jointly by Tom Ellis and Captain Shorts, was launched at Okanagan Landing. The *Penticton* was the first really successful steamship on the lake. She continued to serve lakeside points until the Canadian Pacific sternwheel steamer *Aberdeen* was placed in service in 1893.

Meanwhile, Tom Ellis kept adding to his holdings. He was a ready buyer of abandoned homesteads and preemptions. By 1897 he owned more than 10,000 acres which included the east bench from Penticton to Naramata and the land east of the Okanagan River between the two lakes.

Early in the 1890's it became increasingly clear that the character of the country was changing. Tom Ellis, true to

The above photo shows Penticton in 1907 and the top one the CPR sternwheel steamer *Aberdeen*, launched in 1893. She started a scheduled service on Okanagan Lake and helped transform the economy from cattle to fruit. The first trees were planted by Tom Ellis and today the Okanagan is world-famous for its orchards, characterized by the apple trees at left near Naramata.

The photos on the opposite page are of St. Saviour's Church shortly after its completion in 1892, and a commemorative marker to Tom Ellis in Penticton.

St. Saviour's, built by Thomas Ellis in 1892, was the first Protestant Church in the Okanagan. On November 6, 1892 it was consecrated by Bishop Sillitoe who arrived from New Westminster on horseback. The first organist was Miss Eileen Ellis who later became Mrs. Pat Burns of Calgary. The first wedding was that of Miss Lily Allison, daughter of the pioneer Allison family of Princeton, to George Norman. By a tragic quirk of fate, the first person buried in the consecrated ground was Thomas Arthur Ellis, second son of Mr. and Mrs. Ellis. He was thrown from a horse he was breaking and died February 9, 1900, at the age of 23.

his nature, was well prepared for the change. Mines opening along the International Boundary at Camp McKinney and at Fairview, while providing an expanding market for beef cattle and hay, also brought an influx of settlers. In 1892, the first Ellis land was subdivided by the Penticton Townsite Company. It was on the east side at the southern end of the lake. Here supplies, merchandise, and machinery were unloaded from the *Aberdeen* for forwarding either by land or water to Okanagan Falls where it was reloaded to four- and six-horse rigs for delivery to various mining camps as far east as Greenwood.

At that time Okanagan Falls was a distribution center and headquarters for freighters. A townsite had been surveyed and lots sold in the early 1890's, a newspaper published, and a school with twenty-one pupils opened on August 10, 1896. Meanwhile, the Ellis children were taught by a governess and later by Reverend Thomas Green, first rector of St. Saviour's Church. Not until 1903, and then only after age stretching, were the necessary eight pupils mustered at Penticton to justify a school.

In 1895, Tom Ellis came into possession of the Judge Haynes estate. It included more than 20,000 acres, together with cattle and ranch equipment. This increased the Ellis empire to more than 30,000 acres. His cattle, bearing the "69" brand, ranged from the International Boundary through and along the east side of Okanagan Lake to the foot of Okanagan Mountain and to isolated holdings around Kelowna. Although the meadows of the Haynes estate were more extensive and productive, the Ellis family continued to live at Penticton rather than move to the picturesque Haynes house on the east shore of Osoyoos Lake.

For nearly three decades the Ellis ranch was the only refuge between Okanagan Mission and Osoyoos or Keremeos. At their table there was always room for one more, forage and shelter for horses was never refused and travellers always welcomed. In addition, Tom found time, busy though he was as manager, accountant, and supervisor of ranch operations, to help anyone in need. And Mrs. Ellis, skilled in practical nursing, was always ready to minister to the ill at any time, be they Indian or white.

On many occasions church services were held in the Ellis home. Then in 1892 Mr. and Mrs. Ellis built and furnished the first Protestant Church in the Okanagan Valley, St. Saviour's on Fairview Road, just south of the main gate of the Ellis homestead. It was small, seating only fifty, but completely furnished with nave and chancel, oak lectern, stained glass window, drapes and carpet in the sanctuary. The first service was held on April 26, 1892 and Bishop Sillitoe consecrated the sanctuary on November 6, 1892. The earliest grave in the churchyard is that of Thomas Ellis, junior, who was thrown from a bucking horse and died on February 9, 1900.

By the early 1900's Tom Ellis realized that the day of the large cattle ranch in the Okanagan was ending, especially after U.S. and Canadian agricultural experts declared that only irrigation was necessary to bring the rich glacial silts into production. In 1905 he sold his ranch to the Southern Okanagan Land Company. Next year subdivision, flume and storage dam construction began and soon young orchards extended along the east bench from Penticton to Naramata and south from Ellis Creek along the shores of Skaha Lake.

After the sale, the Ellis family moved to Victoria. Tom Ellis' retirement, however, was marred by the sudden death of his wife, Wilhemina, who had borne him nine children. Of this tragedy, one of his daughters, Kathleen, later wrote in the Fourteenth Report of the Okanagan Historical Society: "My father met this great sorrow with fortitude, as he had done all others, but those near to him knew that the light went out of his life with her passing. The World War, too, and the early reverses in it were shocking disillusionments to him and his generation. However, his interest in living and in his family responsibilities continued until his own call came on February 1, 1918."

The little white Thomas Ellis Church does not stand on Fairview Road any more. It was moved bodily alongside the new, larger St. Saviour's on Winnipeg Street, sheathed with matching stone veneer and dedicated the Ellis Memorial Chapel in 1934. In addition, a school, a creek, and an important Penticton street commemorate the Okanagan's well-known pioneer resident.

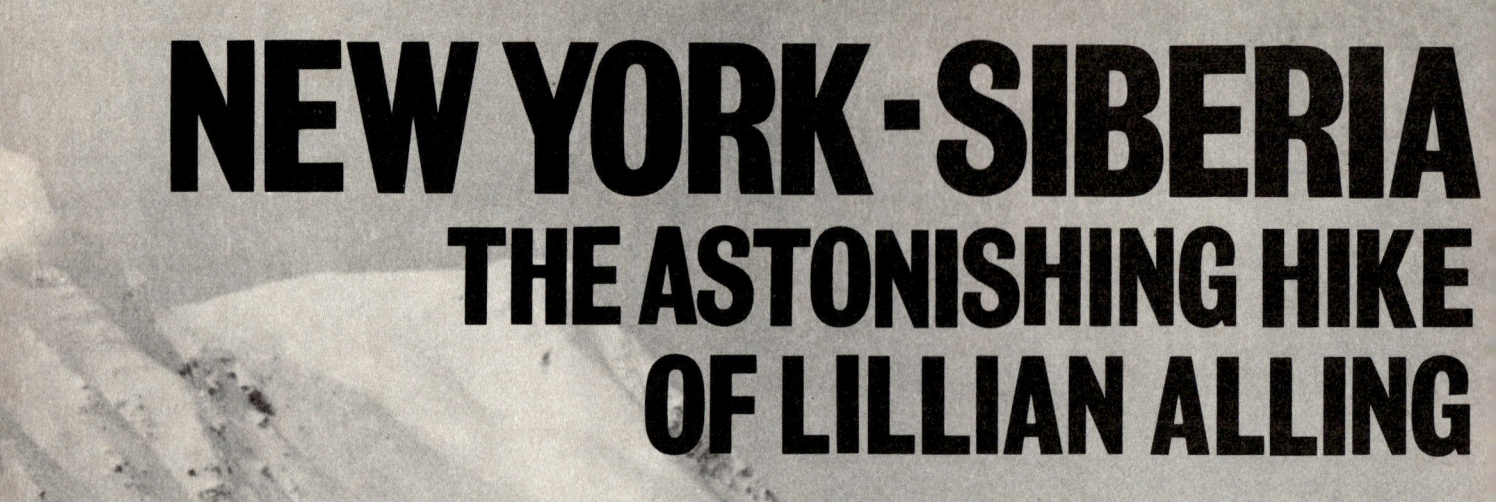

NEW YORK - SIBERIA
THE ASTONISHING HIKE OF LILLIAN ALLING

by FRANCIS DICKIE

In the photo on the opposite page Charlie Janze and his pack dog start down the slope on the divide between the Nass and Skeena River watersheds on the Yukon Telegraph Trail. This was a severe slide area and at times avalanches buried up to a mile and a half of the telegraph wire.

The opposite photo is of Lillian and Bruno, the dog lent to her by lineman Tommy Hankin. The Telegraph Trail crossed several mountain ranges, at one point near 8th Cabin climbing over an 8,000-foot summit.

She hiked 5,000 miles across North America to the Bering Sea. She slept under the stars, ate roots, leaves and berries and answered questions with four words "I go to Siberia." Did she succeed?

Recorded in police files, old newspapers, and the memories of old-timers in the north are fantastic accounts of endurance and determination. Possibly the greatest of these sagas, easily the most unusual, and certainly the most pathetic, was that of a Russian girl, Lillian Alling, who walked some 5,000 miles from New York City to the Bering Sea. Her incredible hike took her through Chicago, St. Paul, Winnipeg and Vancouver. Then she trudged up the Cariboo Wagon Road, through Prince George, then west to Hazelton. From here she walked northwestward for 1,000 miles across mountain passes via the Yukon Telegraph Trail to Dawson City, then down the Yukon River to the Bering Sea. "I go to Siberia," was the answer she gave to all questions about the reason for her trek. In all, she was four years on her solitary journey and whether she finally triumphed or perished in the mist-shrouded Bering Sea, or on the coast of Alaska or Siberia, no one knows.

Her past, and the strange compulsion which drove her to continue this venture of madness against every obstacle of man, plus nature at its worst, remains wrapped in mystery. Throughout all the days, months, and years of her walking, mystery surrounded her. People ranging from telegraph linemen to policemen, magistrate to prison warden tried to help her, or in her own best interest, hinder her from continuing her fantastic trek. She confided in none of them, and refused to listen to those who tried to convince her that the trek was foolish and very likely would be disastrous. "I go to Siberia," she told them all, simply and with conviction.

At the very outset, among the hurrying millions of New York City from where she started, only these sparse facts are known: She was twenty-five years old and came from Russia, but why she came, how long she stayed, why she started for Siberia, we know nothing. We know she worked as a maid, spoke good English, and despite her occupation, apparently was well educated. She told the B.C. Provincial Police that, when after months of work she was still unable to save enough for steamer fare back to Russia, she decided to walk. She explained that she had studied books and maps in the New York Library and had drawn a rough outline of her journey, an outline which the Police thought a remarkable example of cartography on the part of one untrained. When the Police Officer at Hazelton told her of the impossibility of her plan, she replied: "There is only one big difficulty; the fifty miles of Bering Strait. I cannot walk that, but I will cross."

Apparently she must have left New York early in the spring of 1927, because on September 10 she arrived at 2nd Cabin on the Yukon Telegraph Line which angled northeastward through mountain wilderness some 1,000 miles from Hazelton to Dawson City. On the first portion of her journey she had walked an average of thirty miles a day, a gruelling pace that was repeated even in the rough going of woods and mountain. In fact, her stamina and determination continually amazed the experienced telegrapher-linesmen, whose cabins every twenty to thirty miles guarded the wire. Her determination also amazed the Provincial Policeman who tried to bar her path.

During the earlier portion of her trek she was plainly and neatly dressed in brown skirt and shirt waist, plus stout walking boots. She also wore a scarf head-dress, common to Russian peasant women, and carried a small knapsack on her back. As she trudged across hundreds of miles of prairies and rolling rangelands, through the Rocky Mountains, over the Cariboo Plateau and into Northern B.C., her clothing became more and more trail worn. When she finally reached 2nd Cabin on the Telegraph Trail north of Hazelton, her skirt was in rags, shirt waist torn, and boots replaced with running shoes through which her bare feet showed.

With hospitality for which they were famous, the telegrapher at the cabin fed her from his own provisions, then asked her where she was going. "Siberia," she replied without hesitation. The operator realized that she was in no condition, physical or clothing-wise, to continue her trek through nearly 1,000 miles of mountainous country to Dawson City and the end of the line. He sat down and wired Constable J. A. Wyman at Provincial Police headquarters in Hazelton and informed him of the woman's condition. "And she says she's going to Siberia!" was his incredulous comment.

Wyman was an officer experienced in the wilderness. He knew September marked the beginning of bad travelling weather on the mountain trails. Winter was fast approaching, north winds were waiting to swoop down from Alaska with death-bringing blizzards, and fog already hung low over the mountains beyond 9th Cabin, a region where even hardy linesmen could get lost. The constable instructed the telegrapher to keep the woman at 2nd Cabin until he arrived.

Wyman brought her back from 2nd Cabin, although she pleaded to be permitted to continue, then defiantly protested, but finally she yielded without the officer having to use force. At Hazelton headquarters, Wyman turned Lillian over to the District Officer, Sergeant W. J. Service. Again, in answer to a question about her destination, she promptly replied, "Siberia."

Service gazed almost in awe at the woman. She was ragged, wraithlike from the effects of little food and her 3,000-mile hike. Her gaunt features and frame cried aloud of malnutrition. Kindly, Service strove to dissuade her. He pointed out the nearness of winter, and warned her that she endangered her life in going on. When she repeated her intention, he said, "In the clothes you are wearing you will freeze to death; and you are without food."

Her reply was astounding. "I have three loaves of bread and some tea. I must go. Please do not stop me." As she spoke, her eyes pleaded compellingly, suggesting to the seasoned frontiersman a motive akin to madness.

Sergeant Service was in a difficult position. Had he the legal right to prevent a peaceful citizen walking in a free country? Out of the kindness of his heart towards this strange foreign female, to prevent her from committing certain suicide, he hit upon a plan — he arrested her for vagrancy. In a cell the Police matron searched Lillian. She had two $10 bills, and under her skirt dangled a thin iron bar eighteen inches long. When, a few minutes later, the Sergeant remarked to Lillian the bar would be useless against wild animals, she answered curtly, "It's protection against men."

She little realized then how considerately and gallantly in the near future the telegrapher-linesmen on the lonely British Columbia-Yukon Telegraph Trail would treat her, and that the bar was the last equipment she needed.

Brought before Justice of the Peace W. Grant in Hazelton Police Court on September 21, 1927, Lillian was charged with vagrancy. However, the very fact that she had $20, and was on a peaceful walk, made doubtful the strict legality of the charge. However, Magistrate Grant, moved by the same humane intention as the Provincial Police to prevent the woman's folly at this time of year, overcame the legal technicality in her favor by one of his own. He fined her $25 and costs for carrying an offensive weapon!

As her bankroll was limited to $20, making it impossible for her to pay the fine, he gave her the alternative sentence of two months in Oakalla Prison at Vancouver.

Thus Lillian was saved her $20, and assured of free, reasonably decent food and lodging until even she would realize it was impossible to continue, at least for the time being, the hazardous trail leading across British Columbia and Yukon to Siberia. Also, in the mind of the magistrate, was the hope that in the months of confinement Lillian would have time for reflection and forego her folly. But such wasn't the case.

When released from Oakalla Prison the second week in November she obtained kitchen work in a Vancouver restaurant. By the end of May she apparently had saved enough money since she again headed northward. By now the story of the girl's hike had spread throughout the Provincial Police force and at the end of June 1928, Sergeant A. Fairbairn at Smithers received a wire that Lillian was heading his way. To his astonishment she reached Smithers on July 19. Fairbairn made a rough calculation and realized that she had averaged between thirty and forty miles a day. "Did people give you a ride in their cars," he asked?

"I walked all the way," she answered with proud dignity. "I go to Siberia," she added, in an emphatic tone.

Fairbairn looked out of the window. There remained half of July, August, and early September that she might expect good weather. By then, he reasoned, she would probably be over the worst of the mountain passes on the Telegraph Trail and into the Yukon. Since there was no ground on which he could prevent her, he let her continue, but asked her to report to each of the Cabins on the Yukon Telegraph.

"I will do that," she said, with great fervor, and with thanks went on her way.

After she left, Fairbairn wired the personnel on the Telegraph Line, requesting that they keep a watch for her. Consequently, each operator reported her progress from Cabin to Cabin, carefully checking her pace and always amazed at her progress. The trail wound up and down valleys, across mountain sidehills, through mud and swamp and rough terrain in general, but the wiry girl maintained an average of twenty to thirty miles a day.

Cabins 1 to 7 reported her safe arrival and departure, and shortly after she reached 8th Cabin. Here two men, Jim Christie and Charlie Janze, were stationed as linesmen and telegrapher, and occupied a cabin each. They were appalled at Lillian's appearance. Her clothes were in shreds, shoes very worn. Her face was swollen from continuous bites of mosquitoes, bulldog, black and no-see-um flies, and badly burned by sun and wind. Yet it was the manner in which she dropped her nearly empty packsack and slumped into a chair which conveyed to the men how exhausted and hungry she was.

But despite her worn-out condition and beaten look, she shrugged off the men's attempts to persuade her not to continue. Finally they realized that the only thing that could stop her was death itself, and they gave her every assistance they could. In the next three days while she rested in the cabin which Christie had turned over to her and ate enormous meals, the two men achieved a miracle of outfitting.

They remodelled a pair of Janze's breeches which were of toughest cloth. Janze, the smaller of the two men, gave her two shirts, his best, and a new handkerchief for the head-dress she had always worn, and a felt hat over it to keep off the rain. He also gave her a pair of his stout boots, which with two pair of socks, Lillian could comfortably wear.

At this point, the popular accounts of Lillian Alling's hike differ from what actually happened. Many stories state that just before she left, Christie gave her his black and white dog, Bruno, as a companion. The same accounts state that she was deeply affected by the dog and remarked, "My first companion, he will always remain with me." Later, when she arrived at Atlin she carried on top of her knapsack the hide of the dog, lightly stuffed with grass. Supposedly, it had drowned while crossing a stream and she was keeping her promise to Christie that "... he will always remain with me."

One man who disagrees with this version is Cyril J. Tooley, who was relieving Bob Quinn at Echo Lake during the time of Lillian's hike. Because of a tragedy which befell his partner, Scotty Ogilvie, who had set out to help Lillian, Mr. Tooley became deeply involved in the sad drama that was about to unfold and remembers it well.

"I have read several articles relating to the dog incident," he wrote, "and in all cases they have errors in continuity and other things. For instance, Christie never had a dog called Bruno. His was called Coyote but he did not give it to Lillian; another lineman gave her one. But let's go back to 8th Cabin and take things in sequence.

"When Lillian left 8th Cabin, Christie accompanied her over the Naas Summit on past 9th Cabin to the cabin twenty-seven miles south of Echo Lake. Meanwhile, Scotty Ogilvie and I at Echo Lake were preparing to offer what assistance we could. Scotty loaded up his two dogs and went to meet her. I tidied up the cabin and was then required to go north on some line trouble.

"After clearing the trouble I called Echo Lake from a cabin which was about eight miles north of the Station but didn't get an answer. I then contacted Jack Wrathall, the Wire Chief, at Telegraph Creek. He advised me that Scotty had not reported in since leaving Echo Lake in the early morning and I had better hit the trail as early as possible the next day.

"I became very concerned about my partner. Conditions were the worst possible since it had poured with rain all week and the streams were in flood. Even with the greatest of care accidents could easily happen and, tragically, this proved to be the case.

"I headed out early next morning for the 7-Mile Refuge Cabin south of Echo Lake. On arrival I found Scotty's two dogs huddled on the stoop, their packs still on but soaking wet and torn. I attended to the dogs but they would not accompany me so I proceeded up the Ningunsaw River to our usual crossing place. Scotty's and the dogs' tracks were easy to follow to where Scotty had tried to cross the river. Here the bank had caved in and it looked to me as if he and the dogs were catapulted into the river when the bank collapsed. I went back to 7-Mile, called Telegraph Creek and then Jim Christie. I eventually got Jim and told him I thought I could make it over the river, and for him to leave the girl at 27-Mile and I would meet him at what we called 'Misery Cabin' the next morning. We met as agreed and proceeded north to the Ningunsaw River. Because of the flooding there were several channels and we had to make bridges by falling trees and moving logs.

"While looking for bridge-building material, I was shocked to see Scotty's body wedged against a cottonwood tree in one of the channels. With heavy hearts, Jim Christie and I moved the body to a small island in mid-stream. Scotty had apparently struck his head when he fell in and had broken his neck. We wrapped him in a Hudson's Bay blanket and canvas, made a stretcher and with difficulty carried him to the bank. Here, with a prayer and great sadness, we committed his remains to the grave.

"It was now quite late in the day and pouring with rain. We headed for 27-Mile Cabin and arrived late at night, looking like a couple of drowned rats. Luckily, Lillian had a good fire going and with a hot meal we felt better, although neither of us could get Scotty off our minds.

"The next morning at 27-Mile, Jim Christie and Lillian Alling said goodbye, Jim heading back for 8th Cabin, Lillian and I turning north for the river crossing and 7-Mile Refuge Cabin, where we arrived late in the afternoon. Early the next morning I left for Echo Lake since I was needed to instruct a Trail-and-Line crew where necessary repairs were required. One of the crew went to meet Lillian and bring her to Echo Lake Station where she rested overnight. Like us, she was deeply moved by the tragedy.

"The next morning she had much help and instruction from the men assembled there. It was at this time that Tommy Hankin loaned her his black and white husky lead dog, Bruno. Tommy gave explicit instructions on how to put the dog's pack on properly, and also stressed that under no circumstances must she let him run free between 27-Mile north and the Iskut River. This was a trapping area and there were quite a number of poison sets out for wolverine. Bruno must have eluded her just south of the Iskut because he just made it to the Iskut River, took a drink and keeled over dead. This news was telegraphed to us at Echo Lake by Moose McKay who witnessed this additional tragedy from the north shore of the Iskut River.

"Lillian stayed at the Iskut Cabin for a day and then headed north but she didn't have Bruno's hide. It would have taken a skilled person several days to prepare a hide since it would have had to be tanned so that it could be carried during several weeks of hot weather.

"From Iskut she apparently made good progress once she reached the open country north of Telegraph Creek. We listened on the line and were able to follow her progress from Cabin to Cabin, and we all wished her the best of luck.

"I hope that this account will set the historical record straight," Mr. Tooley concluded.

Lillian arrived in Atlin some time in August and then headed to Whitehorse. On August 31, 1928, the following news item appeared in the *Whitehorse Star:* "A woman giving the name of Lillian Alling walked into town Monday evening and registered at the Regina Hotel. Lillian was not given to much speaking but as near as can be gathered from information she gave at different places she had walked from Hazelton to Whitehorse, a distance of about 600 miles, following the government telegraph.

"However nothing is reported of her until she reached Atlin, where she tarried only long enough to buy a pair of shoes. At Tagish she was taken over the river by Ed Barrett. On Saturday last she arrived in Carcross and had a meal at the Caribou Hotel.

"She left Carcross the same afternoon, travelling in a northerly direction. On Sunday afternoon Mr. and Mrs. George Wilson overtook her between Carcross and Robinson and she rode in the car with them as far as Robinson, where she got out, saying that she was going to rest a while. Beyond saying that she was going a little north of Whitehorse she had very little to say. She did say, however, that for a part of her journey she had a pack dog but that he was drowned in crossing a stream. When warned that she would have streams to cross between here and Dawson she said that she would cross them on a log. She told Mr. Erickson that she did not have much money, and she seemed to be conserving her resources but paying her way. She had no means whatever of killing wild game and was

Lillian was last seen beyond Teller, above, a coastal community near the point where Alaska and Siberia are closest.

The top photo shows 8th Cabin where Lillian rested three days while Christie and Janze made her new clothing. The center photo shows Echo Lake Station with lineman Tommy Hankin at right. From this Station, Scotty Ogilvie headed to meet Lillian and death in the Ningunsaw River.

144

carrying very little food. If she knows her destination she is not telling but she started north from Whitehorse on the Dawson trail Tuesday forenoon."

As she trudged toward Dawson, the newspaper carried reports of her progress, referring to her as "The Mystery Woman."

"SEPTEMBER 7, 1928. The last report of the mystery woman was that she was seen by H. Chambers some distance east of Tahkinna several days after she left here. Mr. Chambers offered to give her a ride to the fork of the road but she declined."

"SEPTEMBER 14, 1928. Word reached Whitehorse that the mystery woman passed through Carmacks but she maintained her silence. Some time later she arrived at Yukon Crossing where she allowed H.O. Lokken to put her over the river. She still had the Pelly and Stewart rivers to negotiate."

"OCTOBER 19, 1928. Mystery Woman Reaches Dawson. From the time of the first account of the Mystery Woman in the Whitehorse Star, the people of Dawson have been looking forward with an unusual degree of curiosity for her arrival there.

"At Carmacks she made some meagre purchases and continued her journey; at Yukon Crossing H. O. Lokken put her over the river in a small boat; at Pelly Crossing A. Shafer performed a similar service for her; at Stewart T. A. Dickson's survey party was camped and the boys cared for her for three days during a bad storm, and from this point she went down the river in a small boat to Dawson, arriving there in the morning of October 5th. She left Whitehorse on the morning of August 28 and as far as was known the only provisions she had was a loaf of bread, which she had cut in three pieces, as she said she was not carrying a knife.

"Thirty nine days were spent between here and Dawson and practically all that time she must have slept in the open. Upon reaching Dawson she had a different style of men's shoe on each foot."

How she survived the trek from Whitehorse to Dawson without adequate food, clothing or shelter is another mystery for in the Yukon October nights are short and the days cold. In Dawson she found employment as a waitress, living alone and confiding in no one. Somewhere she got a cheap, battered skiff and occupied herself repairing it and waiting impatiently for spring.

At break-up she loaded her flimsy craft with provisions and blanket roll. Then she launched it and bobbed down the mighty Yukon — a wraith-like wisp of a woman embarked on a 1,600-mile journey to the Bering Sea.

She reached the mouth of the Yukon safely, then on the windswept coast of the Bering Sea she left her boat on the beach and trudged into the Arctic vastness. Months later an Eskimo reported meeting a woman beyond Teller, a coastal outpost near the point where Alaska and Siberia are closest. She was slowly tugging a small two-wheeled cart. After that encounter there was silence.

Did Lillian, by Eskimo or other boat, cross Bering Strait to at long last reach her Russian destination? Or somewhere on that bleak shoreline, or in the icy waters of an Arctic Strait, did she perish, writing *finis* to a saga unique in northern annals? No one can say.

Then, in 1972, I wrote an account of her hike for *True West* magazine. One of the persons who read it was Arthur F. Elmore of Lincoln, California, who wrote the following letter to the editor:

"After reading the article I decided to write because of a very peculiar incident that occurred back in 1965 when I was a visitor in Yakutsk, Eastern Siberia.

"I had been invited by a Russian ex-Army man, with whom I had become quite good friends in Mukden, Manchuria during the closing days of World War II, to come and visit if ever I got the chance. The opportunity finally came in April 1965 when the Cold War had thawed, so I went to San Francisco where I secured passage to Moscow. In Moscow I then flew to Yakutsk where I located my friend.

"It seems he, like I, enjoys mysteries, and one day while exploring around (as much as one was permitted to do) he suddenly asked what I considered a very strange question. 'If I were in America, how would I be treated?'

"Somewhat taken aback, I replied, 'In what way do you mean? What makes you ask that?' Then he told me the following incident.

"As a very young boy — somewhere around fourteen or fifteen — he had lived in a very small community in the Soviet Far East named Provideniya, which is about 170 or 180 miles from the present town of Wales, Alaska across the Bering Strait. He stated that late one afternoon while on an errand for his mother he saw a crowd gathered on the waterfront and several official-looking men were present, questioning a woman and three Eskimo men. He said he recognized that the Eskimos were from the Diomede Islands in the Strait by their dress but the woman was differently dressed, like a European or American.

"He remembered the woman telling the officials she had come from America where she said she had been unable to make a living or make friends (of necessity I'm condensing much of what I was told to save space). She said she had had to walk 'a terrible long way because no one would lift as much as a finger to help me in any way because they didn't want to — or couldn't understand — my feelings. I tried to make friends at first, but everybody wanted no part of me — as a foreigner — and that so deeply hurt me I couldn't bear it and so I began to walk. I knew it was far and would be hard but I had to do it even if no one understood. And I did it!'

"He told me he saw the girl and the Eskimos led away — he never saw them again — but the memory was to linger with him always. He also stated all this took place in the fall of 1930 — he was very positive of the date because he stated his parents and his family were moved two years later farther westward to a place named Ust Yansk where his father fished commercially.

"For several years all of this sort of haunted me — all mysteries do, in one way or another — but I never could figure out any answer. Then this past week I happened to pick up your magazine, and saw the article.

"Now I'm really curious! Is it possible that that girl with the three Eskimos could have been Lillian Alling? The Eskimos were definitely dressed as the Eskimos of the Little and Big Diomede Islands do. The only thing is — no black and white dog was visible or I'm very certain my friend would have said so. Anyway, knowing the people and the country as well as I do — I've spent nearly two-thirds of my life in Alaska — I'm very, very sure Lillian Alling made it! (Though, of course, I have no proof.)"

DAVID DOUGLAS ...pioneer botanist

after whom the Douglas fir is named. He is one of our least known explorers, yet between 1825-27 he walked over 7,000 miles through the unexplored wilderness of the Pacific Northwest.

by ROBERT F. HARRINGTON

Monuments are of many types. Some are sculptured stone, others are hammered brass, still others are gold leafed. They are usually substantial where men of importance are concerned and they tend to be few in number. But David Douglas, the son of a Scots stonemason, is commemorated by monuments that are neither stone nor gold, nor few in number. Almost every garden in Europe and North America is a tribute to the man, as is much of the forest of the Pacific Northwest since the Douglas fir is named after him.

What did a man of so humble birth do to earn this honor? For one thing in a life that was to be tragically short he became one of the leading botanists of his day; for another, he walked, usually alone and in a hostile land. On one of his North American expeditions he walked, according to itemized accounts in his journal, a total of 7,032 miles in the collecting seasons of 1825-26-27. He walked in cold rains in the spring along the coast. He walked in brilliant sunshine and blasting heat over desert sands and was nearly blinded. He walked up through B.C. to Fort St. James and was nearly drowned. He walked over mountain passes and through river valleys, and while he walked he collected thousands of plant specimens. Much of the time he walked alone with Billy, his terrier, as a companion.

Of his dog, Douglas wrote: "My old terrier, a most faithful and now to judge from his long grey beard, venerable friend, who has guarded me throughout all my journeys, and whom, should I live to return, I mean certainly to pension off on four pennyworth of cat's meat per day."

On his walks he collected plants by the hundreds and shipped them to England. Cones, seeds, even birds were also collected, carefully labelled and sent to the Old World. The result of all this is perhaps best expressed in the words of an admirer of Douglas who stated, "to no single individual is modern horticulture more intended...." Some 215 plants were introduced to cultivation by the doughty Scots botanist, plants which include

David Douglas and, opposite page, a stand of Douglas fir in Cathedral Grove Park on Vancouver Island.

the white fir, noble fir, vine maple, Douglas fir, Oregon grape, hawthorn, salal, three species of honeysuckle, twenty-one species of lupine, native tobacco, Sitka spruce, sugar pine, Western white pine, sand cherry, black raspberry, bear grass and evergreen huckleberry.

David Douglas was born on June 25, 1799 in the village of Old Scone, Perthshire, Scotland. At an early age he was regarded as a high-spirited child, displaying his dislike for confinement by playing truant from school. His natural inclination led him to prefer the study of nature to the dull lessons of the classroom. Collecting plants, birds' eggs, live birds and other treasures of nature were stimuli enough to cause him to suffer the schoolmaster's lash on more than one occasion.

His formal education, as such, came to an end before he was twelve, but his interest in plants earned him an apprenticeship at Scone Palace gardens. His aptitude there provided him an opportunity to obtain a position on the staff of the Glasgow Botanic Garden. Here he became a

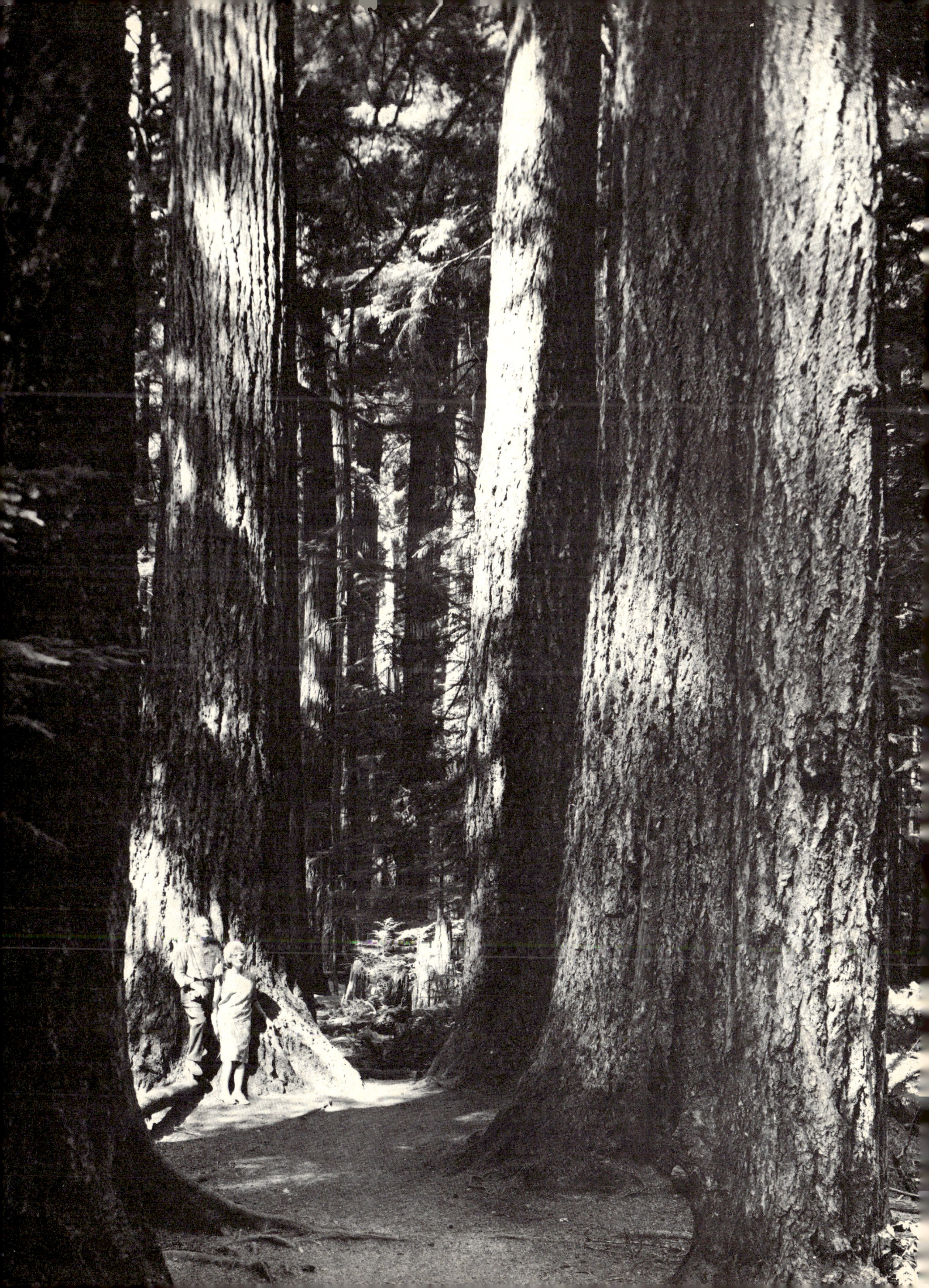

pupil and lifelong friend of Dr. William Jackson Hooker, Regius Professor of Botany at Glasgow University. Hooker observed Douglas closely during collecting trips to the Scottish Highlands and Islands, and was sufficiently impressed to recommend his pupil to the Royal Horticultural Society of London for a plant-collecting trip to the United States and Upper Canada as far west as Amherstberg. The wealth of specimens and information gained by Douglas on this first six-month trip in 1823 caused the official publication of the Royal Horticultural Society to report: "This mission was executed by Mr. Douglas with a success beyond expectation." The pattern of Douglas' future life was set.

Life's great adventures perhaps began for Douglas when on April 7, 1825, the Hudson's Bay Company's ship *William and Ann* crossed the dangerous sandbar at the mouth of the Columbia River and anchored in Baker's Bay. Even before landing, Douglas noted hemlock, balsam fir, and "a species which may prove to be P. Taxifolia." This species, later to be known as Douglas fir, had been known in England since 1795 from twig specimens brought back by Archibald Menzies, surgeon-naturalist with Captain Vancouver. It remained for Douglas, however, to collect cone specimens and seeds from which the tree was grown in England.

To the young botanist the country was awesome. He found the scenery "sublime" and marveled at "mountains covered with perpetual snow." In his words: "The most remarkable mountains are Mt. Hood, St. Helena, Vancouver and Jefferson, which are at all seasons covered with snow as low down as the summit of the hills by which they are surrounded."

For six months he collected along the Columbia between the river mouth and Celilo Falls, 220 miles inland, as well as on the Multnomah (now Willamette) River. Evidence of his diligence is the fact that in this period he collected 499 different specimens, including Camas, the root of which was used by Indians as an important food item (among other uses, camas root was ground into flour). He also collected over 100 varieties of seeds, including Clarkia and various species of Penstemon and Ribes.

Throughout his wandering he continued to come across the tree later to be his namesake. Sometimes these trees were of prodigious size and he found difficulty in reaching the cones with the buckshot as he attempted to collect them by shooting them off the trees. One fallen tree that he measured was 227 feet long and 48 feet in girth at a height of three feet above the ground. He referred to the (Douglas) fir as "one of the most striking and truly graceful objects in nature." His appreciation of its commercial utility is evidenced in his comment: "The wood may be found very useful for a variety of domestic purposes; the young, slender ones exceedingly well adapted for making ladders and scaffold poles, not being liable to cast; the larger timber for more important purposes, while at the same time the rosin may be found deserving attention."

Not the least of his efforts on this first trip to the western part of the continent was his search toward California for the sugar pine. Douglas had found Indians along the Willamette eating nutlike seeds of a pine they said grew further south. A cone presented to him by Baptiste McKay excited his interest even more as the cone was seventeen inches long and ten inches in circumference at its greatest width.

An opportunity to visit the area where it grew, in company with a group under Chief Trader Alexander McLeod, provided him with the chance to see the tree himself. On a tributary of the Umpqua River, Douglas found a new golden leafed chestnut, Western Chinquapin. The sugar pine proved hard to find and his first venture after the elusive tree ended in dismal failure. When the chance to find the sugar pine finally did come, near present day Cleveland, Oregon, it was not without danger of losing his life. His shooting attracted eight Indians who seemed menacing and as Douglas states: "I stood eight or ten minutes looking at them and they at me without a word passing, till one at last, who seemed to be the leader, made a sign for tobacco, which I said they should get on condition of going and fetching me some cones. They went and as soon as out of sight I picked up my three cones and a few twigs, and made a quick retreat to my camp, which I gained at dusk."

By mid-March 1827, Douglas was ready to begin the return trip to England. He set off overland with the Hudson's Bay express for Hudson Bay from where he could

In 1833 Douglas walked 1,150 miles from Fort Vancouver, at top in 1853, to Fort St. James, shown above when Douglas visited it. The Fort was typical of those built by the H.B.C. throughout the northwest.

return to England by ship. At Fort Colville, enroute, Douglas was chagrined to have dogs destroy two grouse which he had collected and preserved. As he remarked in his journal, one of them had been carried on his back 457 miles and the other 304 miles.

From Fort Colville the express proceeded toward Athabasca Pass via the Arrow Lakes. Dangerous Dallas des Morts (Death Rapids), was passed and the party continued to Boat Encampment where they cached the boat and proceeded on foot. Icy streams had to be forded as the journey progressed toward the famed pass in the Rockies. Enroute, Douglas was able to preserve a bird which he later named Franklin's grouse *(Tetrao Franklini)* in honor of the Arctic explorer, Captain John Franklin. The bird he preserved in Athabasca Pass is presently in the Royal Scottish Museum at Edinburgh.

While in the Rockies he made the first recorded ascent of any of the peaks in the Rockies, climbing a mountain he named Mt. Brown, after Robert Brown of the botanical department of the British Museum. Another mountain nearby he named Mt. Hooker, after his teacher and friend, William Jackson Hooker. Because of the fact that he greatly overestimated the height of Athabasca Pass (at 12,000 feet instead of the actual 5,720 feet), the elevations he assigned Mts. Hooker and Brown caused them to be shown as gargantuan peaks on a number of early maps. By foot, horse, and canoe the party proceeded on to Hudson Bay, and Douglas sailed for England on September 15th.

In England, he was welcomed by the Horticultural Society in somewhat the manner of a returning hero. Already he had introduced into England more plants than any one individual had ever introduced from a single country. Furthermore, they were such plants as could thrive in the climate of England. It was reported to the Council of the Society "that Mr. Douglas has throughout his mission acted in the most satisfactory manner and that nothing could surpass the zeal and spirit with which he had executed the trust that he had undertaken." The Society was perhaps happy also to note that Douglas' entire trip had cost less than $2,000, including his wages.

In all, Douglas spent two years in England, during which time he was feted and honored with membership in learned societies. Toward the end of this period his friends noted that he was becoming nervous and irascible. There is little question that he welcomed a new assignment which enabled him to return to his work in North America, this time better equipped to determine geographical positions and elevations. On June 3, 1830, he returned to the Columbia, remained nineteen months, went back to England, and returned again in October, 1832.

His ambitious plan at this time was to go north to Fort St. James and then proceed west to Siberia and return to England across Siberia and Europe. Although he realized that his proposed venture might be doomed to frustration, he set out on March 20, 1833 for Fort St. James, an 1,150 mile jaunt from Fort Vancouver. His trip took him first with the H.B.C. express to Fort Okanagan, then by horse up the Okanagan Valley to Fort Kamloops. At Fort Kamloops fresh horses were secured and the trip continued to Fort Alexandria on the Fraser River. The remainder of the journey was by boat up the Fraser, Nechako and Stuart Rivers.

The trip northward was not without incident. Douglas didn't agree with the policies of the H.B.C. and was not afraid to express his thoughts. Samuel Black was then in command of Fort Kamloops. While enjoying the lonely hospitality of his brother Scot, Douglas, who was more fiery than politic, exclaimed: "The Hudson's Bay Company is simply a mercenary corporation; there is not an officer in it with a soul above a beaver-skin."

Black was aroused in a moment. He informed his guest that he was a sneaking reprobate and challenged him to fight. As it was then dark the duel was postponed until next day. Bright and early in the morning, Black tapped at the pierced parchment which served as a window to the guest chamber and cried out: "Misther Douglas! are ye ready?" But the man of flowers declined the invitation. Black later lost his life tragically, being killed by an Indian.

At Fort St. James, the difficulty of proceeding to the Russian fort at Sitka on Baranoff Island became apparent to Douglas. To reach Sitka would require 500 miles of travel along poorly known trails and rivers to reach Fort Simpson at the mouth of the Nass River and another 300 miles from there to Sitka. Realizing the great rigors that would be involved, Douglas turned back toward the Columbia, staying a day or two at Fort George and then beginning the descent of the Fraser.

Enroute down the Fraser, Douglas nearly lost his life when the canoe which he and William Johnson were using was wrecked on a small rocky island in Fort George Canyon. Douglas was carried into a whirlpool and swept about for an hour and forty minutes before being washed out onto shore. Some 400 species of plants he had collected were lost, as well as food and blankets, a genuine tragedy to a man of his nature.

The remainder of his journey back to Fort Vancouver was without incident. Although he apparently saw Samuel Black again, no evidence of the earlier quarrel is presented in his diary. About the interior of B.C. he recorded: "The interior, north of the Columbia, for the space of nearly 4° of latitude and 7° of longitude is a beautiful and varied country; the soil is generally fertile; and even to a much higher latitude is well worth looking after."

Although Douglas still entertained the possibility of going on to Sitka via ship, he decided instead to return home via the Sandwich Islands. He arrived in Honolulu in December, 1833 and spent the next few months exploring the island of Hawaii. He was probably one of the first men to climb the peaks of Mauna Loa and Mauna Kea. A large amount of his time he spent collecting some 2,000 species of ferns, 90 of which were new to science.

In August of 1834, while crossing the island with his dog, Billy, he fell into a wild cattle pit and was gored to death. His body was found by natives passing the pit later in the day. Billy was found guarding his equipment a short distance away on the path to Hilo. Some speculation of murder was entertained, but no conclusive evidence indicated that death was caused by a human agent.

The scientific world of the time was horrified by his death. Although he was only thirty-five when he died, his contribution to science is on display in gardens across the world. More fitting, the Douglas fir, the tree which he felt was "one of the most striking and graceful objects in nature" and which "may be found very useful for a variety of domestic purposes" has fulfilled the predictions he made for it some 150 years ago. ∎

Tales The Totems Tell

Contrary to common belief, totem poles have nothing to do with religion. The carved figures are taken from the mythology and legendary history of the various tribes.

by B.C. GOVT. TRAVEL BUREAU

For many centuries before its discovery by Europeans, the coast of British Columbia was the home of a large population of native Indian people. Kept in isolation by great mountain ranges and broad expanses of ocean, they were little affected by the rise of civilizations elsewhere. But they were a vigorous and inventive people, living in an environment of great richness, and they readily developed an advanced and complex pattern of living distinctively their own, unique in its values and outlook, rich in the material and artistic products of its energies. Probably the best-known accomplishment of this culture was its grotesque but highly sophisticated art style, which has come to be recognized as one of the great primitive art styles of the world. A wood-carver's art, it found its most striking expression in the great carved and painted wooden columns commonly called totem poles, made by all the coastal tribes of British Columbia and Southern Alaska, and by a few adjacent tribes as well. No other peoples of the world made carvings of identical meaning and conception.

The many Indian groups of the coast of British Columbia fall into six language divisions, which are loosely called tribes.

In the north, the Haida occupied Queen Charlotte Islands and part of Prince of Wales Island. The Tsimshian lived along the Nass and Skeena Rivers and the mainland shores of Hecate Strait. Kwakiutl-speaking groups held the long fiords of the mainland coast from Douglas Channel south almost to Bute Inlet, as well as the northern quarter of Vancouver Island. The Bella Coola, speaking a Salish language related to those farther south, occupied Dean and Burke Channels and the valleys of the rivers which flow into them. Finally, a large number of groups speaking interrelated languages, the Coast Salish, occupied southeastern Vancouver Island and the adjacent mainland inlets, the Lower Fraser Valley, and adjacent areas in the United States. Growing populations of all these tribes still inhabit the old tribal areas, and all of the languages are still spoken.

To appreciate and understand totem poles, one must have a knowledge of the customs, beliefs, and art style of the people who made them. The following is a brief sketch of the origin, economy, technology, social customs, religion, mythology, and art of the Coast Indians.

Perhaps 5,000 years ago wandering migrants, whose ancestors had crossed Bering Strait from Asia, filtered through the interior plateaus or along the coast and became the first settlers on this rich shoreline. They were joined from time to time by later migrants, more recent immigrants from Siberia, who formed the basis of a population more "Mongoloid" in appearance than most American Indians. That these migrants were of diverse origins is evident from the fact that nine Indian languages, or four distinct linguistic families, are spoken on the coast of British Columbia.

These coast dwellers oriented their whole lives to the sea, and reaped a rich bounty from ocean, beach, and stream. In fleet dugout canoes they chased and harpooned

The Thunderbird, above, a powerful and awesome creature of Indian mythology, was a common crest used on totem poles.

At left are totems in the Indian village of Kispiox at the junction of the Kispiox and Skeena Rivers.

151

seals, porpoises, sea-lions, and on the beaches they gathered even (among the Nootka) whales, shellfish and seaweeds. In the bays and streams they caught the teeming runs of fish, using harpoons, hooks, nets, weirs, and traps. They did not ignore the land and its wild products, but trapped and hunted many land animals and birds, and rounded out their diet with wild fruits, roots, nuts, and green shoots. In a rich environment, they had an economy of plenty.

Many inventions did not reach them because of their isolation. They had no agriculture, no domesticated animals (except the dog), no writing, no smelting or casting of metals. They got along without such things as a priesthood, political leaders, footwear, tailored clothing, tobacco, and the axe.

But using the material they found around them, they evolved a superior technology. On the soft, straight-grained wood of the cedar tree they based their highest skill — woodworking. Their large, rectangular houses — the best on the continent — were made of split cedar planks lashed or fitted on a framework of cedar posts and beams. These they located in a line along the shore. Drawn up in front of the houses, they kept their long, graceful canoes. in which they did almost all of their travelling — seasonal movements, fishing and hunting trips, visits, war expeditions. They made many sizes of canoes, all carved out of single cedar logs with fire and adze, and most with the sides steamed and spread to increase their beam and improve their seaworthiness. For storage, cooking, and other containers they made boxes of dressed cedar boards, bent and stitched or pegged with great skill. From the inner bark of the cedar they wove clothing, mats, baskets, sails; from cedar twigs they made rope; from nettle fibre they made lines and nets; from kelp they made fishing lines. Horn was used for spoons and harpoons; bone for fishhooks, arrowheads, awls; stone for knives, chisels, points; and beaver teeth for cutting blades.

Their everyday dress was simple and untailored. Men wore a short apron and a blanket or robe; women, a skirt and blanket. Among the wealthy, the robes were sewn of sea otter or other furs, or woven of mountain-goat wool (or among some Coast Salish, the hair of a special breed of dog). Others wove robes of cedar bark and conical hats with flared brims of spruce roots. Most people went barefoot the year round.

Their complex social system laid great stress on relative rank, which was maintained by displays of wealth,and on systems of kinship and inheritance. The great range of social standing between the highest- and lowest-ranking tribesmen was usually divided into three classes. The rich lineage and clan heads and their close relatives formed a "nobility." More distant relatives and other members of the tribe were "commoners," and captive members of outside groups and their descendants formed a permanent class of slaves. Sometimes the highest chiefs were considered to be a separate class above the nobility. Since rank was inherited and marriages were contracted only with persons of equal rank, these classes had a tendency to become permanent.

Though inherited, rank had to be maintained by displaying great wealth. This was not difficult for the heads of large kinship groups, as they controlled the groups' wealth. Wealth consisted partly of economic privileges — the ownership of salmon streams, clam beaches, berry patches, and so on. But more wealth consisted of non-material privileges — the exclusive ownership of important names, legends, songs, dances, ceremonies, and crests to carve on totem poles and other belongings. To display and pass on ownership of these forms of wealth it was necessary to give great feasts, or public ceremonies, called potlatches, at which large numbers of important guests had to be given gifts for witnessing the event. Thus potlatching brought prestige, and was the main mechanism for maintaining high social rank.

The bonds of kinship were extended to form groups larger than the family; namely, the clans and phratries. The members of a clan believed themselves to be related because they had common traditions tracing back to the same place of origin, from which the clan usually took its name. Each clan had its own stock of names, positions of rank, traditions, songs, and crests, which were passed down within the clan according to strict laws of inheritance. Among the Haida and Tsimshian, for example, a boy belonged to his mother's clan and inherited these things from his mother's brother, not his father. Among other tribes this matrilineal system did not prevail; clan membership and inheritance could be in either line. Phratries, found north of the Kwakiutl, were large groupings of clans which had similar crests. The Haida, for example, were divided into two phratries, the main crests of which were Eagle and Raven. Since members of the same phratry were felt to be related, they were not allowed to intermarry. Every household contained members of both phratries — the husband was in one, the wife and children in the other.

According to the religious thinking of these people, the world was full of spirits — the spirits of animals, plants, and prominent landmarks, and also strange mythical spirit-beings. All spirits could aid or harm man, as they chose. Some, the powerful spirit-creatures, lived in other worlds and were almost deities. By the proper techniques, men could gain power from spirits. Individuals fasted and purified themselves to gain personal power from minor spirits. In this way some became "shamans," or Indian doctors. Groups known as "secret societies" had initiation ceremonies at which members became possessed by the power of the major spirits which patronized the societies. These spirits were represented during society dances by masked figures, although they were not shown on totem poles unless they were also social crests. Totem poles had nothing to do with religion.

It was from the mythology and legendary history of the Indians that the figures carved on totem poles were drawn. Commonly represented were the Raven, Eagle, Thunderbird, Hawk, Bear, Wolf, Whale, Blackfish, Frog, Beaver, and others. Since in the myths these creatures were usually in their human form, they often appear human on the carvings, and can be identified only by certain distinguishing features added to a humanlike face. Actual human characters were also frequently represented. The figures might be well-known mythological creatures which had become the dominant crests of clans or phratries. More often they were characters from traditions

A well-known coastal totem is the Thunderbird at Alert Bay, opposite page. The above photo, taken in 1878, shows the Queen Charlotte Islands village of Skidegate which fronted the Pacific Ocean for nearly half a mile and was a major Haida community. Shown is not only an outstanding display of various totems but also cedar dugout canoes and the Indian houses of split cedar planks.

owned by the family or clan. Some of these were so intimately connected with the clans that they became their crests or identifying marks, but a bewildering variety of other figures was also used since clan members could illustrate any character or incident in the clan's traditions.

It is these crest figures which have been called totems, although in the strictest sense of the word they are not. Most real totems are animals, each of which was thought to have been the ancestor of a clan, which bore its name and revered it.

The art of these people was shaped by all the above factors. Rich resources and a surplus economy allowed leisure time for art to develop. Craftsmanship in woodworking led naturally to experimentation in wood carving and painting. Mythical figures supplied the subject matter; a desire for the social prestige resulting from the display of crests and traditions supplied the incentive. These, combined with man's natural desire for beauty and decoration, led to the development of an art which they applied to almost everything they made — house-fronts, canoes, boxes, screens, masks, staffs, dishes, spoons, blankets, and many other things, as well as totem poles.

A few words should be said about the principles of the art style itself. The whole decorative field was filled up, either by splitting and distorting parts of the figure being represented or by adding "eye," "feather," or other designs as fillers. Certain important features were conventionalized and exaggerated to serve as identifying marks: ears on top of the head identify an animal; beaks identify birds — straight for Raven, curved at the tip for Eagle and Thunderbird, curved back to the mouth for Hawk. The Thunderbird differs from the Eagle (in the art of some tribes) in usually having "horns" on top of its head. Large front teeth and a flat scaly tail identify the Beaver, a blunt face and high dorsal fin identify the Whale, and so on. Faces and heads are usually disproportionately large and carefully carved. Clean, curved lines and "rounded rectangle" forms were preferred. Each tribe had its own substyle, which was to some degree distinctive in treatment and subject matter.

Indians carved and decorated not only totems but face masks, screens, bowls, boxes, dishes and giant canoes such as those above, each hewn from a massive cedar log.

On the opposite page is a replica of a 19th century Kwakiutl House and totem in Victoria's Thunderbird Park. The park and nearby Provincial Museum contain the finest collection of totem poles in existence.

The great variety of totem poles can be classified into types according to their purpose. "Houseposts" were carved posts which supported the main beams of the houses. "House frontal poles" stood flush against the front of houses, displaying crests of the owners and often framing the doorway. "Memorial" and "heraldic" poles usually stood free of the house-front, displaying crests or other carvings of the owner or his predecessor. "Mortuary poles" were constructed to hold the remains of the dead, and stood in front of the houses or in special areas at the end of the village. "Grave-markers" were placed on the burial-sites of important persons.

The different tribes placed varying emphasis on the use of different types of carved poles. In numbers, variety, and artistic skill, the greatest development was found among the Haida. Haida houses were massively constructed and artistically carved. Inside, the main housepost at the rear of the house was carved with crests of the owner. Outside, the front corner posts were sometimes carved as human figures and the projecting ends of the roof beams sculptured in the form of sea-lion heads. Against the front of the house stood the imposing house frontal pole, often more than forty feet high, carved with the crests and legends of the owner and his wife. An oval hole at the base of older poles of this type served as the door. When a Haida chief died, his successor had a mortuary pole carved to hold his remains. This was a massive post with a hollow section near the top for the coffin; the post and the rectangular board in front of the coffin were decorated with the crests of the dead man. Mortuary poles were placed in front of the houses or in a special grave area at the end of the village. Often when a man took over a position of high rank, he raised a memorial pole in front of the house to honor his predecessor. These were usually round poles up to fifty feet high, carved with one or many of the dead man's crest figures, but sometimes they were massive replicas of mortuary poles. In front of a few houses were carved horizontal poles, some of which were memorial figures, some used to support grave boxes. Haida villages of the late nineteenth century contained the finest displays of totem carvings ever made, but today only a few decayed remnants are to be found in these isolated villages.

The Tsimshian are best known for their memorial poles, some of which were close to seventy feet high and the finest of their kind in existence. Many of these still stand in villages along the Skeena River. Tsimshian and Haida poles were artistically the finest on the coast.

Kwakiutl poles, probably the best known, fall into two periods. In the older period a few poles were carved in an art style which was a crude copy of the northern styles. Tall free-standing poles, some bearing only one or two carved figures, showed mythical and human characters and were probably memorial or heraldic poles. Houseposts bore similar figures. About 1890 a new Kwakiutl style was developed, characterized by high-relief carving, carefully adzed surfaces, and bright and complex painting. Tall heraldic poles in this style were placed against the fronts of houses, which were often painted with crest designs, or stood free of the house, proclaiming the owner's wealth of family legends. Inside, four carved houseposts held up the massive beams which were themselves carved or boldly adzed. In the graveyards, serving the same purpose as headstones, were placed memorial poles or large grave figures representing the Thunderbird and Whale or other bird and animal figures. The Kwakiutl also carved many life-sized human figures—some to represent slaves owned by the family; others as "lookout" on the roof, to watch for the arrival of potlatch guests; still others, carved in attitudes of shame or defeat, to ridicule rival chiefs. Several Kwakiutl poles may still be seen at Kwakiutl villages like Alert Bay.

The Bella Coola, Northern Kwakiutl, and Coast Tsimshian tribes made stout house frontal poles with large arched doorways in the bottom. Though little higher than the front of the house gable, they were ornately carved in the family traditions. The Bella Coola also erected gravemarkers, large animal figures or poles with a single painted figure or board on top.

The Nootka have long used carved inside houseposts, rather crude carvings in human form, representing privileges of the owner. They also erected "owner of the beach" poles, long slim poles with a single eagle figure perched on top, placed in front of the house of the man who claimed ownership of the village site. In more recent times they have used carved potlatch, or welcome figures, and tall heraldic poles in a copy of the recent Kwakiutl style.

Of the poles themselves, each shows a series of representations of characters from the mythology and legendary history of the owner's tribe and family. Although often actual human beings are represented, most of the characters are fairly well-known animals which served the natives as crests. Though sometimes shown in human form, they can usually be recognized by certain conventional identifying features that are always present. Thus the informed observer can guess at the identity of the figures he sees on totem poles.

The order of the figures on a pole might also help to interpret its meaning, because in a few cases there was a tendency to place certain types of figures at definite places on the pole. The Tlingit and Haida often, but by no means invariably, placed the main phratry crest at the top of their totem poles; the Kwakiutl did the same with their most important crests. Also, to the extent that the pole told a connected story or referred to a sequence of family myths, the order was usually from the top down. It has to be added, however, that considerations of artistic composition and the whims of the owner or carver often had as much to do with the order of the figures as their places in the family traditions.

Certain obstacles make it virtually impossible for an outsider to fully interpret totem poles. The maker had an almost limitless choice of characters to choose from, and few clear-cut rules governed his choice or the order of the figures on the pole.

The only persons who fully understood and appreciated a totem pole, then, were the owner and the people to whom he recited the traditions represented on the pole, as was done when the pole was raised. As outsiders who do not know in detail all the traditions represented, and who have not been brought up in the appreciation of the value of such displays as a form of wealth, we can never fully appreciate the carvings.

Totem poles were invariably carved from logs of red

cedar. The tree was felled and trimmed by means of chopping-adzes or hammers and chisels, then towed to the village, where it was carved with adzes and knives. On the earlier poles only essential features such as eyes, mouths, and ears were painted. The pigments were mixed with salmon roe and applied with porcupine-hair brushes. Iron ores gave a rusty red, copper-impregnated minerals gave a blue-green, coal or charcoal gave black, and burnt clam shell gave white. Most existing poles have been painted with commercial pigments which the Indians have long obtained from traders.

A man seldom, if ever, carved his own totem pole.

The photo on the opposite page shows totems which are still standing in the village of Kitwanga on the Skeena River.

Below: At the reconstructed village of 'Ksan near Hazelton a modern generation of Indians continue the tradition of their forefathers, carving totems, face masks and other symbols of Indian culture. 'Ksan is built in original Indian style with totem poles and such native implements as fish traps, smokehouses and canoes.

Instead he hired others, usually chiefs of other clans, who in turn supervised the carving and erection of the pole. For these services the owner was expected to pay generously at a great potlatch when the pole was erected. At this time he proclaimed his right to the ownership of the crests on the pole by telling his family traditions.

Once erected, a totem pole could not be altered or repaired without the expense of another potlatch to explain the action. It was almost as cheap to erect a new pole, which would bring more prestige. This explains why the old poles in native villages have usually been left to decay.

Before Europeans came to this coast, there were few totem poles. Judging from the accounts of the earliest explorers, they were smaller and simpler, and of fewer types. In 1780 Captain Cook saw carved houseposts at Nootka Sound; in 1808 Simon Fraser saw this type and carved grave figures in the Lower Fraser Valley. In the north the earliest visitors saw carved houseposts and simple mortuary poles. Painted house-fronts were seen, but no poles standing in front of the houses. In short, over the whole area the association of carved figures with house construction and burial customs had already been established, but because of a shortage of efficient cutting tools and of wealth, only a few of the richest chiefs could afford carved columns.

It was not long before the ambitious natives, bartering furs for steel blades and other forms of wealth, could afford to carve and raise more numerous and elaborate totem poles. New forms were developed as rich chiefs and sub-chiefs sought to outdo each other in the conspicuous display of their crests. For example, the painted and carved door-slab in front of the house grew taller and more elaborate and became the house frontal pole. This type still has a flat or hollowed back, uncarved, which betrays its origin. Mortuary poles and grave markers grew more elaborate. New types, the memorial and heraldic poles, grew out of developments of the old ideas.

This rapid proliferation of large poles began about 1800 on the Queen Charlotte Islands and perhaps a little later on the Nass River. From these active centres the development spread rapidly northward into Alaska, east to the Upper Skeena, and south along the coast.

In these areas the Golden Age of totem carving was the latter half of the nineteenth century. By 1900, missionary influence and a changing way of life had brought the custom to an almost complete halt. Today, few existing poles anywhere are more than a century old because in their original locations they usually fall and decay in a little over fifty years. There are, fortunately, some fine collections of poles and other Indian carvings.

The group at Thunderbird Park in Victoria, along with others in the Provincial Museum collection, form the finest assembly of totem poles in existence. Other poles still stand in front of Indian villages, particularly those such as Kispiox, Kitwancool and other communities along the Skeena. Then at the Indian Museum and Craft village of 'Ksan near Hazelton a new generation of native artists is now producing masks and carved columns that rival — and in some cases surpass — the best of those carved by their forefathers. Since no other peoples of the world make carvings of identical meaning and conception, it is reassuring to know that a rich and unique heritage lives on.

The **Pioneer Days in British Columbia** series

"Pioneer Days" is a blend of words and photos which prove that British Columbia's history is as interesting as that recorded anywhere else in North America. Every article is true, many written or narrated by those who, 100 or more years ago, lived the experiences they relate. Each volume contains 160 pages, plus four-color covers, some 60,000 words of text and over 200 historical photos, many published for the first time.

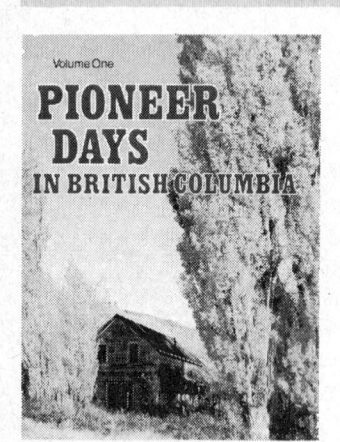

VOLUME ONE

Included among articles in Volume One is the story of Okanagan pioneer Thomas Dolman Shorts who in the 1880's started commercial marine transportation on Okanagan Lake by rowing up and down the sixty-nine-mile-long lake in a twenty-two-foot boat.

Those Cariboo Stampedes is a humourous account of the first stampede in Williams Lake in the 1920's, while **The Taku Tram** describes the Atlin Southern Railway in northwestern B.C. This unique line had only two miles of track, a passenger car that was also home to nesting swallows and an engine that went forward to one terminal, backward to the other.

B.C.'s Worst Marine Disaster describes the tragedy of the *Princess Sophia* which foundered with all 343 men, women and children on board, while **The Voyageurs** provides background on the canoemen who made the B.C. fur trade possible. For these hardy French-Canadians day began at 3 a.m. and ended some eighteen hours later. During this time they travelled upwards of eighty miles, each man paddling over 50,000 strokes.

Other articles are **Pioneer Days in Hazelton, Tales of the B.C. Coast, Pioneers of the Jackpine Forest, Golden Cariboo, Cataline — B.C.'s Famed Frontiersman, Surveying Central B.C. in 1910, Billy Barker of Barkerville,** and many others.

VOLUME THREE

Among the twenty-four articles in Volume Three is **Those Gold-Rush Saloons,** a look at a frontier establishment that considerably influenced western history. In 1896, for instance nuggets shown over a bar in one staried the famed Klondike stampede. Pioneer hotels were also interesting places, although some weren't exactly harbors of comfort. In **Frontier Hotels in Kootenay Country** a traveller in 1889 notes: "Some set up good grub and some don't, some have beds with spring mattresses and some have beds without mattresses."

Bull Teams, Skid Roads and Timber Beasts describes logging when a twelve-hour day, six-day week brought $40 a month. Then there is **The Stikine Trail,** the route in 1898 billed as "the easy way to the Klondike." But men wondered as they travelled up to nineteen miles to advance their supplies one mile. Another herculcan task is described in **Building the Long Road North,** the modern world, ranking ahead of the Eiffel Tower, Golden Gate Bridge and Empire State Building.

There is **Ghost Towns of Lardeau-Slocan, First Car to Hazelton 1912, Pioneer Days in the Chilcotin, By Stagecoach to Cariboo . . . 1877,** and fifteen other features.

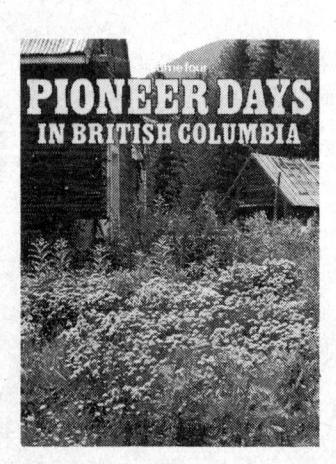

VOLUME FOUR

Pioneering in the Okanagan relates the experiences of the first family in the Summerland area in 1887. For ten years they lived in a sod-roofed cabin, their broom birch twigs and their evening light a string in a saucer of grease. Pioneers in Interior B.C. faced equal hardships. As related in **Early Days in the Nechako Valley,** settlers in the Vanderhoof-Fraser Lake region were 400 miles from the railway and a 250-mile round trip by sleigh or wagon from their nearest major supply point.

City life was equally spartan. As noted in **Life in Trail . . . 1897,** the normal work day was thirteen hours, six days a week. As a consequence, breaks like Christmas were celebrated with gusto — at times with unexpected results. **An 1890's Christmas in the Kootenays,** for instance, describes one Christmas at Fort Colville when ". . . the cook somehow dropped his pipe and tobacco into the soup and everyone went to bed early, feeling sick."

The hardship and isolation of pioneer life created independent people. Paddy and Sammy Carroll at Ootsa Lake in Central B.C. wanted to travel but had only their dogs for transportation. They set out anyway. **The Bannock Trail** describes their experiences during a 6,000-mile dog-team trek across North America.

Among many other articles are **Forty Years a Country Doctor, Diary of Despair, Day of the Hand Troller,** and **A Cowboy's Grand Hotel.**

Heritage House
Publishing Company Ltd., 5543 - 129 Street, Surrey, British Columbia, V3W 4H4

INDEX

Aberdeen 137
Alaska Highway News 125
Alling, Lillian 140 to 145
Anahim Lake 27
Anarchist Mountain 115
Anderson, James 128-135
Ashcroft Manor 68
Atlin 55, 57 to 59

Baillie-Begbie, Sir Matthew 65, 82
Barkerville 68, 80-81, 128 to 135
Barnard's Express 84, 87, 89, 130-131
Beaver, The 127
Big Eutusk Lake 10
Blackwell family 11-12, 15
Bonnington Falls 46-47
Bowron, John 129, 133
Boyd, John 81 to 89
British Columbian 65-66
Buffalo Lake 127
Bulkley, Col. C. S. 33-34
Bulkley Valley 8, 12, 33, 99
Burke, Paddy 55 to 59
Burns Lake 10-11, 15, 97, 102-103
BX 22

Cadenhead, Capt. John 124, 126-127
Calbraith, John 61-62
Camborne 17, 19
Camels 60 to 69
Cameron, J. J. 18
Canadian Pacific Railway 46
Cape Beale 110 to 114
Cariboo 27, 29, 80 to 89, 129 to 135
Cariboo Road 23, 37-38, 60, 62, 65, 68, 81 to 89
Cariboo Sentinel 80, 133-134
Carrich, K. F. 112
Charlotte 24
Chief Sam 118
Chilco Ranch 27 to 29
Chilcotin 27 to 31, 37 to 39
Christie, Jim 142 to 144
Clearwater 117 to 118
Clerf, Sam 58
Coal-Oil Johnny 44-45
Cold Creek 107, 109
Collins Telegraph Line 33-34
Colonial Hotel 37
Comaplix 19
Cook, Capt. James 48-49, 157
Cottonwood Canyon 24-25
Cottonwood House 37, 65, 80 to 89
Craddock Bridge 34-35

D. A. Thomas 120 to 122, 124 to 127
Dawson 144-145
Decker Lake 99 to 103, 105
De Smet, Fr. Jean 95
Dewdney Trail 69, 137
Discovery 48 to 50
Douglas, David 146 to 149

Ellis, Thomas 136 to 139
Esche, Otto 60

Ferguson 17, 19
Fernie 21
Float 18
Flying Dutchman 63, 65
Fort Edmonton 95
Fort George Canyon 25, 97
Fort Graham inside back cover
Fort Kamloops 149
Fort St. James 22 to 24, 146, 148-149
Fort St. John 121 to 123, 125, inside back cover
Fort Steele 68-69
Fort Vancouver 95, 148-149
Fort Vermilion 121-123, 127
Francois Lake 9, 11 to 13
Fraser Lake 24
Fraser, Simon 157
Friendly Cove 49, 51-52

Galbraith, Robert 67, 69
Grande Prairie 60, 69
Grand Trunk Pacific Railway 11-12, 35, 90, 97 to 105
Greenwood 21
Grouard, Bishop 120, 123
Guillod, Harry 65
Gunner from Galway 45-46

Hagwilget 32 to 35
Hawall 149
Haynes, Judge 137, 139
Hazelton 7-8, 11-12, 23, 33, 35, 90-91, 97, 99 to 101, 105, 141-142
Henkel, Jake 9
Herridge, H. W. 40-41
History of Washington, Idaho and Montana 69
Houston 11-12
Hudson's Bay Company 24, 68, 121-122, 125, 127, 149
Hume Hotel 42
Hurdy-gurdies 131

Ibex Mine 71
Indian tribes 151 to 157

Jacob Henkel 12
Janze, Charlie 142 to 144
Johnson, Capt. 111-112
Jowett, A. E. 92 to 94

Kading, Emil 55 to 59
Kamloops 68-69, 107, 109, 117
Kamloops Daily Sentinel 109
Kaslo Claim 17
Kaslo Kootenaian 17
Kelly, Robert 35
Kemano 9
Kispiox 157
Kitwancool 157
Kootenay Lake 46
'Ksan 157

Lac La Hache 67 to 69
Laumeister, Frank 62, 66
LeBourdais, Louis 66-67

Ledge, The 18
Liard River 54 to 59
Lillooet 64-65
Lower Post inside back cover
Lowery R. T. 16 to 21
Lowery's Claim 18
Lucky Jack Claim 17, 20-21

Mackay, John 49
McBride 101
McLeod, Don 66 to 68
Malbouf, Antoine 83-84, 87
Manhattan Saloon 42-43
Maquinna, Chief 51, 53
Martinez 51
Martin, Robert 55 to 59
Meares, John 49, 51
Mileposts in Ogopogoland 115
Moodie, Inspector inside back cover
Morris, John 67-68
Muirhardt, Henry 74

Nakusp 18
Nasookin 44, 46
Nelson 18, 21, 42 to 47
New Denver 18
New Denver Ledge 21
Newton's Ranch 28
New Westminster 63-64
Nootka Sound 48 to 53, 157
North West America 51
North West Mounted Police inside back cover
North With Peace River Jim 123
Nugget, The 18

Office Saloon 43
Ogilvie, Scotty 143-144
Okanagan Lake 137
Omineca Hotel 90
Ootsa Lake 7 to 11, 13, 14, 15
Osoyoos 115, 137, 139

Queen Charlotte Islands 48, 151, 157
Quesnel 22 to 25
Quesnel, Commercial Center of the Cariboo Gold Rush 129

Paddlewheels on the Frontier 123
Peace River 120 to 127
Peace River 120, 123
Penticton 137 to 139
Penticton 137
Phoenix 20-21
Poplar 16 to 21
Poplar Nugget 17-18
Port Douglas 63
Port Essington 78-79
Port Simpson 91, 98
Prince Rupert 35, 97, 104-105

Ray, John Bunyan 116 to 119
Resolution 48, 50
Rhondda, Lord 124

159

Sandon 71 to 75
Sandon Paystreak 18
Santiago 48
Sawney's Letters 129, 131-132, 134
Sculthorpe, Gordon 125, 127
Shelford, Jack 7 to 15
Shorts, Capt. T. D. 137
Siberia 141 to 145, 149, 151
Silver King Mine 46-47
Skeena River 77-78, 90, 97 to 99, 141, 151, 156
Slocan Drill 18
Smithers, 100, 142
St. Charles 123
Strathcona Hotel 44
St. Saviour's Church 138-139
Stuart Lake 23

Tahsis 53
Telkwa 99 to 101
Teller 144-145
Tete Jaune Cache 100
Three Forks 72, 74
Tingley, Stephen 82, 87
Trout Lake 17, 93-94
Tweedsmuir Provincial Park 10

Valencia 110 to 114
Vancouver, Capt. George 51-52
Vancouver Province 65
Victoria 61 to 67, 89
Victoria Colonist 61-62, 64, 66

Waddell, J. L. 33

Walsh, Joe 55, 57, 59
Washington Historical Quarterly 69
Washington Statesman 66
Wasson, Everett 55, 57, 59
Watson Lake 127
Weenusk 127
Wells Gray Park 117-118
Whitehorse 59, 144-145
Whitehorse Star 144
Williams Creek 83, 86, 88
Windsor Hotel 94
Wistaria 9, 13-14

Yale 130
Yukon Telegraph Trail 141 to 144

Zeballos 52-53

PHOTO CREDITS

B.C. Government — Front, Inside front and back covers, 6, 10, 28, 30, 35, 80, 112, 115, 138, 147, 150, 151, 155, 157.
Boss, R.M. — 10.
Clemson, Donovan — 21, 26, 29, 30, 36, 38, 39, 40, 41, 135, 156.
Ellis, F. H. — 54, 55, 57, 58.
Fort St. John Photo Shop — 125.
Glenbow-Alberta Institute — 54, 102, 121, 126.
Harrington, Richard — 31.
Hudson's Bay Company — 124, 148.
Knox, B. & W. — 58.

McClelland, Jim — 22.
National Film Board — 133.
Nelson Museum — 47.
Pooley, Nigel — 117, 118.
Provincial Archives of B.C. — 8-10, 16, 22, 24, 25, 33, 34, 37, 40, 42-47, 50, 60, 63-68, 70-74, 77-82, 87, 88, 90, 93-95, 97, 101, 103, 104, 113, 122, 128, 130-134, 136-139, 141, 144.
Provincial Museum & Archives of Alberta — 104, 120, 121, 122, 126, Inside back cover.
Public Archives of Canada — 9, 73, 91, 100, 104, 153, 154.

Shelford, Arthur — 7, 12, 13, 14.
Sutherland, J. W. — 56, 140.
University of B.C. Library — 85
Vancouver City Archives — 32, 45, 63, 64, 108, 130.
Vancouver Public Library — 18-20, 75, 92-94, 152.
Washington State Historical Society — 110, 114.
Wenger, Ferdi — 106, 107.
Wrathall, W. W. — 13, 91, 98, 100.
Wright, R. — 36, 95, 109, 116, 118, 119, Inside back cover.
Young, Peggy — 48, 51, 52, 53.

ARTICLE CREDITS

The articles in this volume are reprinted from BC Outdoors, a magazine which was born in the Cariboo in 1945 and which has grown into the largest publication of its kind in Canada. Editorial content ranges from fishing to conservation, wildlife to travel. History also is popular with readers, and over the years the magazine has published hundreds of historical articles. Additional information is available from #202, 1132 Hamilton Street, Vancouver, B.C. V6B 2S2